Jesus Descending From The Golden Gates Of Heaven:

A Divine Revelation With Jesus And Four Biblical Heroes

Pamalyn Lalor

Copyright © 2024 Pamalyn Lalor

Copyright © 2024 Pamalyn Lalor

This book or any portion thereof may not be reproduced or used in any manner whatsoever without the author's and publisher's express written permission except for the use of brief quotations in a book review.

Printed in the United States of America

First Printing, 2024

Independently published.

ISBN 979-8-9909659-2-8

Unless otherwise noted, all Scripture quotations are taken from the King James Version (KJV) Study Bible Copyright © 2013 by Holman Bible Publisher.

Scripture quotations marked *NIV* are from the Holy Bible, New International Version, Copyright ©1973, 1978, 1984 Biblica. Used by permission of Zondervan. All rights reserved.

Scripture quotations marked ESV are from the Holy Bible, English Standard Version, Copyright © 2001 by Crossway Bible, a division of Good News Publishers, Used by permission. All rights reserved

Scripture quotations marked NLT are from the Holy Bible, New Living Translation, Copyright © 1996, 2004, 2015 by Tyndale House Foundation. All rights reserved.

Merriam–Webster Online Dictionary Copyright © 2012 by Merriam–Webster, Incorporated

Cover designer and creator: Robert L. Ruff Jr.

Endorsements

"Therefore, my beloved brethren, be ye steadfast, unmovable, always abounding in the work of the Lord, forasmuch as ye know that your labour is not in vain in the Lord."

--1 Corinthians 15:58 -

This book: *Jesus Descending From The Golden Gates Of Heaven: A Divine Revelation With Jesus And Four Biblical Heroes* reveals a powerful encounter with Jesus, Abraham, Moses, Elijah, and David. Pamalyn Lalor, whom I have the privilege to call my Mom, will give you a glimpse of what God showed her in a dream that will tug at your heartstrings. This read will empower those that are saved to stand flat-footed for God yet encourage unbelievers to know God in a personal way. Not only will you feel a deeper connection with God after reading this book, but Mother Pam also implores us to appreciate the gifts that God has given us and to use our gifts for His glory. This book will invite you to get into a secret place of prayer with our Heavenly Father as it was through prayer that this encounter began. Get ready to have your spirit ignited, your gifts stirred, and your heart rejoicing after reading this miraculous revelation.

--Sivanaise Anthony/ Entrepreneur, Concord, North Carolina.

God honors those who seek to have a personal relationship with Him with life-changing encounters. This book vividly portrays the author's supernatural experience with Jesus Christ, a direct response to her relentless pursuit of an intimate relationship with Him. It also gives its readers an in-depth account of the value of establishing and maintaining a relationship with Jesus Christ. So, prepare to embark upon the beautiful spiritual journey of an unapologetic herald of the power of God's love, forgiveness, and power.

--Dr. Cherié N. Graham. Concord, North Carolina.

Endorsements

Glory Hallelujah to God Almighty! I thank God for my sister, Pamalyn Lalor, who is lovingly called Mama Pam. As a Missionary, I had the pleasure and first-hand opportunity to see her witness and pray warfare prayers for many people near and far. I will always value and cherish our mission field experience on the seashore of Montego Bay, Jamaica, working together to win souls for God's kingdom. She has a loving heart for God's children and a burning desire for souls to be saved.

Several years ago, she told me about her profound encounter in a dream of seeing Jesus descending from the Gold Gates of Heaven. Through the help and motivation of the blessed Holy Spirit, she was able to write and demonstrate the awesomeness of this divine Heavenly experience. I highly recommend this amazing book which will stimulate your mind and encourage your soul. A must-read read which includes some poems that illustrate and highlight the journey of some of the biblical heroes seen in the dream.

-- Missionary Sheila Robinson. Montego Bay, Jamaica.

In Genesis 6-8, God gave Noah instructions on how to build the Ark. Yet, Noah was ridiculed for following God's instruction. We all have dreams; some we remember, some we forget, and some may reoccur. **This book titled, "***Jesus Descending From The Golden Gates Of Heaven: A Divine Revelation With Jesus And Four Biblical Heroes* "will give you an insight into how to follow God's instructions and plans for your life when it is delivered via a dream. The vivid details of these dreams will build your faith and bring you into a closer relationship with our Heavenly Father. Reading about the lives and journeys of these biblical heroes will encourage you to stay steadfast and strong in the knowledge of God. I strongly recommend you read this uplifting book. I can assure you that your heart and soul will be ignited by some of the unimaginable things that God is preparing for us in Heaven.

--Jeanetta Francis BSN, RN. Hartford, Connecticut.

I have known my dear Daughter Pamalyn from her childhood days in the church. I have witnessed her focus and commitment to serving Christ from that time until now. *Jesus Descending From The Golden Gates Of Heaven* is a remarkable book about the goodness of our Lord Jesus Christ and how He speaks to us, not only through his words but also through dreams. In the Bible, God spoke to some of his servants through dreams, a way of sending messages to His people. This is a wonderful way to evangelize to others and let readers know that we serve a Mighty God who loves and cares for all of us if we only believe; a God that can do the impossible. A very thoughtful work indeed.

>--Sister Rosalee McCormack, Bethel Mennonite Church, Grey Ground, Jamaica.

God made you special. I remember clearly like I could touch it, as if it was yesterday, Sis Pamalyn's days at church, teaching in Sunday School, and being actively involved in the Youth group. Sis Pamalyn and other older folk in the Bethel Mennonite Church have set a godly example for me to follow in fully committing and wholeheartedly dedicating a life of service to Jesus Christ, our soon-coming King. She has raised the bar high for younger folk like me to maintain the same high standards in living a life of integrity so that I too can be a witness to young Christians and to those who have not yet committed to Christ.

Sister Pamalyn's life, work, prayers, and encouragement have helped to shape me and all those who have come in contact with her. As Paul charged young Timothy, so is this same charge from her today (*see* 2 Timothy 4:1-5). She would have received similar encouragement from her late mother, Sister Murdel, who was so gentle, yet a woman with great fortitude. I am grateful for this opportunity to give thanks to God for her achievements. The life she lives is for Christ only, and I know that this wonderful book will certainly bless your hearts and increase your faith journey as you anticipate the return of the Lord.

>--Sister Charleen Daley, Bethel Mennonite Church, Grey Ground, Jamaica.

Have Heavenly Thoughts and Desires

"If ye then be risen with Christ, seek those things which are above, where Christ sitteth on the right hand of God. 2 Set your affection on things above, not on things on the earth. 3 For ye are dead, and your life is hid with Christ in God. 4 When Christ, who is our life, shall appear, then shall ye also appear with him in glory. 5 Mortify therefore your members which are upon the earth; fornication, uncleanness, inordinate affection, evil concupiscence, and covetousness, which is idolatry: 6For which things' sake the wrath of God cometh on the children of disobedience: 7 In the which ye also walked some time, when ye lived in them. 8 But now ye also put off all these; anger, wrath, malice, blasphemy, filthy communication out of your mouth. 9 Lie not one to another, seeing that ye have put off the old man with his deeds; 10 And have put on the new man, which is renewed in knowledge after the image of him that created him: 11Where there is neither Greek nor Jew, circumcision nor uncircumcision, Barbarian, Scythian, bond nor free: but Christ is all, and in all. 12 Put on therefore, as the elect of God, holy and beloved, bowels of mercies, kindness, humbleness of mind, meekness, longsuffering; 13 Forbearing one another, and forgiving one another, if any man have a quarrel against any: even as Christ forgave you, so also do ye.14 And above all these things put on charity, which is the bond of perfectness.15And let the peace of God rule in your hearts, to the which also ye are called in one body; and be ye thankful. 16 Let the word of Christ dwell in you richly in all wisdom; teaching and admonishing one another in psalms and hymns and spiritual songs, singing with grace in your hearts to the Lord. 17 And whatsoever ye do in word or deed, do all in the name of the Lord Jesus, giving thanks to God and the Father by him." --Colossians 3:1-17 KJV

Dedication

TRUST ONLY IN GOD'S WISDOM, AND IT SHALL BRING YOU BLESSINGS!

"Trust in the Lord with all thine heart; and lean not unto thine own understanding. In all thy ways acknowledge him, and he shall direct thy paths. Be not wise in thy own eyes: fear the Lord and depart from evil. It shall be health to thy navel and marrow to thy bones."

--Proverbs. 3:5-8 *KJV*

First, I want to dedicate this book to my Heavenly Father, who sent His only begotten son, Jesus Christ, to die for my sins—recognizing Jesus, my Savior, as the Author and Finisher of my faith in whom I put my complete trust to lead me in every area of my life. Father, I acknowledge that it is from You that we gain the spirit of wisdom through the indwelling of the Holy Spirit who resides in us. Holy Spirit, thank You for being an Advocate, Comforter, Teacher, and Counselor. Most importantly, thank You for the supernatural recall of these beautiful dreams.

Father, You are the Creator of Heaven and Earth, who grants me wisdom, knowledge, and understanding to go forward by trusting only in You. **The Bible says, "For in him we live, and move, and have our being; as certain also of your own poets have said, For we are also his offspring" (Acts 17:28).** Therefore, I recognize that as I yield to Your command, statutes, and precepts, Your Almighty power nourishes every bone in my body. I am thankful to be called Your offspring packaged in Your image! My bones are healthy to combat the adversary's attack when I stay steadfast, bold, and strong in You, dear Lord.

Thank you, Father, for giving me the gift of dreaming so many

Dedication

meaningful dreams. The Bible says, *"Every good and perfect gift is from above, coming down from the Father of the heavenly lights, who does not change like shifting shadows. He chose to give us birth through the word of truth that we might be a kind of first fruits of all he created" (James 1:17-18 NIV).* Thank You for the dream of seeing Heaven's Golden Gates and another dream giving me an assignment to write this book.

Second, I would like to dedicate this book to my beloved mother, Murdel, who never hesitated to tell me to BELIEVE in God and to put my TRUST and FAITH in the Lord. She repeatedly reminded me, "God will never fail you, nor will He leave you." She would say, "No matter how crooked your life seems, only God can make it straight."

Third, to my phenomenal daughter, Sivanaise Anthony, who continues to inspire me in so many different ways. Thank you for being the best daughter that a mother could ever ask for. You are a great example of Ephesians 6:2 which says, "Honour thy father and thy mother; which is the first commandment with promise." Thanks for walking and exemplifying this promising commandment to your life. Praying that God's abundant blessings will be your portion along with a long life.

Finally, I would like to dedicate this book to all prayer warriors worldwide. I implore you to keep praying and interceding for your family, relatives, friends, and every nation in the universe. PRAY FOR ISRAEL! In Psalm 25:22 (*KJV*), the Bible says, "Redeem Israel, O God, out of all his troubles." God wants us to PRAY one for another; there is no distance in prayer, so keep the prayer line burning with unceasing prayer. Do not get weary in spreading the gospel to all nations. Our Heavenly inheritance will be great when the Bridegroom comes and finds us ready to partake in the marriage supper. In everything you do, WATCH, PRAY, and be READY!

Review

"Jesus Descending From The Golden Gates Of Heaven: A Divine Revelation With Jesus And Four Biblical Heroes" is an encouraging read for the Believer and Non-believer alike. Pamalyn Lalor, Mother Pam as she is affectionately called, releases a true masterpiece surrounding her unique encounter with the Christ. This intricate piece provides illustrative detail of the majesty and beauty of Heaven, along with descriptive attributes of some biblical heroes such as Abraham, Moses, Elijah, and David. This revelation pushes the believer to yearn for an experience akin to Pamalyn's. It challenges the non-believer to want to know this Jesus who so beautifully served as a heavenly tour guide for her journey. The love He showed her during this visitation and the delicate care given will warm any human heart and unlock euphoric feelings of joy.

Pamalyn sets the tone for the book with this statement concerning Jesus Christ, "He is the passport for our access to Heaven." This not only summarizes her book, but it serves as a mantra for a life in Christ. She stresses to the reader that this access is only afforded through acknowledging Christ as the Redeemer. Throughout this work, many highlights point to the reality of Christ along with numerous scriptural proofs to support this revelation. Scripture says "Forever, O Lord, thy Word is settled in heaven" (Ps. 119:89). Ms. Lalor's use of Scripture sprinkled throughout her account serves as a foundation for the fact of her unique experience in the heavenly realm. Weaving in the biblical heroes along with details about their appearance speaks to the preservation that Heaven brings. Throughout her writing, there is a trail of how young and strong each of these men appeared. After connecting these heroes to the vision, Christ brings things back to her through the unicorn's expression. Pamalyn shows the reader how concerned Christ is for them by releasing a special sign to prove His love for her as He has for the reader now.

The Apostle Paul states, "Lest I should be exalted above measure through the abundance of the revelations, there was given to me a thorn in the flesh, the messenger of Satan to buffet me, lest I should be exalted above measure" (2 Cor. 12:7). Mother Pam expresses the physical pain she endured prior to, and still carries to a degree, surrounding the release of this book; however, the same promise God made to the Apostle Paul He makes to the modern-day believer, "My grace is sufficient for thee: for my strength is made perfect in weakness" (2 Cor. 12: 9a). The baseline of this book calls for the believer to take an introspective look and examine their lives to ensure that their walk aligns with Christ. The author has a recurring theme surrounding God's plan for each of His Children today. She writes this with an eye toward the return of the Christ. Truly, He will come looking for a Bride to receive unto Himself and release to His Church the rewards detailed throughout this story. This book challenges the non-believer to be saved and causes the Believer to echo the words of John the Revelator, "Even so, come, Lord Jesus" (Rev. 22:20b). God bless.

Bishop Bertram D. Hinton, Jr.

Bethel Temple Faith Church

Senior Pastor / Founder

Concord, NC

Foreword

I am honored and happy to write a Foreword to this wonderful, eye-opening book, *Jesus Descending From The Golden Gates Of Heaven: A Divine Revelation With Jesus And Four Biblical Heroes.*

It has been my pleasure to have known Pamalyn Lalor since 2016. Interestingly enough, our relationship began with me being her realtor, blessed with the responsibility of assisting both her and her family with the purchase of their next home. We have since grown from a realtor-client relationship to a Minister and Member relationship, serving under the same Ministry Bethel Temple Faith Church, located in Concord, NC, under the Leadership of Bishop Bertram D. Hinton, Jr., and the First Lady Nickie Hinton, to a now deeper relationship, under the same Ministry and Leadership, as Elder and Mother. It has been a pure joy over the past several years watching Christ manifest Himself through Mother Pam, whether it be through her exhibited attitude, her loving kindness, or through her life-changing testimony. Known to be a Prayer Warrior and a Praiser, **Mother Pam has proven to be one of God's Chosen, handpicked by Him for His service.** Mother Pam, a humble servant of Jesus Christ, has been gifted by the Father in so many areas; the area that comes to mind is her talent for writing. Mother Pam has dedicated her life to the Father, and keeps a sensitive, submitted ear open to His voice allowing her to flow in her writings, whether it be through a play or **as we're seeing, writing a book; you can be assured that the Lord was the true Author.**

When Mother Pam first showed me a "sample" of her book, I was overwhelmed with the transparency of her experiences and the high level of detail that the book presented to help readers understand what can come out of the purity of Praise, the willingness to Worship and the press to Pray. God, who is the King of Kings, feeling the igniting pull of His daughter, chose to reveal Himself, His Son, and

Foreword

His Spirit to the author in such a way that we the readers will be drawn closer to Him. Through Mother Pam's dream and her interpretation of it, you will be able to walk through her journey with the Trinity, gaze into the revelation given to her of Heaven's design, and feel the elation felt when she encountered Four Biblical Heroes from the Bible. This book can take you from hurt to wholeness. Like our author, you too can be healed, set free, and delivered.

The Bible says in John 15:16, "Ye have not chosen me, but I have chosen you, and ordained you, that ye should go and bring forth fruit, and that your fruit should remain: that whatsoever ye shall ask of the Father in my name, he may give it you." Mother Pam is an author who has been chosen by God for a time such as this. She shall be remembered by her fruit because it shall remain.

--Elder Toney B. Black, Sr.

Bethel Temple Faith Church, Concord, NC.

Acknowledgments

First and foremost, I want to give the highest honor and praise to God, my Father, as I acknowledge him as the Chief Cornerstone of my life.

I would like to extend my gratitude to all my community supporters for being who God said you would be in my life. Unfortunately, I am unable to address everyone by name; however, I want to thank you all for all the prayers, texts, emails, calls, and consistent encouragement throughout this writing phase. This accomplishment would not have been possible without the divine intervention and leading of the blessed Holy Spirit, and the love and support from you all.

I would like to say a hearty thank you to my mother, Murdel Johnson (*d.*), my grandmother Enid McIntosh (*d.*), my father Arthur Laylor (*d.*), and my stepfather Cleveland Johnson (*d.*). Special thanks to my daughter, Sivanaise Anthony, who has been my prayer partner for many years. Your daily encouragement, thoughtfulness, and editorial guidance throughout the writing of this book have been exceptional. Many thanks to my son-in-law, Orlando Anthony, for always encouraging me. A wonderful thank you to my three beautiful granddaughters Serenity Anthony, Sariah Anthony, and Shaelyn Anthony. The Lord placed you all in my life when I needed an outlet from my days of sadness, pain, and being distraught, to a joyful place of peace and tranquility. Days of receiving an embrace, a kiss here and there, and most of all, prayer from you all during this assignment were so much needed. Solomon encouraged us that, "Children's children are the crown of old men; and the glory of children are their fathers" (Proverb 17:6 *KJV*). I thank God for blessing me with the crown of grand motherhood. It is a priceless gift of honor that I am privileged to be granted such a role to govern and love every child set under my care.

Acknowledgments

To my six beautiful sisters: Yvonne Hussey (*d.*), Sandra Johnson, Ena Laylor, Janet Laylor, Sheila Robinson, Violet Spinks. My five wonderful brothers, Gregory Johnson, Phillip Ray Johnson, Franklin Laylor (*d.*), John Laylor, and Linton Morris. To other family and friends who constantly keep in touch during the writing phase: Claudette Chambers, Jeanetta Francis, Mercedes Oliva Garcia, Claudette Jones-Graham, Juilette Grayson (*d.*), Rayman Kanhai, Seymour Lalor, Janet Maragh, Lisa and Frank Morgan, Marva Smith, and Loretta Stone. To all my spiritual daughters around the world, just to name a few who keep encouraging me throughout this journey: Audrey Tyner-Gilzene, Lucretia Fleeting, Shamira Lee Woodward, and Takaira Johnson. Additionally, to all my uncles, aunties, nieces, nephews, cousins, and many other relatives who have been motivating me along on this journey.

Special acknowledgment to my Bethel Mennonite Church Family and friends in Heartease District, Manchester, Jamaica. Thanks, Pastor Stanley and MaryJane Shirk, Pastor Tyson (*d.*), and Mrs. Tyson (*d.*). To Mrs. Isolene Lewis (*d.*), a phenomenal Headteacher at Bethel Mennonite Christian School, also a great Sunday school teacher and mentor throughout my childhood journey. I have so much appreciation for all the other great Bishops, Preachers, Teachers, and Mentors who played such an important role in my life. Thanks for encouraging me from a tender age to write poems and skits which helped to propel me into the writing world.

It is such an honor and privilege to acknowledge my Trinity Community Church of God Family, friends, and all my spiritual children in Hartford, Connecticut. To Bishop P. Taylor and First Lady Taylor, I am truly grateful for the twenty-six years that God has allowed me to be a part of this awesome ministry. Also, this is the first church that I was privileged to share my dream of Heaven in February 2012.

To my Crossroads Community Church family and friends of two wonderful years of encouragement in East Hartford CT, under the leadership of Bishop and First Lady Wiles. My sincere appreciation to Pastor Emily Spongberg for your thoughtfulness as you encouraged and mentored me to continue writing this book.

To my Bethel Temple Faith Church family, friends, and all my spiritual daughters in Concord, North Carolina since March 2017, under the leadership of Bishop Bertram D. Hinton, Jr., and First Lady Nickie L. Hinton. I cannot express how grateful I am for all the support, inspiration, and continuous prayer for me and my family during the writing phase. Bishop Hinton, I thank you for writing such an astounding review. To Elder Toney B. Black, Sr. for his prayers and encouragement and for writing such an inspiring foreword. To your dear wife, Minister Gwendolyn Black, thanks for being the spiritual daughter that God would want you to be in my life. To the wonderful crew of Church Mothers who connect every Tuesday night for warfare prayers. Thanks for your continuous prayer for the success of this book.

Special acknowledgement to Elder Cherie Graham. Many thanks for your labor of love and all your editorial input during this writing journey. Your constant prayer and advice are invaluable.

Thanks to everyone who took the time to write these great endorsements. Thanks for your contribution.

To my publisher for her patience, understanding, expertise, and a good sense of humor. Thank you for a work well done.

Finally, I am grateful to this great and compassionate God for having you all in my life. We came this far by faith. To God be the glory, honor, and praise!

Contents

Endorsements iii

Have Heavenly Thoughts and Desires vi

Dedication vii

Review ix

Foreword xi

Acknowledgments xiii

Introduction xix

Please, Join me in Saying This Thanksgiving Prayer! xxix

Part I: Life Before the Dream 1

Chapter 1: Jesus—God's Precious Gift to Man 2

Let Us Pray, Thanking God for the Outpouring of His Spirit! ... 16

Chapter 2: Growing Up in Jamaica with a Praying and Virtuous Mother . 18

Prayer of Thanks for Caring Hearts! 27

Chapter 3: Trusting the Mighty and Powerful Creator! 29

Prayer to the God of Abundance! 35

Chapter 4: Different Surgeries and Healing Testimonies 37

Let Us Pray This Prayer of Healing! 44

Chapter 5: Humbling Myself in Fasting and Prayer 46

Prayer--Surrendering All to Jesus! 56

Part 2: The Night of the Heavenly Dream 57

Chapter 6: Prayer and Intercession on a Cold Winter Night 58

Chapter 7: Hours Just Before the Dream 65

Chapter 8: The Dream and Who I Saw in the Dream 67

Chapter 9: Seeing Jesus in His Pearly White Robe 76

> **Poem: When I See My Savior's Face!** 83

Chapter 10: The Golden Pearly Gates of Heaven 86

Chapter 11: The Beautiful Swaying Curtains Above the Gates 91

Chapter 12: Seeing Four Biblical Heroes 96

    A: The Appearance of Father Abraham 98

    Poem: Abraham, the Father of Faith at Heaven's Gate! 104

    B: The Appearance of Moses 107

    Poem: Moses! Moses! Take Off Your Shoes! 114

    C: The Appearance of Elijah 117

    Poem: Elijah The Praying Prophet! 121

    D: King David Appeared with a Huge Golden Harp 123

    Poem: David! The Musician After God's Own Heart! 131

Chapter 13: Changes in my Thought Process................................... 134

Chapter 14: I Had No Memory of The Past, No Sadness or Pain............. 142

Chapter 15: Jesus Walking Beside Me and He Gave Me a Unicorn............ 148

Chapter 16: The Lord Uses Animals to Illustrate His Majesty 164

    Poem: The Mystical Bronze Unicorn! 180

Part 3: Second Dream: Seeing Jesus With A Book in His Hand 182

Chapter 17: Yes! To the Call of God's Assignment After the Second Dream
.... 183

Prayer--Seeking God's Direction and Guidance for the Assignment! ... 196

Chapter 18: Jesus' Voice! My Strength, Power, and My Guide 198

Prayer--Thanking God for Being My Strength, Power, And My Guide!
.... 210

Chapter 19: Every Gift from God Has a Significant Meaning............ 211

Prayer of Thanks for Gifts and Talents! 219

Part 4: Inspiration of Biblical Heroes in the Dreams 221

Chapter 20: Faith Exercised by Jesus and Biblical Heroes 222

Prayer– Thanking God For Biblical Heroes! 232

Chapter 21: Appreciating the King of Glory 234

Acknowledgments

Meeting The Queen and The Duke of England 240

Chapter 22: Preparing to Meet the Returning King 244

Poem: Are You Ready to See Jesus The King?............................**259**

Prayer--The Great Day of Separation!..**261**

Song: King Jesus Is Coming 265

About The Author 266

From the Author 268

Introduction

THE GIFT OF REDEMPTION THROUGH JESUS CHRIST!

> *"For the grace of God that bringeth salvation, hath appeared to all men, teaching us that, denying ungodliness and worldly lusts, we should live soberly, righteously, and godly, in this present world, looking for that blessed hope, and the glorious appearing of the great God and our Savior Jesus Christ; who gave himself for us, that he might redeem us from all iniquity, and purify unto himself a peculiar people, zealous of good works. These things speak, exhort, and rebuke with all authority. Let no man despise thee."*
>
> --Titus 2:11-15 *KJV*

Do you know that God loves us so much that He gave us His only begotten Son, JESUS CHRIST to die to set us free from sin? God granted the world His most precious and glorious GIFT, so we will not perish if we believe Jesus Christ is Lord. Yes! Our Heavenly Father made that ultimate sacrifice for you and me to have abundant life through His Son! Having said that, how can we not love and appreciate the gift and the gift giver? (*see* Ephesians 2:8 and Psalm 130:7). God, our Father of all Fathers, commands us to love Him and have no other god before Him. God's word tells us, "By grace are ye saved through faith." We cannot save ourselves! Therefore, let us love the gift of God, Jesus Christ, who gave Himself for our sins so we are free from all iniquities. Christ, our only blessed hope of glory, plenteous in redemption, extends His mercy toward us. Jesus came willingly to bridge the gap between Heaven and hell, giving us a free PASSPORT to enter Heaven by God's grace! Jesus Christ, our only hope of glory is worthy to be praised!

He is the Messiah who, in obedience to His Father, came down to Earth to bring salvation's plan to save us from the claws of the adversary. Oh yes! Jesus left His home in Heaven and came down in

Introduction

human form to take up our sins, guilt, shame, and disgrace by dying for us on Calvary's cross. Such divine and holy love came to us from the Father above! Jesus is the perfect and most special GIFT to humanity. He is The Priority Package sent to redeem and rescue you and me and set us free from the dark world of sin. The Word of God said in Romans 6:23, "For the wages of sin is death; but the gift of God is eternal life through Jesus Christ our Lord." Jesus, I thank You for bridging the gap between Heaven and hell for my salvation because your love for me is amazing! We need to love God the Father, God the Son, and God the Holy Spirit. Together they are the Holy Trinity and we cannot live without them.

Friends, Jesus humbled Himself and died for us, and was buried in a borrowed tomb owned by Joseph of Arimathea (John 19:38-42). Jesus took our guilt to the grave but arose on the third day to set humanity free from sin, giving us access to live with Him if we believe and trust Him only. Because of Jesus' POWER, STRENGTH, and AUTHORITY, no grave could keep Him down or hold Him captive! HALLELUJAH! The Messiah got power over death, the tomb, and the grave! Now, we are rejoicing in the glorious resurrection power of Jesus' shed blood to set us free from sin to salvation! Jesus was crucified, resurrected, and ascended to His Father. However, He didn't leave us comfortless. Instead, He sent the Comforter to live inside of us. The Holy Spirit is the Comforter, and He is here to stay with us until Jesus returns from the place He is preparing for us. Are you anxiously anticipating the return of the Messiah, our glorious gift from God our Father? The Bible tells us in 2 Corinthians 9:15, "Thanks be to God for his unspeakable gift." Hallelujah!

I was around eight years old when I started to write songs, poems, skits, and prayers which I would share with family, friends, and sometimes my teachers. At that time, I didn't even know that these gifts would make room for me to share with others later in life. As I grew older, my passion for writing increased, which became one of my favorite things to do. Most of all, my alone time with my Abba Father helped me to depend on Him for everything as my intimacy with Him grew closer. I never published any of that material because

Jesus Descending From The Golden Gates Of Heaven

I kept putting it off. I guess it was not the time--maybe God was preparing me for this moment, time, and season. Sometimes, we don't realize or understand God's plan for us; it is not what we want for our lives but what God wants for us. His plans are always best, perfectly designed to lead us into our destiny and divine purpose.

It is so important to LISTEN to the voice of God and not make hasty decisions without the direction of the Holy Spirit. Sometimes, we need to be SILENT and LISTEN to what God wants to speak into our hearts. God will give us the desires of our hearts, but we need to listen keenly to the visible and invisible God. The Almighty God can do the practical, the natural, and the supernatural in our lives.

Looking back, I must admit that I was guilty of making several hasty decisions that weren't in the will of God at the time. I have learned some mighty good lessons from choosing the wrong path when I was younger. I am so glad that our Heavenly Father is so loving and kind; most of all, He is so forgiving. We serve a God who is generous in grace and mercies. However, I have discovered over the years that it doesn't matter how old or young you are; even a seasoned and mature Christian can learn something new in the knowledge of God once you crucify the flesh!

Regardless of how saved or sanctified we feel as Christians, we need to walk in HUMILITY because this FLESH can put us to shame anytime and anywhere. We MUST be HUMBLE and SUBMISSIVE to the voice of God through the direction of the Holy Spirit. God's plan is the ultimate plan for us to follow, not our plans or man's. His ways and thoughts are purer and higher than ours (*see* Isaiah 55:8-9). We are weak and powerless without the direction of the Holy Spirit. Therefore, we are encouraged to worship God in Spirit and Truth as we build a mind of Christ in our daily walk.

If we follow and seek God's direction from His love letter to us, then we are walking in God's will and plan for our lives. Even when the adversary wants to tell us lies to distract us from the will and promises of God, we need to stand firm on the Word of God and believe in His promises for our lives. God had the authentic plan for our lives before we were born, sealed, and engraved in His hands (*see* Isaiah 49:15-16). God's love for us remains the same; we are continually on His mind. Isn't that amazing? It is so encouraging to know that our Heavenly Father has so much love and compassion for us and that He knows our names. **HALLELUJAH!**

The Lord also gifted me with some profound **dreams,** some I did not understand, so I always sought my mother's advice when I was younger. We would pray about seeking God's direction as we waited on God for the answer. There were times when I was left bewildered by God's greatness and His revelation in different ways, especially revelations about myself! There were changes I needed to make in my relationship to get closer to God. Even as Christians, sometimes some baggage in our lives needs to be removed so the light of Christ can shine in us.

That's why it is so important to build a stable relationship with the Holy Spirit, our Advocate, to help us stand flat-footed for God so we can serve Him wholeheartedly. We must purge ourselves of the sins that will hinder us from fulfilling our purpose in God, asking Him to search us so that He can purify our hearts, minds, bodies, and souls. The Bible tells us, *"But in a great house there are not only vessels of gold and of silver, but also of wood and of earth; and some of honour, and some of dishonour. If a man therefore purge himself from these, he shall be a vessel unto honour, sanctified, and meet for the master's use, and prepared unto every good work" (2 Timothy 2:20-21).* God is preparing us as clean vessels to be used for His glory and to honor Him! Are we willing to open our hearts for spiritual purification and purging? That should be our daily desire!

Would you like to drink clean water from a dirty cup? Oh no! Why not? Because we would be exposing ourselves to all the germs and bacteria that would enter our bodies which could cause us to have an infection, with so much pain and discomfort, making us sick. We want to drink from a clean cup to stay physically clean and healthy. So too, God wants us to be spiritually clean and ready to receive more of Him! He cannot pour new wine into old bottles. Mark 2:22 says,

"And no man putteth new wine into old bottles: else the new wine doth burst the bottles, and the wine is spilled, and the bottles will be marred: but new wine must be put into new bottles." Therefore, we should kill the flesh daily, allowing the Spirit to walk and function in holiness with the Spirit of God.

This is the Word of the Lord in the parable of the cloth and the wineskins. Our hearts must be in the right place with God so He can trust us and use us for His glory. God showed me things I had to change in my life through several dreams that I could not ignore if I wanted to be in good standing with my Abba Father. Now, my relationship with God is much better, and I am still seeking Him and depending on Him to give me the strength to carry on as I crucify this old flesh daily. I have to constantly seek Him in fasting and prayer to detox me from known and unknown sins and carnal weaknesses.

It is a wonderful experience to have different dreams, especially if you can remember them. Even though I look forward to dreaming, I am sometimes puzzled by them and choose not to tell anyone unless the Holy Spirit directs me. For years, I have been writing down most of the dreams that stood out in my memory; I would pray and let the Lord have His way.

Over the years, I have had several wonderful and happy dreams of Heaven. I also had many sad dreams of seeing people in hell crying because they were in gruesome pain, with strange voices begging for help. It was heartrending to hear the wailing cries as if no one could rescue them or release them from the impending doom and torment. Unfortunately, it seems as if it is too late, who will listen to your cry? Saints of God, the Bible tells us in 2 Peter 2:4-5, *"For if God spared not the angels that sinned, but cast them down to hell, and delivered them into chains of darkness, to be reserved unto judgment; And spared not the old world, but saved Noah the eighth person, a preacher of righteousness, bringing in the flood upon the world of the ungodly."* The Word of God tells us that God did not spare the angels who sinned; why should we think we would be spared from the wrath of God because of disobedience?

Introduction

Sadly, if we do not REPENT and live for God, we will end up in hell, where it will be too late to repent. Remember the days of Noah; the people hardened their hearts, and only eight souls were saved by the water (*see* 1 Peter 3:20). Seek Jesus now, before it is too late. The next moment, neither is tomorrow promised to anyone! NOW is the acceptable time to turn your lives to Jesus Christ, the King of Glory! We ask the question, "Where will I spend eternity?" We have two choices! Heaven or Hell. God gave man free will, but He also commanded us to seek Him first. Seeking God first will grant us access to live with Him in Heaven forever. However, if we refuse God, we'll end up in hell forever with the devil--a place of unrest, with the sadness of everlasting doom and gloom, all because we disobeyed the command and truth of God! Most of the time, I tell my family and friends about my dreams, and I have to apply them to my personal life. These dreams, however, draw me closer to God as I prepare for His return.

Of all my dreams, none stood out as much as the dream of seeing Jesus bursting out from the right side of Heaven's golden gates on February 12, 2012! Even though it has been over eleven years, I cannot forget, nor do I wish to forget, that breathtaking and supernatural encounter with Jesus, my Lord, in the Heavenly dream of a lifetime! Can you recall dreaming of Heaven or seeing Jesus Christ the Messiah bursting out of Heaven? Such a dream can be one of the most phenomenal encounters you can ever experience. A dream of Heaven is mind-blowing, astonishing, and supernatural. It can also be a profound spiritual awakening to revolutionize one's spiritual life, perception, and relationship with the Supreme God of the Universe! Either way, I think the experience is wonderful and inspiring to get closer communication and a deeper spiritual connection with the Omniscient God of the world!

The Bible tells us that HEAVEN is God's throne, His resting and dwelling place (*see* Isaiah 66:1). Some of Merriam-Webster's meanings for the word Heaven are *(a)"the dwelling place of the Deity and the blessed dead." (b)"a spiritual state of everlasting communion with God."* Here, we realized that it is God's Kingdom, the House of God, His

Jesus Descending From The Golden Gates Of Heaven

Domain, a City, a better Country, a Sabbath rest for God's people; a beautiful place where he lives and where the angels and Jesus also live; a place where we shall have everlasting communion with our Father. The Bible makes mention of all these beautiful names of God's Home, His resting place that He spoke about in His love book to us; a place that we inherit through the adoption of our Lord and Savior. This beautiful HEAVEN which we are looking forward to is beyond human comprehension and imagination. That's the promise that Jesus made to His disciples before He left Earth, and that promise is for us also, if we only believe (*see* John 14:1-5). Are you anticipating living with God in Heaven? I hope you do! **A place where there will be no pain, sickness, sorrow, or death!** Jesus said it is a place where our lowly bodies will be transformed so we can be like His glorious body, a place where we will have our eternal citizenship to live with our Father (*see* Philippians 3:20-21). Isn't that amazing? I am eagerly awaiting to be with my Lord and Savior, to live in peace with Him forever in HEAVEN.

Heaven is a real place and so is hell, these two places that Jesus talked about several times throughout his ministry here on Earth. The word 'hell' from Merriam-Webster has more than one meaning. I will refer to these: 1. *a (2):" the nether realm of the devil and demons in which condemned people suffer everlasting punishment." (2)"a place or state of misery, torment, or wickedness."(b) "a place or state of turmoil destruction, "(c) a severe scolding."* Here, we see that hell is a real place of turmoil and everlasting destruction. It is a doomed place that Jesus doesn't want us to go to and He warns us against it. Jesus spoke about the anguish and torment that you will feel in hell (*see* Luke 16:19-31). He also spoke about the unquenchable fire and worms that never die (*see* Mark 9:43-48). Jesus spoke about the weeding out of His kingdom, the blazing furnace, where there will be weeping and gnashing of teeth (*see* Matthew 13:40-43). God wants us to see, hear, and understand His words, His commandments, His precepts, and His statutes. Let us obey, so we can produce good fruits and live with our Father who is in HEAVEN.

The word HEAVEN is mentioned over **SEVEN HUNDRED** times in the Bible. God spoke about Heaven which is mentioned in over forty books from the Old and New Testament. Therefore, God wants us to know about HEAVEN and the things He has in store for us there. Things that money cannot buy such as, "the glory of God in the face of Jesus Christ" (2 Corinthians 4:6). Oh! How marvelous and glorious it will be to sit at Jesus's feet, basking in His solemn sovereignty, enjoying being in the presence of our Heavenly Father! Jesus taught His disciples, when you pray say, "Our Father, who art in HEAVEN..." (*see* Matthew 6:6-13). So, if we are talking to our Heavenly Father and praying to Him daily, why are we **uncomfortable talking about Our Abba Father's home which one day will be our PERMANENT HOME?** It is God's everlasting kingdom where all domains shall obey Him! HEAVEN should be one of our daily topics (*see* Daniel 7:27). After all, we are not going to be on this Earth forever because it is our TEMPORARY HOME. Therefore, we should start preparing for the permanent and everlasting home that Jesus went to prepare for us, which I got a glimpse of in this phenomenal encounter. Are you excited about your PERMANENT home which is in Heaven?

There were some spectacular moments throughout the dream that I continue to hold dear to my heart, which I will share in more detail in future chapters--**moments such as seeing the Heavenly glow of light that illuminates around Jesus. His powerful glory that filled the Heavens and the Earth! I continue to feel shivers of adrenaline rush through my body when I think about this supernatural encounter with my Lord.** I know many people have dreams of Heaven and speak of their Heavenly experiences in different ways. As for me, I know this is the most divine highlight of my entire life, which is unexplainable and unimaginable! However, I am so humbled and thankful to God for granting me this favor and assigning me to share it with you. Through the help of the blessed Holy Spirit, I will describe and explain the vividness of this dream in more detail which will include Heavenly scenery, different scriptures, biblical characters, and some of their life experience. Also, I will describe some of my testimonies of what the Lord would have me share through the direction of the Holy Spirit! The Holy Spirit is the Spirit of Truth to lead and guide us as we travel on this pilgrim highway to Heaven (*see* John 16:13).

In the Bible, we read of several biblical characters who had dreams in which God spoke a revelation to them in different ways. A pivotal time in their lives when they depended on God's wisdom to catapult them into their destiny assignment and propel them to their purpose. As for me, it was a time when everything seemed to be in disarray, confused and out of line. I was in a chaotic zone of many unanswered questions surrounding my life and the lives of some of my family members. Furthermore, I was experiencing some medical complications from a recent surgery. A crucial time when I least expected such a divine encounter with God my Father in this awesome dream of seeing Jesus descending from the Golden Gates.

For example, Jacob, in a dream, spoke about the house of God and the gate of Heaven! (*see* Genesis 28:10-22). It is so amazing that even when you have stones for your pillows, God will visit you in your sleep with a dream to revolutionize your life. Our God never sleeps, and He continues to minister to us through visions, dreams, and different encounters for His glory and to share with others. We don't know the answers to God's plans for our lives. However, we are happy that God chose to give us insights and assignments for this generation and future generations, just like He did several thousand years ago with many biblical heroes.

The Bible tells us that *"Jacob awaked out of his sleep, and he said, 'Surely, the Lord is in this place; and I knew it not.' And he was afraid, and said, 'How dreadful is this place! this is none other but the house of God, and this the gate of Heaven"* (Genesis 28:16-17). Now I understand a little how Jacob felt in that dream; he was shocked and afraid! How can we not feel shocked, amazed, and tremble at the awesomeness of God's power and authority even as we look around to see and experience His handiwork, seeing the sun, moon, stars, rivers, oceans, valleys, and mountains? **Most of all, the miracle and birth of babies, a channel which we all came through. The miraculous hands and**

Introduction

eyes of God are everywhere!

In the dream, I saw so many amazing things that I cannot compare to anything on Earth that can measure up to that extraordinary encounter and beauty in the presence of the Lord. Attempting to would be an injustice to God's creativity and authentic handy work. My dream was a magnificent, unforgettable revelation, a favor, and an assignment from God to share as a spoken and written testimony as directed by the Holy Spirit! My desire for you is that as you read this book the Holy Spirit will inspire you to STAND up for Jesus as you anxiously await His royal return. Also, your soul will be stirred up and come **alert to know more about God's kingdom, His dwelling** place, which is your future home.

The Bible also tells us, as spoken by Solomon, "For those who find me find life and receive favor from the Lord" (Proverbs 8:35 *NIV*). God is so amazing and chooses to grant us favor by pouring out His spirit upon all flesh, allowing the Holy Spirit to allot to us different gifts to edify the body of Christ and glorify God. I am grateful that God looked beyond my fragility and inadequacy and chose me for this wonderful assignment, and He will use you too. Solomon says, *"Wisdom brings blessings."* He says, *"Trust in the Lord with all thine heart; and lean not unto thine own understanding. In all thy ways acknowledge him, and he shall direct thy paths"(Proverb 3:5-6).* The wisdom of God will bring you eternal blessings!

Jesus Descending From The Golden Gates Of Heaven

Please, Join me in Saying This Thanksgiving Prayer!

Dearest Father in Heaven, the Great and Mighty Creator of the Universe. The maker of all good gifts around us and through us. I thank You, Father, that You are the All-Sovereign God. Today, I humbly bow before You to give You glory, honor, and praise because You are the only true King who rules and reigns forever. There is no other King before You and none after You. You are the Alpha and Omega, the Beginning and the End; hence, we worship You with every breath that we take and the mobility of every limb.

I thank You for this breath that You lend to me, oh Lord! I am forever appreciative of Your unmerited favor and love during every season of my life. Father, I am so grateful that You pulled me out, emptied me of my sadness, heartache, and pain, and filled me with your strength, joy, peace, and happiness. I thank You for the joy of placing this Heavenly dream of seeing Jesus my Lord at the Golden Gates of Heaven. Thank You, Holy Spirit, for partnering with me to remind me of every detail as seen in the dream. Your supernatural recall inspired me with wisdom, knowledge, and understanding to write this assignment as shown to me by God my Father. The Bible tells us, "We are laborers together with God: ye are God's husbandry, ye are God's building" (1 Corinthians 3:9 *KJV*). Thank You for directing and counseling me on this writing journey to put FAITH before fear as I stand firmly in the full **ARMOR OF GOD.**

Father, I thank You for every eye and hand that will see, read, and touch this book. I pray that they will be immensely blessed. To my friend who is reading this book right now, I speak blessings in every area of your life for a supernatural breakthrough as every chain is

Please, Join me in Saying This Thanksgiving Prayer!

broken in Jesus's name. I pray that the Lord will grant you the desire of your heart by His will. If they are going through some difficult season of their life, Father, my sincere desire is that their souls will be blessed. I pray and believe that **their spirits will be lifted to a measure of increased hope, joy, peace, and happiness in You.** I know You can give them peace, confidence, hope, and assurance in You if they put their faith and trust in You as their Father, that everything will be all right! I pray for a supernatural change in the dynamics of their situation from bad to good, from negative to positive, in the Mighty Name of Jesus!

I pray that they will ask You, dear Holy Spirit, to come into their heart, and live within their soul! I pray that Your divine inspiration will ignite a fire of total surrender to Your love and Your mercies in the mighty name of Jesus! They will see You, Jesus, as Number One in their life, and as they put You first everything good will be added to their lives and the lives of their loved ones. Praying that their life will line up with Your words and that they will keep their focus and their eyes upon You as they anticipate Your royal return. I thank You, oh God, that they will not be distracted by the plans of the enemy, nor will they be blindfolded by his schemes and tricks. Let their mind stay on You at all times as they grow to know more and more about You and Your love for the world! That if they believe in You, they shall not perish but live with You forever (John 3:16 *KJV*).

Jesus, I thank You that You declare in Your words that You are coming back for Your children to bring us home to that magnificent place that You are preparing for those who do Your will. Jesus, You said in the Bible that You are coming back to a church without blemish, wrinkle, or stain (*see* Ephesians 5:27 *KJV*). Thank You, Father, for preparing our hearts for Your royal return so that we will live according to Your will and ways. Father, please remove every unholiness from us as we live and separate ourselves from the distractions and sins of this world. Wash us with hyssop and purify our hearts to line up with Your Word so that we will be doers and not hearers only.

Thank You, Abba Father, for entrusting me with this Heavenly assignment, that I will stay within the path of Your leadership and guidance. Thank You for Your divine alignment to make all the crooked paths straight under the leading of the Holy Spirit. Father, I give You praise for all the destiny helpers that You send to assist and support me on this writing journey. Thank You for keeping me focused so I can stay stable to discern and see with the eyes of my heart what You want me to write in this book. My will and desire are to please You all the way! Holy Spirit, help me to write only what You want me to write, say, and present to Your people in Jesus's name. Let me focus on Your leading and Your direction that I will not add or subtract from what You appointed me to share.

Father, I thank you for increasing my faith to lean on the wisdom of the Holy Spirit as I keep my mind centered on You. Thank You for the revelation of this Heavenly Bliss, a place that you are preparing for us. Please, let our eyes of discernment stay distinct on the road that leads to salvation.

Thank You for helping us to walk this FAITH journey as we depend on You totally for daily instruction and guidance. Thank You for the open Heavens of blessings that You pour down on Your people every day. We thank You for being our Abba Father, and our God of Abundance. Dearest Father, we thank You for giving us Your only begotten Son, Jesus Christ our Lord. Jesus, we thank You that You came to save us through the shedding of Your blood on Calvary's cross. Jesus, You are the perfect gift of ETERNAL LIFE!

We love You and adore You. We give You thanks in the matchless name of Jesus, a name which is above all names! Amen.

Part I: Life Before the Dream

Chapter 1: Jesus — God's Precious Gift to Man

God said, "I will pour out my Spirit upon all flesh!" The Prophet Joel tells us about a pouring out of God's Spirit:

> *"And it shall come to pass afterward, that I will pour out my spirit upon all flesh: and your sons and your daughters shall prophesy, your old men shall dream dreams your young men shall see visions: And also, upon the servants and upon the handmaids in those days when I pour out my spirit. And I will show you wonders in the heavens, the earth, blood, fire, and pillars of smoke. The sun shall be turned into darkness, and the moon into blood, before the great and the terrible day of the Lord come. And it shall come to pass, that whosoever shall call on the name of the Lord shall be delivered: For in mount Zion and in Jerusalem shall be deliverance, as the Lord has said, and in the remnant whom the Lord shall call."*
>
> --Joel 2:28-32 *KJV*

Peter's explanation of Pentecost:

> *"But this is that which was spoken by the prophet Joel; And it came to pass in the last days, saith God, I will pour out of my Spirit upon all flesh: and your sons and your daughters shall prophesy, and your young men shall see visions and your old men shall dream dreams. And on my servants and on my handmaidens I will pour out in those days of my Spirit; they shall prophesy: And I will show you wonders in heaven above, and sign in the earth beneath; blood, and fire, and vapor of smoke: The sun shall be turned into darkness, and the moon into blood, before that great and notable day of the Lord come: And it shall come to pass, that whosoever shall call on the name of the Lord shall be saved."*
>
> --Acts 2:16-21 *KJV*

Are you aware that God is still pouring out His Spirit upon ALL flesh? Do you believe we are living in the Last Days? Are you anticipating the return of the King of Glory? The answer to those questions is, "Yes!" You may have a different answer, but if you take a good LOOK, OBSERVE, and LISTEN to all that is happening with wars and nations against nations and chaos everywhere, then you will understand that we are living in a perilous time.

God's prophecy must come to pass as told in the Bible from the beginning of time to the end of times. The Bible tells us that *"...nations shall rise against nations, and kingdom against kingdom: and there shall be famine, and pestilences, and earthquakes, in divers places" (Matthew 24:7 KJV)*. Nevertheless, we as Christians are encouraged to keep our focus on God and forget not His promises, His benefits, His grace, and His mercies towards us. He is God and He is still sitting on the throne. He is still allowing His Spirit to fall upon all flesh! WHY? Because God's love for us is unconditional; it is unwavering, unlimited, and it is everlasting. Even when we do not merit this kind of love, He still gives it to us freely. Our human mind and thinking cannot comprehend why God loves us so much, but He does because He is God Almighty and everything about Him supersedes human comprehension. Man cannot fathom the mystery and powers of God, no matter how hard we try. We cannot imagine the awesomeness of the characteristics of the Omniscient, Omnipresent, and Omnipotent God that we should love, appreciate, worship, adore, and serve every day of our lives! Paul's prayer that the love of God is appreciated." (*see* Ephesians 3:14-19).

This unselfish love that we receive from our Father above is without measure. No breath, length, depth, or height can compute or calculate the level of love from God! Such magnitude of LOVE is beyond our imagination! Not only does God love us so much, but He will allow His Spirit to fall upon ALL flesh. Can you imagine? Yet, we often show how we do not appreciate Him by disobeying His commands, His statutes, and His will. How can we experience the fullness of God's love if we continue to live in sin and refuse to repent and turn

Chapter 1: Jesus—God's Precious Gift to Man

from our wicked ways? Friends, there is a great day coming when we all must give an account of all the sins in our lives that separated us from the love of God if we do not repent. This great and mighty God who wants to dwell in our hearts so that we can be rooted and grounded in His love is so generous, patient, and kind towards us. We can only experience **the magnitude of God's power, strength,** love, and might if we give Him access to dwell within us. He wants us to have a repentant heart so our vessels can be clean so that He can pour out His Spirit upon us.

The Prophet Joel spoke of what would take place in the last days—explaining about the fullness of God and how God would pour out His Spirit upon all flesh. Even though Joel had prophesied this to happen, it is also clear that for this to happen, everyone must repent from their sins and seek God first and foremost. Joel is encouraging us that in the last days, God will judge all men after which He will heal the land and allow His Spirit to fall upon all flesh.

However, man needs to surrender, submit to God's commands, and live according to His Word. Here, we see where the Apostle Peter endorsed what was said by the Prophet Joel, reminding us to call upon the name of the Lord. The Apostle Peter repeated what Joel **prophesied centuries ago. God's prophecy MUST be fulfilled!** Even though it is in a different era, the Word of God remains active and alive for all generations. Therefore, we are encouraged to apply God's living and breathing words daily to our lives. The Word of God stands forever and will remain from everlasting to everlasting! **There is so much POWER in the name of the Lord through His Living Word for us to experience daily! There is the power to heal, save, deliver, restore, refresh, renew, revive, name it and you can claim it in the name of the Lord.**

Throughout history, the Almighty God has communicated with His children in different ways. The Bible also tells us that God will allow His Spirit to fall on ALL flesh distributing all kinds of gifts for us to use for His glory. God loves us so much that He does not show favoritism and He chose to bless us according to His will and His purpose. The Bible tells us God allows prophecy, visions, and dreams to fall on ALL flesh. He is the one who makes the decision when to bless you with these special gifts. We just need to be prepared to use these gifts to encourage each other and to glorify God as they are allotted to us. **God is the Chief Executive Officer (CEO) in the universe, and He is the head of our physical and spiritual credit account.** Hence, He has the authority to make all the decisions in our lives according to the plan He has for us. **He got all access to our wealth, gifts, talents, and life achievements before we knew of them or even attained them.** Therefore, all the credits that we obtain and receive in life really belong to God, but He gave us access to utilize and occupy until He comes.

My friend, remember, whatever plan God has for our lives is always a good plan because, in the end, all credited glory goes back to Him, none other but the Almighty God who owns everything! The CEO of our lives is none other than God, our Father! He regulates and delegates our daily lives using His plan according to His order and whatever way He chooses! That's why it is important to put Him first in our daily agenda. We should not hesitate to do so because **He has the Master Plan and the Master Key to open and close the different DOORS of our destiny and our purpose. God is the Chief Magistrate in the Courts of Heaven and Earth with final jurisdiction, verdict, decision and authority.**

The Word of God tells us on several occasions how God talks to His people through **dreams.** God's Word continues to be alive, active, and effective in the life of man day after day. There are many Bible characters who have received messages from God through dreams and visions, and with the direction of God, they were commanded and inspired to fulfill God's assignment for His glory. Let the Spirit of God lead you to your destiny and your purpose in the things of God as you use your gift for His glory. We should continue to seek God in prayer and hope that the lens in the eyes of our heart will stay focused on the light of Emanuel, **"God is with us."** He will never leave you destitute nor forsake you in times of trouble or need.

Chapter 1: Jesus—God's Precious Gift to Man

It is time to focus on availing yourself of the possibility of God's plan in your life; take on the responsibility in faith and God will work out the impossibility. God can exceed all that we think of for our life, and He will do the absolutes abundantly if you exercise the power of **Faith** over the spirit of Fear. The Apostle Paul reminds us in *Ephesians 3:20-21, "Now unto him, that is able to do exceeding abundantly above all that we ask or think, according to the power that worketh in us, Unto him be glory in the church by Christ Jesus throughout all ages, world without end. Amen."* This is the word of the Living God, and we are standing on His promises until He returns that He can do the abundant and the impossible in us! **We are all servants of God and are called to serve Him in holiness and righteousness through our faith and belief in Him.**

There is an **assignment** from God for you to tap into. It may be a vision, a dream, a gift, a talent, an aspiration, or a prophecy that was spoken over your life. Whatever it is, remember, God is still pouring out His Spirit on ALL flesh, and the Holy Spirit continues to distribute gifts to all of God's children! You are a member of God's wonderful family with destiny's purpose knocking at your door, waiting to be let in the plan that God has for you before you were born! TAP INTO IT TODAY!

Will you avail yourself of the assignment, plan, or purpose of God for your life?

There are times when we are so busy, we cannot identify or hear the voice of our Savior! Be silent so that you can listen to the keen voice of God as you sit around the conference table directed by God, as He sets out His plan for your life! It may be a dream or a vision that can become a reality because God said so at that specific moment! God started the work, and He will finish it until the day He returns (*see* Philippians 1:6).

Sometimes, we may not know the answer to a particular assignment idea or a dream at a given time, but God knows how to prepare His children to fulfill His plans for His glory. For instance, Joseph had wonderful dreams which he shared with his father and his brothers. However, his brothers were jealous of him; they hated him so much and did not believe him. They mocked and teased him, called him a dreamer, saying that they would not bow to him. They envied and despised Joseph with such intent that they planned to get rid of him, and they did so in a cruel and evil way. They lied to their father that Joseph was dead, which grieved their father deeply for many years. How could they live with such guilt and hatred for so many years? The heart of man can be desperately wicked even against his own brother. Living in the flesh will drive you into sin's poisonous highway which will lead you to destruction. The Bible tells us, *"The heart is deceitful above all things, and desperately wicked: who can know it?"* (Jeremiah 17:9 *KJV*). Joseph's father was sad and cried for several years, mourning the loss of his most beloved son when he was told that Joseph was dead (*see* Genesis 37-50). How can your very own children be so cruel? They did this evil act against their brother, and they didn't care that they broke their father's heart for so many years.

This kind of hatred, wicked desire, and jealousy is still happening in our world today, but we need to keep our focus on the Omniscient God to change our hearts. We will make the necessary sacrifice to stand on the solid rock of Jesus, so we can get our hearts in the right place as we feed and connect with the word of God every moment. We are talking about the spiritual heart that needs spiritual food to sustain it, so we fall not into sin. Psalm 119: 11 reminds us, *"Thy word have I hid in my heart, that I might not sin against thee."*

Joseph's relationship with his father came forcefully to a pause because of the evil plot set up by his brothers, but that's not the end of his story. God's plan for our lives stands forever, no matter who tries to stop it. God will always come through for us, and He is always on time. We need to have confidence, trust, and believe in God that He is faithful, and He will never abandon us at any time. Even when we are going through a storm, He will steady the boat and speak peace and calm to the sea. The great and mighty God who walks on

Chapter 1: Jesus—God's Precious Gift to Man

the water is our Jehovah Mephalti. He is our Deliverer! He is our solid Rock, our Fortress, our Foundation, He is our Daniel God. He will deliver!

Joseph's earthly father thought he was dead, but his Heavenly Father kept Joseph and Joseph's dream alive. God is doing the same for us today. Keep on trusting the Omnipotent God! He is keeping us and our dreams alive when others may think we are dead. **He is preparing your heart to get you ready for His plan, purpose, and assignment! Don't worry when you are experiencing wilderness separation, rejection, and setbacks.** There were many patriots before us who had those experiences and disappointments, but God delivered them out of them all! God is up to something great in you, and sometimes He wants to set you aside to prepare you for His kingdom assignments.

It is through your trials and tribulations that you can travail and triumph on the finishing line leading to glory! Can you study and prepare for a test or an exam in a noisy environment? The answer may be yes or no! I know I cannot focus if there is too much noise and distractions around me. For example, I love to read, write, and meditate, and I can do so sometimes anywhere. However, I will center my thoughts, ideas, and attention on a project so much better if I am alone in a quiet place, especially if it is an assignment from God. Sometimes, we need that alone time with our Savior and He knows what is best for us, so let Him lead as we follow His lead and His direction.

Furthermore, there will be times when God chooses to separate us from the noisy distractions so He can get our full attention. Remember, He has the final say as to where He wants us to be at a certain time in our lives; just keep on trusting God. He will and always makes a way! He plans our lives daily, so we don't make bad decisions and crazy mistakes. Even when we have a mother and father around, sometimes they cannot help us out of certain situations; but God will. Our parents can't always help us because they too depend on God for direction and guidance. God is our Abba

Father, and He will always be with us, even when we are going the wrong way. He will turn us around and lead us on the path of righteousness. That's why we need to put complete trust in God, believe in Him, and stand on His promises. **We cannot believe in man who has only natural power; we must believe in God who has the natural and supernatural power to save us above and beyond human imagination.**

We are so fortunate to have a Father who has the power to fix, change, and create the chemistry of the Heavens and the Earth and everything beneath the Earth, and the power to change every and anything in our mundane life also! Just stay focused on God and do not be derailed or get distracted by the adversary! The adversary has been around for so many centuries and he has been trying to kill, steal, and destroy humans, and he will never get tired of what he is doing! **Be alert and vigilant; the devil is busy hanging around the corner trying to destroy you and your family, telling God of sins that you already asked forgiveness for. The devil is a sly, cunning old liar who is always busy planning how to kill you, your loved ones and your dreams! But, in the Mighty Name of Jesus, we crush his head under our feet, and he is powerless and trembling at the POWER of Jesus!**

Friends, the enemy was busy then and he is still busy trying to destroy and kill us now. He will use our closest family members to do his bidding to attack and derail us. The adversary will use our spouses, friends, coworkers, and others we may never know or meet to destroy us. That's why it is of paramount importance that we put on the Full Armor of God daily, reminding ourselves that it is not our mommy, daddy, sister, brother, aunt, uncle, or neighbor who is fighting against us. It is the different spirit of principalities and power that is floating and roaming around in the atmosphere seeking to come at you through your loved ones! The Bible tells us, *"For we wrestle not against flesh and blood, but against principalities, against powers, against the rulers of the darkness of this world, against spiritual wickedness in high places" (Ephesians 6:12 KJV).*

Chapter 1: Jesus—God's Precious Gift to Man

We must keep the eyes of our hearts open and the lens of our understanding alert to know and see the attack of the adversary coming from the four corners of the Earth. We need to fully depend on the strength and guidance of God Almighty to face each day. **Now is not the time to be weary or weak on this Christian journey. We MUST be fully clothed every moment of the day and all through the night.** We should be ready and waiting in the army of the Lord so we can be spiritually equipped and prepared to fight against every attack coming from the enemies. We must be spiritually alert, bold, oriented, and fully prepared and ready to always punch the enemy in the face so he can flee from us. How can we do that? By clothing ourselves in the righteousness of God, so that even when we are in the fire we will not get burned because we are in the protection of the Omnipotent God of the Universe.

We cannot stop the tests of time, with trials, wars, chaos, and tribulations in this world that are coming at us from every direction because we are living in a world that is full of sins and sorrows. Nonetheless, we have all the army gear to fight off the attack of the enemy. Most of all, we have Jesus, the Warrior of all warriors, who never lost a battle! We just need to call the name of JESUS and all weapons of mass destruction coming from the enemy will fall down. They MUST come down in the Name of Jesus! There's so much power in the BLOOD of Jesus to set us free from all harm and danger. Isaiah 54:17 tells us, *"No weapon that is formed against us shall prosper; and every tongue that shall rise against thee in judgment thou shalt condemn. This is the heritage of the servants of the LORD, and their righteousness is of me, saith the LORD."* The WORD of God is our weapon; use it with power and authority in the Name of JESUS!

Our Shepherd will protect us from every fiery dart of the avenger coming from every direction so we can fulfill our purpose in life. Jesus saved the three Hebrew men, Shadrach, Meshach, and Abednego, who did not bow down to King Nebuchadnezzar's image, so too will He save us (*see* Daniel Chapter 3). Jesus is protecting us from the seen and the unseen arrows coming from the enemy to kill us and our dreams! These young men stood up for Jesus whom they believed to be the only true King. Jesus not only saved them, but He was the fourth man in the furnace which was seven times hotter than the usual heat. There's no power that is greater than the **DYNAMITE POWER** of the Almighty God who is the ONLY GOD of the cosmos world! He controls the world and every living thing with his PLAN in the palm of his MIGHTY HANDS! His name is JESUS! The Son of the Living God who has ALL the answers to man's questions.

God's plan for our life is for us to prosper and our God is not slack concerning His promises! His word stands forever, and that is why it's important to stand on the promises of the True and Living God. Therefore, whenever God commands you to do His work or give you an assignment, do not hesitate or question God concerning what He wants you to do. Remember, He is the one who selects, anoints, appoints, and favors you to complete His will through you for His glory. We have to seek Him in prayer, fasting, reading, and meditating on His words with confidence that He will guide us through to the finish line. We will face some roadblocks and obstacles but press on in FAITH, believing in the God of Abraham, Isaac, and Jacob. Prayer is the key to unlocking the doors and windows of Heaven to release the answer to our breakthrough. The Bible says, "Pray without ceasing" (1 Thessalonians 5:17 *KJV*). That doesn't mean you will be on your knees all day and all night. Instead, you should have such a prayer life in which you are communicating with God constantly, that you should not hesitate to pray to Him anywhere and anytime. I could be talking with you and also whispering a prayer to God. He hears us and He understands what's in our thoughts and our hearts.

Paul wants us to have such a relationship with God that we should not worry about anything but tell God everything (*see* Phil 4). The more you practice doing anything, the more it becomes easier and a part of your daily living. Keep on praying; God will make a way and provide all the tools needed according to His plan for your life. TRUST GOD! Breakthrough is just around the corner!

God will not give you a vision without maximum provision and a

Chapter 1: Jesus—God's Precious Gift to Man

destiny position to complete what He starts in you. So many biblical warriors and heroes were faced with adversities and obscurity on their mission field for God. However, they never gave up; they depended on the STRENGTH of God to see them through the wars, the fights, and the setbacks. **Through their unfailing faith, they persevered and held on to the hands of God to the end.** Now, they are rewarded with the Heavenly inheritance in the Kingdom of Heaven! **God's plan for us never ends; He will always complete what He starts in us and take us to the perfect end in His own time because He is the Alpha and Omega, the Beginning and the End** (*see* **Revelation 1:8). Therefore, He will complete the work He starts with us.**

Joseph's brothers planned to eliminate him from the circle of the Earth through envy and jealousy. Their plan failed and it was short-lived because God had a plan for Joseph's life that no man could alter, not even his brothers. Friends, remember that God has a plan for your life too! No matter what you are experiencing or going through, don't forget that God is bigger than the mountains that are distracting you. These cruel brothers thought they had got rid of Joseph forever, but God protected him so that he could fulfill the assignment that was set before him. Joseph survived by the grace of God. He suffered some trials and tribulations at the hands of his brothers and the lies that Potiphar's wife told against him. Yes! He suffered for several years in prison; he had two years of famine but seven years of plenty before he saw his brothers again. Joseph had not seen his brothers for over twenty years (*see* Genesis 37-43).

I believe during that time, God was softening Joseph's heart towards his brothers so he could forgive them for all the wrong they had done to him. His brothers planned his death, but God planned to prosper him and favor his life so he could feed his enemies. **Joseph was thrown into a pit, then he experienced several years in prison but he was promoted to a palace.** God was still with him in prison, preparing him for the journey ahead just like He is with you. God's favor and anointing were upon Joseph, not only to dream dreams but he was called to interpret a dream for the King (*see* Genesis 41).

Shortly thereafter, he was made ruler of the Palace in Egypt. Joseph experienced severe abuse and challenges on his journey, which was painful and debilitating. However, he refused to succumb to the situation, and he endured relentlessly through faith to the end.

Joseph was rejected and laughed at by his brothers, but he held on to the promises of God and stepped out in faith with a forgiving heart. The gift of having dreams and the Holy Spirit guided him to interpret **the King's dream propelled Joseph to walk and excel in the plan and calling of God in his life. You may be a JOSEPH today! I want to remind you that God's plan for your life stands forever! Hold on! God** can change our messy life into a life of blessings, not only for us but also that others may be encouraged by our lives and testimonies. God will choose to prepare a table before you in the presence of your enemies. Also, He can anoint you until your cup runs over, and it should be all to His glory (*see* Psalm 23). Such a mighty and considerate God whose love for us failed not.

God has gifts and assignments for all His children to fulfill and that's why it is important to trust in the plan of God over our lives and not the plan of man. Do not be upset or angry as you go through the different seasons of your life. Remember, it is a process and God will see you through the unpaved road, the hills, and the valleys, because He will strengthen and restore you along the rugged side of the mountain. Do not forget that the hands of God are on you to protect you and propel you into your destiny so you can accomplish what He already started in your life!

The Bible tells us in Genesis 37 about Joseph's dream, and how he was excited to share his dream with his brothers. However, they hated him and did not believe him. In the long run, Joseph's dream came true, and his brothers bowed down to him. Joseph forgave them and gave them plenty of food supply and even gave them back the money they had used to pay for the food! He showed them love even though it was painful to do so at first. God's power allowed him to have a forgiving heart towards his brothers; it was a heart that held no animosity or grudges. We can only be free when we learn to

FORGIVE through the strength and power of God! Our great and Mighty God will remove the bitterness to make us a better person for His glory as He prepares us for His Kingdom. Only a strong relationship with God can bring us to such spiritual maturity of forgiveness!

Today, if you are experiencing rejection of any sort from anyone, remember God will always love you, and He cares for you. He will not forsake you! Psalm 27:10 tells us, *"When my mother and my father forsake me, then the Lord will take me up."* The Lord is always there to deliver us and set us free, even if we are rejected or abandoned by our biological family. Don't give up; try not to hate anyone or hold any grudge! Leave all vengeance to God. Let Him take full charge of the battles because they are bigger than us and God is bigger than all the battles put together! Your family and friends don't define your life; neither did they die on the cross to wash away your sins. Therefore, put your life in the hands of God, the one who can save you, restore you and revive you. He is the only one who can give you eternal life! Let the Holy Spirit lead and guide you because we are in a spiritual battle that we dare not fight alone! **We can only win these fights by leaning on the strength of God, totally depending on the only Mighty and Powerful Warrior, who is Christ the Lord.**

The Bible tells us of *"The Mighty Warrior."* It says, *"The Lord thy God in the midst of thee is mighty; he will save, he will rejoice over thee with joy, he will rest in his love, he will joy over thee with singing"* (Zephaniah 3:17 KJV). God's love is unfailing and knows no boundary. For that reason, my friend, rest in the joy of the Lord; you are not alone! He is the Warrior of all Warriors, and He is constantly fighting our battles, seen and unseen, as He continues to pour out His Spirit upon all His children!

Now, we see where Joel, the Prophet, is explaining how God will pour out His Spirit upon all flesh, allowing His children to prophesy, old men to dream dreams, and young men to have visions, He will also pour out His Spirit upon the servants and the handmaids. **No matter what role you hold in life, from being a King to being a**

handmaid, never think you are not precious in the sight of God. We are God's MASTERPIECE, made straight from His authentic blueprint created by the Potter's Hands. We are not cloned, copied, imitated, or duplicated! Isn't that a wonderful thing to know that we are all unique, created in the marvelous image of God with a great plan and a purpose for our lives? Therefore, when God makes promises to us, He never lies, and He cannot lie. He will come through to the end and He will honor His words. We are all born with a special gift that we can use for the glory of God and He desires us to use it to edify others and build His Kingdom.

I encourage you today to find your gift and ask the Holy Spirit to guide you on your journey. Seek the knowledge, wisdom, and understanding of God and how to excel in your gift for the glory of God. Saints of God, be encouraged that the Spirit of God is also upon you to reveal His power over your life in many different ways. **Make God your priority and allow Him to lead and guide you through this puzzled and chaotic world.** We are standing on God's Word which is the breath of the Omniscient God to blow peace to the storm we are facing, so you will never drown in the raging dark sea.

Sometimes, you will go through the fire, but you will never get burned nor look dusty with ashes, nor will you smell of smoke. It's a Hallelujah praise right there! For instance, **when you see what God has done for you and you are still alive, you can testify of God's goodness, grace, and mercies. It is a time in our lives when we should glorify and honor this loving God who is our Father.** I am still here to tell the story of how Jesus brought me out from the FIRE, and I did not get burned because He is the fourth Man in the fire! You can't help but sing praises to God for His goodness, His grace, and His mercies. Such a loving and compassionate Father! He is our Deliverer and the giver of all good gifts around us!

Let Us Pray, Thanking God for the Outpouring of His Spirit!

Dear Heavenly Father, the Creator of the Universe and everything in and around us. We give You all the glory, honor, and praise for who You are in our lives. Father, You are the great giver of life, health, strength, and our daily food. Abba Father, You continue to supply ALL our needs according to Your riches in glory. We worship and adore You, Great and Mighty God!

Father, we thank You for allowing Your Spirit to fall upon ALL flesh. Please help us to be grateful to You and to use these wonderful gifts to Your honor and Your glory. Abba Father, we appreciate every gift that You placed into our lives. We promise that we will not abuse it because of our selfish thoughts, ideas, desires, or pride. Father, help us to crucify the flesh so we can fulfill the calling that You placed in our lives as we try to live a life that will measure up to Your will, statute, and command. Father, help us to exercise the fruits of the Spirit in every area of our lives as seen in Galatians 5. Holy Spirit, we thank You that You will guide us into the knowledge of truth and that we will not frustrate You at any time. Help us to be obedient to Your Lordship as we honor You every day with a repentant heart.

We acknowledge that You are the Great and Mighty God who will show wonders in Heaven and also on Earth at any time. Therefore, we will continue to seek You with the eyes of our hearts to live a life that will line up daily with Your word. Father, You are the Great and Almighty God that can change the moon, the sun, and the stars to whatever size and shape You want them to be. You can move mountains and make them plain and change the shape of the valleys, land, and sea because You are the God of the mountains, hills, and valleys. Your greatness is dynamic, forceful, and ever so strong! There is no other God like You and none can compare to Your Righteousness and Your Holiness. **We seek You first and place You as the only true God and Creator of Heaven and Earth whom we will serve with all our heart, mind, body, and soul until eternity comes! Father, we are forever grateful for the gift of life, and the amazing breath that You blew into us, and now we are living souls.**

Holy Spirit, thank You for teaching us to walk in the Spirit of Truth, righteousness, and holiness. I pray that we will stand in humility as we share these gifts that You chose to place in our lives. Father, we are committed to fulfilling every task and assignment that You placed before us by the direction of the Holy Spirit. We are forever grateful to the Holy Spirit for playing a partnership role in our lives. We will depend upon Your wisdom to take full control of every step we make in the path of righteousness as we encourage others with the gifts that You placed into our lives.

Father, again we thank You for Your Son Jesus Christ, such precious gifts that You placed into our lives to set us free. Jesus, we love and adore You for standing in the gap for our salvation, giving us access to the throne of grace, so we can live forevermore with Thee. Most of all, we are grateful to be called Kingdom Kids as we are joint heirs with You Sweet Jesus.

Abba Father, we give You all the glory, honor, and praise in Jesus' Holy Name.

Amen!

Chapter 2: Growing Up in Jamaica with a Praying and Virtuous Mother

"Who can find a virtuous woman? For her price is far above rubies. Strength and honor are her clothing; she shall rejoice in time to come. She openeth her mouth with wisdom, and in her tongue is the law of kindness. She looked well to the ways of her household, and eateth not the bread of idleness. Her children arise up and call her blessed; her husband also and he praises her. Many daughters have done virtuously, but thou excellest them all. Favor is deceitful, and beauty is vain: but a woman that feareth the Lord, she shall be praised. Give her of the fruit of her hands; let her own works praise her in the gates."

--Proverb 31:10, 25-31 *KJV*

I join with King Lemuel as he describes a virtuous woman because my mother exemplifies so many of these wonderful qualities. She was a stern disciplinarian but was a devoted and loving mother, a mother who feared and loved the Lord with all her heart and wished the best for everyone. Today, the rich fruit of her legacy of wisdom lives on in this generation and in the generations to come. There are days now when I can still hear her sweet voice calling me to daily devotions as we sang beautiful and lively choruses, shared favorite scriptures, and enjoyed the blessings of the Lord. These are precious moments that take me back to much younger days with my siblings, family, and friends and Mom's sweet voice saying:

"Where are you going, Palma?"

"To play before the sun goes down."

"Okay! Remember that you have some work to do!"

I can hear my mother's sweet but commanding voice as I rush down the garden to play with my siblings and cousins.

"Yes, Mom!"

The hot sunshine spread several unique shadows beside me as I skipped my way past my neighbor's fruit trees and their beautiful flower garden. I could see the rays of sunshine around me as I twirled around, enjoying the unique but different shapes my shadow took on as I hopped from one leg to the other in the evening sun. This was one fun thing that I enjoyed doing on my own as well as with others: playing with my shadow in the bright and hot sunshine on the beautiful Island of paradise. I would twirl until I fell and lay on the ground, trying my best to gaze into the rays of the sunlight! So much fun playing in the evening sun which was bright but cooler than the midday hot temperature.

Finally, I reached where three of my brothers, one of my sisters, and two of my cousins were playing all kinds of games. I immediately joined in the fun, making use of the sunshine before the sun went down at around seven thirty p.m. This gave me about two hours to play outdoors. I remember looking forward to this kind of recreation almost every evening, especially when our parents would join in and play games with us. Most of the time, we ended the evening eating different kinds of fruits, and delicious roasted corn while our parents would tell us stories under the beautiful moon and shining stars!

So, you asked the question, eh? Where am I from? I am from the ever-so-beautiful Island of Jamaica. (With nuff, nuff love! Yes, man!) I am the fourth of seven children. Even though my biological father was living in England, we still managed to maintain a wonderful relationship. When I was twelve, he passed away from a sudden heart attack. This left me severely sad and devastated for a long time. I was heartbroken for years because I had met my dad twice for six weeks each time when he came home to visit us. He was actually on his way

Chapter 2: Growing Up in Jamaica with a Praying and Virtuous Mother

home to Jamaica when he experienced a massive heart attack on his way to the airport in England and died. I thought I couldn't make it after he passed away, but Jehovah Shalom, "The Lord Is Our Peace." He gave me the peace and strength to keep my faith alive, and I had a good support system. **God knew how to give us peace and comfort us during the storm; no matter where you are or how old you are, Jesus is our Rock, and He is our PEACE.**

I was living with my mother and my stepdad who has played a vital father role in my life since I was the age of five. My parents and six of my siblings, my maternal grandmother, along with two of my cousins all lived together in one family house. We weren't rich, but we had enough to meet our basic human needs and because we were very happy we never thought we were poor either! We had a strong family unit and bond that kept our love for each other to stand firm in faith for the good times and the not-so-good times. Mother would remind us to give God thanks for what we have, and that we should be content and be appreciative for all our blessings. Praise and worship were one of our daily late evening activities that we looked forward to with great anticipation. We continue giving praise to Jehovah-Jireh for supplying our everyday needs. Since my stepfather played different kinds of instruments, we were pretty much a musically inclined family, enjoying each other's gifts and talents whenever we got a chance to have our concert at home.

We were a close-knit family that found pleasure in embracing each other in different areas of achievement, failure, and loss. My stepfather was a great farmer; everything he laid his hands on seemed to flourish and produce bountifully. He took much pride in his farming and never hesitated to give his best crop to the church harvest, family, and friends. We always had enough for three meals a day and enough to share with others. We were ever so happy just having so much fun with our siblings, cousins, and a host of other relatives and friends who visited us quite often! We had so much pleasure enjoying all the beautiful scenery and wonderful nature that we were surrounded by.

Most of our days we would spend outdoors after school, also visiting family and friends, and attending different church functions in our neighborhood. We looked forward to some amazing scenic sights and trips to various beaches, lots of music, and different types of entertainment all year round! There were times when we had lots of rain and stormy weather, but most of the year the sun was always shining.

My mother was a seamstress and a stay-at-home mom. She made sure that we had devotion every morning and at night, along with other recreational activities. Each night before we went to bed, we would join our hearts together in singing several songs, reciting different poems, and reading different scriptures. My mother, who was always in a choir and loved to sing, kept on teaching us new and lively songs. My stepfather loved music and would often play his mouth organ and his handmade drums.

Our extended family would come together almost every holiday for family celebrations where we would have so much fun listening to each other reciting poems, scripture reading, dancing, singing, cooking, and baking. My mother made sure we showed love and respect to each other at these family gatherings. We looked forward to these special times with eagerness and anticipation to enjoy each other's performance together as we didn't have a television set at that time. Mom was a no-nonsense mother, but she had a heart of gold and she loved us and she loved the Lord wholeheartedly. She was also a mother to two of my cousins, which was more like a sister and brother-relationship to us. She made sure we stayed on top of household chores, homework, and our relationship with God. She would ask us on several occasions, "Did you talk with the Lord today? Did you read your Bible?" to which, she wanted us to tell the truth with a yes or no mom! She was always praying for each of us, calling out our names one by one to God.

A great prayer warrior indeed who never hesitated to pray for anyone, anytime, and anywhere. She was always praying for our soul salvation and for the protection of God to be with us everywhere we

Chapter 2: Growing Up in Jamaica with a Praying and Virtuous Mother

traveled. My mother always prayed some of her favorite Psalms which would be 1, 23, 24, 27, 91, 100, 119, 121, and several other scriptures over our lives. As I grew older and more mature in my spiritual relationship with the Lord, I realized that she was practicing what the Bible tells us to do in 1 Thessalonians 5:17, "Pray without ceasing." I realized that that's the only way to connect and communicate with our Heavenly Father and it is necessary. We need to be committed and persistent in praying to God our Father and through His Son, Jesus Christ.

My maternal grandmother, who we called Mumma, loved us dearly and always came to our rescue when we got in trouble. She spoiled us with gifts and enjoyed telling us stories of our forefathers. She was a mighty prayer warrior also and she would pray over all of us every moment she got. At that time, I used to wonder why she was praying for our safety and protection so much. As I grew older and became a mother and a grandmother, I realized those prayers were so necessary then as well as now. I found myself doing the same to my family and those set under my care. I am so happy my mother and grandmother planted those seeds of prayers over our lives. They were planting the building blocks of keys to the kingdom connection! They were always speaking positive words of encouragement over us and also to all the neighborhood children who would come to our home to visit or play.

Even though we were not rich in material things, I can say we were rich with so much love and affection towards each other. Neither did we have a perfect family, but my mother worked hard to maintain that model among us. As I grew older, I realized that Love and Unity were ordained by God for every family that stands together in one accord. I wish for UNITY among every generation of Father Abraham who, because of his trust, belief, and FAITH in God, was called righteous. We need to live right in the eyes of God. Every family should seek to please God and believe in the God of Peace, even when it seems impossible, we must try to seek after PEACE.

The Bible tells us, *"And he believeth in the Lord; and he counted it to him for righteousness"* (Genesis 15:6 KJV). This family tree would not be complete without the seeds of love that are sewn together with the truth to fight against disunity. We stand firm and flatfoot in the circle of God's compass, knowing that if God is in the midst, our faith will grow stronger and we will get wiser in the knowledge of God. **Together we are standing taller, stronger, wiser, and more determined to keep on fighting the fight of FAITH so the legacy of love lives on as we journey towards the Kingdom of Heaven.**

My mom and my maternal grandmother were my biggest role models in the Christian world. They taught me how to live an upright and Godly life. My mother loved and feared God so much she worked at being steadfast in her relationship with God. Even when she was extremely sick, she kept on singing and worshiping the Lord through the pain and suffering, encouraging us to live for Jesus. She reminded us that the Lord is our PROVIDER, and He will never leave us alone, that God will supply all our needs, just like He did for our Father Abraham.

There were times when my mother would look around and meditate on the wondrous and majestic handy work of God, shouting thanks to God our Father! She would always talk about the great architectural and authentic work of God with a deep admiration of the beauty that surrounds us, admiring and accepting how God beautifies the Universe in such a unique way and it is the same way He made us beautiful! I can remember the first time she came to visit us in Connecticut in April of 1997. One morning we woke up to several inches of snow and boy! Oh boy! She was rejoicing about the wonders of God! My mom stood by the window, and she was praising God so much and admiring the outline and formation of the snow on the buildings, cars, and most of all the trees. She lived the scripture that says *"Let everything that has breath praise the Lord. Praise the Lord"* (Psalm 150:6 KJV).

My mother never hesitated to tell us to love the Lord, put Him first and praise Him for His goodness, grace, and mercies. She would tell

Chapter 2: Growing Up in Jamaica with a Praying and Virtuous Mother

us on several occasions that **"No matter how rich you get in life, never forget to give your best to the Lord,"** always telling us about the parable of "The Rich Man and the Poor Man (Lazarus)" (*see* Luke 16:19-31 *KJV*). She would remind us that whatever stage we are in life, rich or poor, we must always put GOD FIRST, and we should not hesitate to help others! She encouraged us to read the Bible and share it with the world so we can build the Kingdom of God.

It is important to teach our children about the love of God because it stays with them. As I grew older, I realized those stories stayed with me. I learned to appreciate my mother more for sharing those wonderful Bible stories and teaching us those beautiful songs. My mother demonstrated her role as a strong faith-believing dedicated Christian very well. With dignity and fortitude, she taught us well and left a legacy that having a good relationship with God is the most important decision in your life. A legacy I can now pass on to my daughter, grandchildren, and others while applying it to my life.

My mother instilled in all of us to fear God, saying, *"The fear of the Lord is the beginning of wisdom, and the knowledge of the Holy One is understanding"* (Proverbs 9:10 *KJV*). She reminded us several times, "When you think you can fool others, you cannot fool God," encouraging us daily not to put our trust in man but to trust and believe in the Creator of Heaven and Earth, telling us that God has all the wisdom of the world packed away in the Bible, so read His Word and get wise about the mysteries of God (*see* Proverbs 9:8-12).

Sometimes, I am faced with different challenges, and I need to make major decisions or choices in life. I can still remember my mother saying, "Wisdom comes from God. Seek God first in every area of your life and He will lead you in the right direction." From an early age, we all attended the Bethel Mennonite Church, in Manchester, Jamaica where I was baptized at age ten. We were taught biblical principles that groomed and challenged us to live a life that was pleasing to God, the truth of Loving God with all your heart, soul, and mind, and love and care for each other. We were taught to seek

God in everything to make wise decisions and to stay away from the adversary, so we won't make foolish decisions. The topic of LOVE was often preached on, along with several teachings of "The Fruit of The Spirit." We were also taught to obey the commandments, the precepts, and the statutes of God. Also, the life and teachings of Jesus and what we should exercise in our Christian life. I enjoyed my Mennonite school and church life to the max with other family and friends who attended both the school and church during my middle and late childhood. Some of those years were really testing but the Word of God kept me going in faith believing that God is the ONLY way to peace, joy, and happiness.

The Bible talks about the two greatest commandments! (*see* Matthew 22:36-40). As I discovered my newfound love for the Lord, I realized I had many more challenges to face daily. However, I had faith that God was always watching over me and that He would guide me through this big and confused world. God will do the same for you and your family. I joined with some of the other teens and shared different testimonies, which helped us to be more open and learn to pray for each other.

In my early teenage years, I would fast and pray, asking God to reveal things to me in my dreams so I could get a better understanding. God began to show me things in my dreams, and oftentimes, I could not keep them to myself, because I yearned for answers. Sometimes, I would share those dreams with my mother who always prayed with me or encouraged me to wait on the Lord for an answer. She encouraged me that the Lord would make it clear to me when He chose to. The Holy Spirit inspired me to make note of these dreams which I was having more frequently and they were more vivid. I thank God for the gift of dreaming and continue to write down my dreams as I follow the lead of the Holy Spirit if I should share a particular dream or pray and let God have his way.

Over the years, I started to connect the dreams to my life and there were some amazing things that I would see or experience in these dreams. Throughout my adult life, some of these dreams have drawn me closer to God because of some of the revelations that my family or I would experience resulting from those dreams. I can credit some of my spiritual growth and maturity to some wonderful dreams that I have had over the years which pushed me to read and study the Word of God more for His divine revelation. Each day, I kept falling more in love with this great and mighty God, **the Creator of man and this beautiful Universe.** It was during those times that I sought the wisdom of God and depended on the Holy Spirit to direct me as to what to do. Most of the time, I would pray and just think about the goodness of God and the different ways He communicates with His children through visions and dreams.

God is infinite and awesome in power and majesty! He knows how to satisfy the desire of our hearts in every way possible and His truth stands forever. Our God wants us to build a stable relationship with Him, depend on Him, and worship Him in Spirit and in Truth. How do we get close to the one who created us in His likeness? We should read His Word and obey His commands, His precepts, and His statutes and apply them to our lives! If we can listen and obey our earthly father, then we must listen and obey our Heavenly Father who gives us everlasting life! **Reading, praying, fasting, meditating, and obeying God are ways in which we are getting spiritually equipped as we prepare to meet our Savior, who is coming back for a prepared church!** Do you want eternal salvation with Christ the King? Seek Him now, for deliverance and life eternal He brings! He is the only King who rules and reigns forever and He is coming back for His children that are ready and prepared to meet Him!

Jesus Descending From The Golden Gates Of Heaven

Prayer of Thanks for Caring Hearts!

Eternal Father of Heaven and Earth and everything in and under the Earth, we give thee thanks for Your loving and compassionate kindness to us. We glorify Your beautiful and matchless name; a name above all names; a name to which angels bow down and worship; a name that makes demons tremble and flee. Such a marvelous and beautiful name! You, O Lord, are worthy to be praised. Your Word tells us that we should love You with all our hearts, all our souls, and all our minds. Help us to be truthful to Your Word and Your commandments as we live according to Your will and Your way! Dearest Father in Heaven, I give You thanks for the gift of Your Son, Jesus Christ. Jesus, we thank You for the gift of life through Your birth, death, resurrection, and ascension. Now, we gain access to the Kingdom of Heaven if we trust and believe in You always.

Abba Father, we thank You for Your marvelous love and faithfulness to us each day. Today, I give You thanks for life and for all the wonderful people that You send to be the village helpers in our physical and spiritual growth so we can fulfill our destiny and purpose. Dearest Father, we thank You for the mothers and fathers that You placed in our lives and the important role they play throughout our lives. We thank You for spiritual parents near and far that You will bless them abundantly. Father, we thank You that we are a part of this big family of God.

Father, we thank You for the villages all over the world that take the time out to raise children as their own; that's what You want from us. We pray for the hearts of love and bowels of compassion to be

Prayer of Thanks for Caring Hearts!

expressed to others near and far. Father, please take away the cruel spirit of hate, ignorance, and abuse of any nature from your people and replace a heart of flesh and sincere love. Thank you, God, for infusing our hearts with Your love so we can show compassion to innocent babies, children, adults, seniors, and animals around the world. Remove the spirit of cruelty and replace a heart like thine in Your people so that we can love each other with a pure and sincere heart.

Father, I thank You for Spiritual eyes to discern the evil plot of the enemy against Your people around the world. Please give us the strength of Samson to fight against the enemy with Your power in Jesus's name (*see* Judges 15). This battle belongs to You, and we thank You that You are the number One Mighty Warrior.

Abba Father, we thank You for all the beautiful gifts that You place into our lives. Father, please help us use them to glorify You and to edify and encourage others, and I hope that they will do the same. I thank You for Your amazing love, Your multitude of mercies, and Your grace toward us. Thank You for loving us much more than how we know how to love ourselves. Help us to set aside time for You, Father in our daily lives, not cheating You of the time wasted in doing unimportant things that will distract us from our devotion to You. Please, help us to find purpose in You and find time to build a relationship with You, refusing to listen to the voice of the adversary instead of the voice of the Holy Spirit. Father, today we will not get so busy that we can't make time to worship You in Spirit and in Truth. Today, we dedicate a time of worship and praises to You, oh Father. We know that You inhabit our praise, so we welcome every moment with You in the beauty of holiness.

Father, You are such a good and loving Father to us. We bow before You in adoration and praise, knowing that You reside in us as we offer up praises to You. All these mercies we ask in the Mighty and Powerful Name of Jesus.

Amen!

Chapter 3: Trusting the Mighty and Powerful Creator!

Life and faith exercised by my mother!

> *"Blessed be God, even the Father of our Lord Jesus Christ, the Father of mercies, and the God of all comfort; Who comforteth us in all our tribulation, that we may be able to comfort them which are in any trouble, by the comfort wherewith we ourselves are comforted of God. For as the sufferings of Christ abound in us, so our consolation also aboundeth by Christ.."*
>
> --2 Corinthians 1:3-5 *KJV*

> *"Know therefore that the Lord thy God, he is God, the faithful God, which keepeth covenant and mercy with them that love him and keep his commandments to a thousand generations."*
>
> --Deuteronomy 7:9 *KJV*

Do you know that our Heavenly Father is a Father with a multitude of mercies and that He is full of grace? Not to mention His extensive compassion and comfort that He has been giving to us daily. God is so merciful and kind to us that we should not hesitate to serve Him and show affection and love to others. If we learn how to trust, obey, and believe in the mighty Creator, our lives will be so much better. He is the one that makes the moon and the stars shine by night and the sun to shine by day. He numbered the stars and knew them by name. His understanding is infinite because our God is great (See Psalm 147:4-5). **He is the Creator of the sea, hills, mountains, and valleys. Yet, we are hesitant to trust Him with our daily schedule.**

Can you imagine? He created us in His image and breathed His

Chapter 3: Trusting the Mighty and Powerful Creator!

breath of life in us so we can become a living and functional soul. Still, we seek the advice of so many others before we consult Him first about the signs and symptoms in our body, knowing that He is the greatest scientist in the Universe. Our bodies were made by Him! Come on, my friend! Our Creator knows it all! He knows and numbers the hairs on our heads! Tell me who can fathom this merciful and compassionate God of the Universe? No one, because He is Almighty, All-powerful, and All-wonderful. He is the Sovereign God that rules Heaven and Earth and everything under the Earth! Who should we put our faith in?

My mother was a sweetly saved, anointed prayer warrior, who worshiped, praised, and sang like an angel. Her virtues were on display for all to see that she worshiped and praised the true and living God. Most of all, a mother of faith and a strong belief that everyone should serve God because God is so good and gracious to us. She never ceased to talk about the goodness of God. May her sweet soul Rest in Peace. So many times, she would talk about how beautiful Heaven must be and what a joy to be granted the privilege of living with Jesus forever. **She always reminded us to live a life that is clean and holy because "you cannot go to Heaven with sins in your heart." She would tell us that perilous times would come but always encouraged us to hold on to Jesus and never let Him go.**

One of the saddest moments of my life was when my twenty-year-old brother drowned at work in a recreation pool. That was a very devastating time for my mom and the rest of the family, but my mother held on to faith. Two months later, two more family members, ages fifteen and eighteen, drowned one week apart. It was shocking to the entire family and our community, but God was in control. My mother kept the faith as she stayed on her knees in prayer and praising God for life, even through her tears! God understands our tears, a language that only the Creator can translate in His way! This was a sorrowful time for us, but I thank God for a praying, praising, and groaning mother. Just to face each day was a challenge, but God always stuck closer than a brother. Sometimes, we held onto each other crying in disbelief about the whole ordeal of having three young family members drown in such a short time!

At the time, I was eighteen and had to assist with two funeral arrangements which the Holy Spirit guided me through. It was only the strength of God that brought us through, even when we were walking through the valley of death. We had faith in God that we would not die but live through this challenging season! Our Heavenly Father gave us the strength to endure and a praying mother who was strong in her faith to daily encourage us to hold on to the unchanging hands of our Lord and Savior. It is a wonderful thing to trust and obey the All-knowing God! He is the FAITH BUILDER! The STRONG TOWER, the MIND REGULATOR, and the SPIRIT LIFTER!

Mother continued to tell us that God would take care of us because He promised us that He would supply our needs. I can recall when tears were falling down her cheeks, but she would be singing a beautiful chorus that would soothe our hearts and quiet our souls. I can still hear her saying, "Only God knows. One day, all the trouble and trials will be over," reminding us that God never leaves us; He is always by our side and He will give us comfort and peace in times of trouble. **She sang her way through many mountains of trials, seas of tribulations, and valleys of pain. She gave us the courage to keep on fighting and the courage to keep the faith.** God always comes through for us, and He makes a way when things seem impossible and uncertain; He keeps on providing for us. I think God likes to blow our minds at times! So many times, He opened the window and doors of Heaven with multiple abundance of blessings that left us in shock! God is a GOOD, GOOD Father and He is our number ONE PROVIDER and WAYMAKER!

Throughout the years, we faced several challenges of family and friends who died of terminal diseases, accidents, and other crises. Through it all, I saw my mother exercise faith and trust in God as she continued to tell us about the different biblical heroes who experienced some perilous times but kept the faith. We came together as a family during that time and leaned on the Savior's steady hands,

Chapter 3: Trusting the Mighty and Powerful Creator!

trying to comfort each other while gaining strength from God, knowing that He would never leave us or forsake us. Even in my teens, I remember my mother saying that God is our burden bearer and He is the LIGHT through our darkest hour and He will see us through.

Today, I can say without a shadow of a doubt that my God is a promise keeper. I thank God for extending His multitude of mercies and His incredible gift of grace and abundant love to my family and me throughout those challenging years. Abba Father, you are all that we need! The God of Abraham, Isaac, and Jacob is our God! He is our Jehovah-Jireh, Our provider! Jehovah-Nissi, Our Banner! Jehovah-Rapha, Our Healer! Jehovah-Shalom, Our Peace! We can't help but serve a great God like this! **Will you give him first place in your life? Accept JESUS as your priority package today!**

Prioritizing God FIRST in your life is the most important step you can make so He can lead and guide you through life's journey. Doing that will give you the courage to persevere in any season of your life. The assurance that you are not alone will give you the strength to pursue your dreams, your goals, your destiny, and your purpose in the Kingdom of the Lord. I had to make that decision and wished I had done it sooner. Only God knows when the different seasons of your life will appear, and they will come. As we journey through life, we realize that there are some chapters we wish we did not have to experience or go through. However, these are milestones that become a part of our mundane life, history, and testimony. My friend, every season or chapter of our life is to propel us to the next level of growth and development, be it physical or spiritual growth that will sustain us through life's journey. Therefore, **we will not stop at the crossroads of adversities.** Rather, we will pray our way through with Jesus as our leader. We will not BOW to the easy way out. Instead, we will **pursue and fight** to be victorious in fulfilling the plan of God over our lives.

I implore you to stay focused on the Creator who knows about every season of your life. Do not get sidetracked or worry about a problem that is too big to fix on your own. **Remember, God is bigger and greater than all the world's problems and stronger than all the opponents who constantly push and fight us. Do not focus on the disappointments, distractions, or the past; instead, focus on building a good and stable relationship daily with your Savior.** No one should ever be at a stage where they think they don't need God in their lives. WE ALL NEED GOD! No matter who you are or what kinds of credentials you've earned, we need the Creator. Have you ever stopped and thought about who made us? It is God who chose to make man in His image. The Bible says, *"So God created man in his image, in the image of God created he him; male and female created he them"* (Genesis 1:27 *KJV*). God is amazing, and He is worthy to be appreciated and praised. We were made to serve Him. We glorify Him with the fruits of our lips and dare not put anyone before Him.

Our relationship with our creator should be our **first and primary priority;** everything else should be secondary. Only salvation with Jesus will last forever, so why not put Him first? How can we pretend or reject the great and mighty God who chose to create us in His image? After all, He only lent us His breath for a while. During that precious time between birth and death here on Earth, do we acknowledge Him as our Lord and Savior or forsake Him? We should accept Him for who He is and make Him the center of our attention. We all need the righteousness of Jesus Christ to make it through this life. It is impossible to be at peace in this world full of turmoil and so much unrighteousness if we don't have the right relationship with God. We should do a daily self-check because our self-righteousness cannot make it into glory. After all, it is filthy rags (*see* Isaiah 64:6). We need to live right and act right toward each other! Choose to follow God's righteousness!

Therefore, the basic approach to communicating with God is through prayer, fasting, meditating, reading the Bible, and applying His words to our daily lives. Believe in the Lord and put your trust in Him, allowing the Holy Spirit in you to inspire you to make the right choice and decision—killing the flesh and burying the natural man so

Chapter 3: Trusting the Mighty and Powerful Creator!

we can serve the Lord in Spirit and in Truth. These are some of the keys and steps we can practice in our Christian walk with the Lord which can lead us towards eternal life with the Messiah. Jesus' love for us is unconditional; through His birth, death, and resurrection, we are made free from all guilt and shame. Because of His unfailing love for us, which bridges the gap between Heaven and hell, we are now saved and have access to inheriting the Kingdom of Heaven. Such a wonderful and priceless privilege to be in **this royal family of God**, all because of this amazing love that God the Father bestowed upon us.

My mother kept on reminding us that God promised to take care of us, and He will never leave us alone, just like He did for the matriarchs and patriarchs of long ago. God is not slack concerning any of His promises. He is always coming through for you, morning, noon, and night. She continued to tell us that those biblical heroes experienced fears of the unknown, but God delivered them from the hands of the adversary. They accomplished their assignment through the help and direction of God, and now, they are enjoying their Heavenly inheritance in the presence of the Lord.

Friends, God will do the same for us if we trust Him and continue to believe that He can do the impossible. We are all going through a process of endurance and perseverance, and it is not an easy road to travel, but great shall be our reward in Heaven. That magnificent place that Jesus went to prepare for us is far beyond human imagination or comprehension! Hold on to the Solid Rock, which is Jesus Christ our Lord, the Chief Cornerstone! He is the Creator of Heaven and Earth and He is the God of abundance. He is the supplier of ALL our needs. Put your trust in Him! He will never fail us! He is making all the ways to sustain us through the storms of life!

Prayer to the God of Abundance!

Our Dearest Father in Heaven, I thank You for being the Universe's Creator. Heaven and Earth bow before You because You deserve all glory, honor, and praise. Angels bow down and worship You because You are holy! Father, I trust You because You are the God of abundance and plenty and You never fail us. I worship You in the beauty of holiness because You are Great and Mighty. Father, I thank You for the sweet comfort You placed in my heart so I can experience joy and happiness, even through the seasonal phases of my life! Abba Father, I have faith and confidence in You that You will supply my needs and You will bless me according to Your riches in glory. Let me be content with all the good gifts You bestowed upon my family, friends, and me. Father, we are forever grateful to You for Your love and mercy during our trying phases! You never leave us or forsake us.

Greatest Father of all Fathers, I thank You for providing comfort and peace in a time of need. Abba Father, help me to bless others, not out of abundance but out of my need as I daily walk with thee. Father, help me always to have a heart of thanksgiving and praise on my lips to worship and praise You. Father, let me selflessly give of myself to others who need me in whatever way necessary. Father, I thank You for allowing me to live and declare Your works to people near and far. Let my life be a living testimony to others who need an encouraging word, a helping hand, or prayer! Let Your grace abound in me to give bountifully (*see* 2 Corinthians 9:6-11). Abba Father, thank You for Your faithfulness to give us things in abundance so our character can grow in You (*see* Romans 8:28-29).

Dearest Father, let us harken unto Your voice diligently as we seek to OBEY You, so You can set us above all nations. Thank You that You are the God of plenty and You are lacking nothing because You are the God of EVERYTHING! We give You thanks for all Your blessings

Prayer to the God of Abundance!

that You will bestow on us when we trust and obey You in Spirit and in Truth as seen in Deuteronomy 28:1-14. We pray against the curse of Deuteronomy 28:15-68 because we desire to obey You and repent of all unrighteousness so we can live in holiness.

Father, I give You thanks in the mighty name of Jesus, my Lord, and soon coming King! Amen

Chapter 4: Different Surgeries and Healing Testimonies

Cry For The Lord's Mercy During Time Of Trouble

"In thee, O Lord, do I put my trust; let me never be ashamed: deliver me in thy righteousness. Bow down thine ear to me; deliver me speedily: be thou my strong rock, for an house of defence to save me. For thou art my rock and my fortress; therefore for thy name's sake lead me, and guide me. Pull me out of the net that they have laid privily for me: for thou art my strength. Into thine hand I commit thy spirit: thou hast redeem me, O Lord God of truth."

--Psalm 31:1-5 KJV

"Then they cried unto the Lord in their trouble, and he saved them out of their distresses. He sent his word, healed them, and delivered them from their destruction. Oh, that men would praise the Lord for his goodness and his wonderful works to the children of men!"

--Psalm 107:19-21 *KJV*

The above scriptures encourage us to "cry for the Lord's mercy during the time of trouble." I am happy to say our Heavenly Father not only sees our tears but He hears us, saves us, delivers us, and redeems us from all our troubles. Glory to God! Have you ever been there where you know that if the Lord did not take complete control of that situation in your life, you would not be around to tell the story? I can tell you that I cry unto the Lord and my God sent out His destiny angels to take charge of my situation and my circumstances just in time. He sent helpers on assignment to deliver me from my distress and save me from going down the destruction highway! Glory Hallelujah! My Heavenly Father is my All-Time God! The above scripture says God is," ...my rock and my fortress;" God is the one who can pull us out from the net of bondage and set us free. He

Chapter 4: Different Surgeries and Healing Testimonies

will give us the strength to carry on even when we are in the middle of the storm. I must continue to rejoice because His healing hands touched my broken and afflicted body several times. **Glory to God, I am walking in my healing and deliverance testimony because His wounded hands touch my life.**

In October of 2011, I had major abdominal surgery which should have been for four hours but it lasted for over ten hours. I was left with five large abdominal incisions instead of four small ones. Ten days after the abdominal surgery, I was discharged and sent home. Within twenty-four hours I was back in the hospital. It was Jesus that kept me cradled in His protective arms throughout the entire ordeal. I was experiencing severe post-surgery projectile vomiting, chills, and severe pain when my daughter had to call 911 on a cold winter night. During that time, I was silently calling on Jehovah El Shaddai, God Almighty, in prayer to hear my cry and attend to my plea! In the icy winter weather, I lay in the back of the ambulance, inaudibly praying to Jehovah Rapha, My Healer. I felt like every organ in me was on fire, with excruciating pain all over my body, but the Holy Spirit spoke comfort to me that He would never leave me.

I somewhat watched the EMTs doing my vital signs and administering IV. I was unaware of my surroundings and what was really happening to me. I knew there was a comforting presence of angels on assignment in the ambulance, and I had no fear. The Bible tells us, *"Fear thou not; for I am with thee: be not dismayed; for I am thy God: I will strengthen thee; yea, I will help thee; yea, I will uphold thee with the right hand of my righteousness"* (Isaiah 41:10 *KJV*). There I lay in the ambulance, hearing the sirens along with the heavy snowflakes which were rapidly coming down. As the ambulance skidded from side to side, my body shook with unbearable pain, nausea, and vomiting. I cried out, "JESUS, have mercy on me!" I felt the heat of God's presence, telling me to "Hold on. I am here with you!" The ride to the hospital took over an hour due to the inclement weather. Even though I was in severe pain, I had no fear because I knew that Sweet Jesus was with me. I felt PEACE in the midst of it all!

Finally, we made it to the Emergency Room, even though I was unaware of what had taken place or where I was until several hours later. God has been so merciful and faithful in all His promises, and I have confidence that He brought me this far, never to leave me. God will do the same for you. He knows what you are going through. There is nothing impossible for God; He has the answer to every question! Deep within my heart, I know that my Redeemer lives, and because He lives, I kept saying I shall live and not die. Psalm 118:17 tells us, "I shall not die, but I will live, and declare the works of the LORD."

Even though I was re-admitted several times and my recovery seemed long, my God's healing power worked mightily in me. The Bible says, *"But he was wounded for our transgressions, he was bruised for our iniquities, the chastisement of our peace was upon him and with his stripes we are healed"*(Isaiah 53:5 KJV). Also, 1 Peter 2:24 (KJV), says, *"Who his own self bares our sins in his own body on the tree, that we, being dead to sins, should live to righteousness: by whose stripes ye were healed."* Glory Hallelujah for His promises! Jesus Christ died on the cross for our anguish, grief, and pain. Our God is our healer, deliverer and our protector. He is steadfast in His love! No matter what you're going through or what you are experiencing in mind, body, spirit, and soul, JESUS will heal, deliver, and set you free. Sometimes, I still have aches and pains, but I know the devil is a liar, trying to tell me I am not healed, but I claim healing from the healing station of Heaven in the name of Jesus. I know healing is a process, and I refused to believe that old devil, that deceiver, the father of lies that I am not healed. I claim complete healing by the stripes of Jesus Christ!

I went through thirteen surgeries within a couple of years, non-cosmetic, and I am still walking upon my grave. Glory to God! Who could it be but my Abba Father? My great Jehovah Rapha, the mind, body, and soul Healer! His free love prescription and Bible reading direction never run dry because He is the living water! My friend! Take a drink from the living healing water fountain! (*see* John 4:10). The Balm of Gilead is here to deliver and restore our physical and spiritual health if we only BELIEVE. It is written in Jeremiah 8:22, *"Is*

Chapter 4: Different Surgeries and Healing Testimonies

there no balm in Gilead? Is there no physician there? Why then is there no healing for the wound of my people? And because of their unbelief, he couldn't do any mighty miracles among them"(NIV). If we believe, then we shall receive and experience the possibilities and power of God our Savior. Our Deliver and our Healer!

Saints, I have been healed and set free from physical limitations and mental anguish. The Bible tells me that healing is **the children's bread** which I am feasting on. "But I will restore you to health and heal your wounds,' declares the Lord" (Jeremiah 30:17 *KJV*). **I will continue to give God thanks for restoring my health and the health of my daughter who passed out several times.** There was a time when we were both in the hospital at the same time sharing the same room, but God was our present help during that time of our lives and He continues to be present. The adversary wants to kill you and your family, but we have to stand on the promises of God; even though we are afflicted, we are healed by His stripes. The word of God tells us to give thanks for everything. We might question God. How can I say thanks when we are feeling sick? But we can give God praise that we are still alive; praise Him through sickness. God hears your cry, and He will answer your plea. He feels our anguish and pain. In His love for us, God sees and experiences our suffering, and He looks beyond our sins and sees our needs. God is such a compassionate and loving Father!

I am standing on the promises of God that He is my deliverer. You too can stand on the promises of God our Father! Glory be to God! Oftentimes, we wonder why we go through anguish and pain. Only Jesus has all the answers to all our questions, and some sweet day, we will understand why. Right now, I am so grateful to Jesus Christ for keeping me **ALIVE** and that I am in my right mind. Hallelujah! I am so thankful to everyone, including my church family, who constantly pray for our healing and breakthrough.

Even though I went through several years of physical and occupational therapy, I realized that Jesus is my greatest Physician. My Abba Father showed up as the greatest healing Potter, putting back together all the broken pieces in my life, physical, spiritual, and mental! A time in my life when I was experiencing difficulties in my health, extreme sadness, and depression from four miscarriages. I was unable to work for a couple of years due to work-related injuries to my right arm and my lower back. I experienced severe weakness and tremors in my right hand, even now which led to partial disability to man but not to God. No matter what you are going through, God can still use a broken vessel because He is the Potter. Lord, I am **available t**o be used by you, dear Lord!

During those seasons of my life, I also experienced major losses and financial deficits which forced me to sell our home and downsize just to make ends meet. I also experienced grief through the death of several family members within a couple of years including my mother, one of my sisters, my grandmother, two of my uncles, one of my young nephews, and my stepdad. BUT GOD! At the same time, many other family issues were coming from every angle with a force like a tsunami erupting around my life.

I was also facing difficulties in my marriage which led to separation and divorce. But God is a promise keeper who never leaves us alone. **Jesus cradles my MIND and BODY in his nail-scarred hands.** Oh Yes! Jesus's wounded hands and counseling voice gave me more comfort than anyone could give me. I found peace and rest in the arms of my Lord and Savior. I encourage you to trust the God of PEACE, you will find complete comfort in the arms of Jehovah Shalom. **He is the God of my Peace and He is also the God of your Peace. No one can steal Jesus's PEACE from you because He gave it to you** (*see* John 14:27).

The recovery phase was painful and very difficult, but my Savior stood closer than a brother. For a while, I had a cane and two different walkers to assist with ambulation ONLY for a couple of weeks, which I have not used for over six years. I will not hesitate to tell the world that Jesus "...heals the brokenhearted and binds up their wounds." (Psalm 147:3 *KJV*). **It does not matter how far you think you are away from God; He is right there beside you. He is your next BREATH!**

Chapter 4: Different Surgeries and Healing Testimonies

Whether you are experiencing physical, mental, or spiritual pain, Jesus will fix it for you. Call on your Father who is in Heaven; He sees, and He knows what you are going through. Deliverance and healing are in the Bible, and I believe every single word in the Bible. It is our LOVE LETTER from our Father, use it and enjoy it. Do you believe it? If you believe then you too shall receive every good gift coming from the Father above!

Please read with me:

> *"Every good gift and every perfect gift is from above, and cometh down from the Father of lights, with whom is no variableness, neither shadow of turning. Of his own will begat he us with the word of truth, that we should be kind of first fruits of his creature."*
>
> --James 1:17-18 *KJV*

Jesus bore all our griefs and carried our sorrow because of his love for us! Take EVERYTHING to God in prayer!

> *"Surely, he has borne our griefs, and carried our sorrows yet we did esteem him stricken, smitten of God, and Afflicted. But he was wounded for our transgressions; he was bruised for our iniquities; the chastisement of our peace was upon him and with his stripes we are healed."*
>
> --Isaiah 53:4-5 *KJV*

Even though I experienced several heartache, griefs, and pains, Jesus never left me alone. He removed my pain and sadness, and He replaced it with **His perfect healing and serenity of peace.** The Lord told us in Psalm 30:2, "O Lord, I cried out to you and you healed me." Thank you, Abba Father, for Your never-ending love, and Your nail print hands of protection over my body. Jesus, my Healer, continues to shelter my body in His loving arms of protection. I knew that God had stepped out in a mighty and powerful way to restore my health. He conquered death in time of our need. In His compassion, He saved and snatched me from the hands of the adversary. The enemy is at work day and night trying to hinder you and your family's breakthrough. I am encouraging you to stand in authority and speak

LIFE over your family in the name of Jesus. Pray and declare Psalm 118:17 over your life and the life of your loved one.

We have to be ALERT, BOLD, and stand STRONG in the Lord because the adversary is fighting against us daily. Remember in *Ephesians 6:12, "For we do not wrestle against flesh and blood, but against principalities, against powers, against the rulers of the darkness of this age, against spiritual wickedness in the heavenly places."* Pray for healing scripture over your loved ones. The Apostle John tells us, *"Jesus said to her, 'I am the resurrection, and the life: he that believes in me, though he were dead, yet shall he live: And whosoever liveth and believeth in me shall never die. Believest thou this?"* (John 11:25-26 KJV).

Through it all God was present and now I look back and give Him thanks for ALL He has done for me. I SURVIVED because Jesus rescued me and pulled me out of the net of affliction, torment, and worry. Jesus is my Rock and my Fortress! He is the Creator of Israel and He will make a way where there seems to be no way out (*see* Isaiah 43:15-17). There is nothing too hard for God. He wants us to BELIEVE! Jesus raised Lazarus who was dead for four days, by this time he stinketh. God showed His glory and He raised Lazarus from the dead (*see* John 11:1-44).

Our Heavenly Father is a miracle worker. He walks on the sea and He also calms the sea. He sent the flood and He fixed and changed the Earth that was without form and void. We can't help but serve this great and Mighty God, who is our Father. Will you trust and believe in the God of the impossible that He can heal, deliver, and set you free?

Let Us Pray This Prayer of Healing!

Heavenly Father, ruler of Heaven and Earth. I praise Your Holy and Righteous Name. Father, thank You for Your healing power and for hearing my cry. Dearest Father, You said we should call upon You when we are in need, and You said You would answer our call and our cry. So, Father, in the name of Jesus, Your precious Son, I pronounce Mark 5:34 over my life in Your words, "He said to her, 'Daughter; your faith has healed you. Go in peace and be free from your suffering'." Today, I declare I am free from sickness, suffering, and diseases in Jesus' name. I pray for this same faith-healing power over my family and friends in the precious name of Jesus! I declare and decree that healing shall be our daily bread in the name of Jesus!

Loving Father, I thank You for being my Healer, my Savior, and my Deliverer. Today, I am rejoicing because I am free. I live this life only because of Your gracious grace and multitude of mercies. Father, I can feel the anointing of the Holy Spirit going through my body, mind, and soul. I thank You for the spiritual circumcision taking place in my heart as You remove every known and unknown sin. Thank You for Your divine restoration of a heart like thine. Thank You for delivering me and setting me free to work and function in Spirit and in Truth. Thank You, Jehovah, for Your unfailing love and Your endless grace. I can sense Your restoration of healing power running through my veins, arteries, capillaries, and all the organs in my body. You are an awesome and mighty God who comes to heal my physical, spiritual, psychological, and mental wounds. Today, I declare that I am experiencing TOTAL healing in every fiber of my being in Jesus' Holy Name.

Father, I give You all praise with the fruit of my lips as I join in with

Jeremiah the Prophet to say, "Heal me, Lord, and I will be healed; save me, and I will be saved, for You are the one I praise" (Jeremiah 17:14 *KJV*). Father, You are my Rock, Shield, Banner, Fortress, and hiding Place. I praise You for Your divine healing over my life, my family, and my friend's life. This moment, Father, I am shouting Hallelujah for Your divine intervention from the healing fountain of Heaven.

My Dearest Abba Father, we praise You for Your many gifts sent from Heaven above to Your children. Help us accept and acknowledge all good gifts around us, and that we will use them to glorify ONLY You and edify others. Thank You for the compassion You extended to us daily. Abba Father, we love You and we adore You. We give You thanks in Jesus' name! Amen!

Chapter 5: Humbling Myself in Fasting and Prayer

David--Comfort for the Brokenhearted

> *"When I wept and chastened my soul with fasting, that was to my reproach. I made a sackcloth also my garment; and I became a proverb to them. They that sit in the gates speak against me; and I was the song of the drunkards."*
>
> --Psalm 69:10-12 *KJV*

Do you know that you can find comfort in fasting, prayer, and making sacrifices to meditate on the Lord? It is a secret time when you can humble yourself before your Creator in complete humility, even if you think the world is against you. **Try to be steadfast and focus on the Creator, not the distractor who is trying to deceive you.** David is writing from the breath of God, seeking forgiveness and how he found **comfort in God during his brokenness. We, too, experience sorrows and human fragility where we lament, get lonely, afraid, or cry**. So instead of getting depressed and having a complaining and pity party, we can turn to our Heavenly Father in fasting and prayer. Fasting is expressing to our Heavenly Father that we are dependent on Him as we sacrifice quality time to spend with Him in humility, especially when we are experiencing the things that we are facing in this chaotic and troubled world day after day!

Furthermore, we have so much to give God thanks for every day. Especially, the breath of life to move about freely with all our senses fully functioning within normal limits. Being ALIVE is such a wonderful blessing, that alone should encourage us and lead us into fasting and prayer. After all, God grants us life because He loves us unconditionally. We can show him how much we love and appreciate Him through the act of worship as we fast and pray. Fasting is a special time when we humbly bow before the Lord, our maker, **as we refrain from the physical food and other distractions around us so we can focus on the Spiritual food. A time to discipline the physical flesh so we can focus on our Spiritual needs, so God can dwell in us (***see*** Romans 8:9) Fasting is a sacrificial way to show love and appreciation to our Heavenly Father as we celebrate and worship Him.**

Oftentimes, we may wonder and ask ourselves the question: Why should we fast and pray? Then, we can remind ourselves if the Son of God went into fasting for forty days and nights, then why shouldn't we make fasting a part of our lifestyle? Jesus sets the example for us to follow as we travel this Christian path to glory (*see* Matthew 4:1-11) **Jesus Christ is our Number One role model to follow and portray**. The devil tempted Jesus just after He finished fasting but Jesus rebuked him with the Word of God. We cannot enter into fasting with our strength. We need God to guide us throughout the fast and after the fast. God will give His angels charge over us as we dedicate time to prayer and fasting (*see* Matthew 4:1-11). **Fasting is mentioned over seventy times throughout the Bible.** Several biblical characters practiced the sacrifice of fasting for different reasons.

One of the best ways to acknowledge the Father is through humbling ourselves in fasting and prayer. Jesus also tells us in Mark 9:14-29 that something comes by prayer and fasting. It was during, "The healing of a possessed boy." Jesus tells the disciples, "...This kind can come forth by nothing, but by prayer and fasting" (Mark 9:29). We are encouraged by Jesus's teaching even in our modern world that prayer and fasting are still required to combat the trials and tribulation that we are experiencing in the world today.

We can nourish and empower our Spiritual life through effective fasting and prayer if we trust and believe in the God of the impossible. Also, we should spend time meditating **on the engraved word that we find in the Bible, which is a beautiful love letter from our Heavenly Father.** A letter that is so active and alive in us and through us when we feed on it and apply it daily to our lives.

Chapter 5: Humbling Myself in Fasting and Prayer

I found so much strength and comfort in dedicating time to praying and fasting. Even though the flesh sometimes wants to distract and derail me, I have to fully depend on the direction of the Holy Spirit to guide me. We must learn to kill the flesh and put it under subjection so we can walk in the Spirit! It is not easy, but God can, and He will sustain us during fasting and prayer if we depend on Him.

Sometimes, we need to speak to our mouths and say, no food today! I will use my mouth today to read God's word, praise him, and pray to Him. Dear Mouth, you are on vacation from food until my fasting is over. It is not easy, but we have to depend on the Holy Spirit for Spiritual clarification and guidance during this practice. God will give us the strength to follow through if we focus on Him and not on ourselves or our desires. A self-discipline that can only be controlled by the strength of God to kill the flesh.

The Holy Spirit continues to lead me and guide me as I humble myself in several prayers and fasting. There were times when I could not focus and write without physical and spiritual distractions. There were days when I was faced with infirmities, and all kinds of pain over my body, but I know I cannot give up, so I completely depend on the Holy Spirit to lead and guide me. I know my Savior walks beside me and that He will carry me through, so I had to set aside time for sacrificial prayer and fasting.

I thought about the story of Jesus and His disciples when they were praying for the man with the sick son who was a lunatic. The disciples prayed but nothing happened until Jesus turned up and a miracle happened. They were ashamed and asked Jesus why! *"And Jesus said to them, Because of your unbelief: for verily I say unto you, If ye have faith as a grain of mustard seed, ye shall say unto this mountain, Remove hence to yonder place; and it shall remove; and nothing shall be impossible unto you"* (Matthew 17:20). **So, we see that fasting is also about believing and trusting God to do his will in our lives. We have to exercise faith and believe in God's divine intervention as we fast and pray that God can and will do the impossible according to His will.**

It is also very important to seek God's direction as you prepare to go into individual or corporate fasting. I must give thanks and praise to the Holy Spirit for His complete supervision and manifestation in leading me through both kinds of fasting before and during this assignment. God will show you and point you to different people and what directions to take so you can fulfill His purpose in you. He is such a faithful and a Mighty God who sticks closer than a brother to us. All He wants us to do is to BELIEVE that He is the God of the impossible and He will propel you through to the end and it is all for His glory.

During this time, I had several people encouraging me and they were fasting and praying for me and with me. Jesus makes the ultimate sacrifice to die for us and He is daily taking the time to pray for us and intercede on our behalf before the Father. We are also encouraged to carry each other's burden and to love and motivate each other at all times. One of the best ways to do so is to dedicate time to fast and pray to strengthen your Spiritual man to stay empowered and strong in the Lord.

On January 7th, 2018, I went on a twenty-one-day Daniel Fast, seeking more of God and His direction as I continue writing this book. On the last day, January 28th, **the Holy Spirit told me to apply Psalm 51 to my life. WOW! Such a wake-up call! I experience total conviction from the Holy Spirit, which is the Spirit of Truth. I realized that I needed that epiphany to search my life and see if I was in the right standing with God!** Realizing that I was NOT completely at the right place where the Lord wanted me to be, I said, "Lord! I thank You for this eye-opener exposure in my life. **Thank You, Holy Spirit for your PERFECT EYES OF DISCERNMENT to reveal my sin-sick soul."** Who would think that I would have this insight during fasting and prayer? One of the works of the Holy Spirit is to convict us and bring us to the knowledge of truth regarding our relationship with God. Thank You, God, for the blessed Holy Spirit to open my eyes in so many areas (*see* Isaiah 11: I-5).

I repented immediately! Asking God my Father to forgive me for everything and anything that would hinder my breakthrough, as I

Chapter 5: Humbling Myself in Fasting and Prayer

kneel before the Lord in brokenness! Have mercy on me, wash me, and help me to make it right as I kill this flesh and seek more of You, dear Lord! I felt such a relief and complete joy running through my body after that confession! I said, Father, "I thank You for Your divine revelation that You awakened in me."

Let us read Psalm 51 together:

Confession and Prayer for God's Pardon–A Psalm of David

> *"Have mercy upon me, O God, according to thy lovingkindness: according unto the multitude of thy tender mercies blot out my transgressions. [2] Wash me thoroughly from mine iniquity, and cleanse me from my sin. [3] For I acknowledge my transgressions: and my sin is ever before me. [4] Against thee, thee only, have I sinned, and done this evil in thy sight: that thou mightest be justified when thou speakest, and be clear when thou judgest. [5] Behold, I was shapen in iniquity; and in sin did my mother conceive me. [6] Behold, thou desirest truth in the inward parts: and in the hidden part, thou shalt make me to know wisdom. [7] Purge me with hyssop, and I shall be clean: wash me, and I shall be whiter than snow. [8] Make me hear joy and gladness; that the bones which thou hast broken may rejoice. [9] Hide thy face from my sins, and blot out all mine iniquities. [10] Create in me a clean heart, O God, and renew a right spirit within me. [11] Cast me not away from thy presence; take not thy holy spirit from me. [12] Restore unto me the joy of thy salvation; and uphold me with thy free spirit. [13] Then will I teach transgressors thy ways; and sinners shall be converted unto thee. [14] Deliver me from blood guiltiness, O God, thou God of my salvation: and my tongue shall sing aloud of thy righteousness. [15] O Lord, open thou my lips; and my mouth shall shew forth thy praise. [16] For thou desirest not sacrifice; else would I give it: thou delightest not in burnt offering. [17] The sacrifices of God are a broken spirit: a broken and a contrite heart, O God, thou wilt not despise. [18] Do good in thy good pleasure unto Zion: build thou the walls of Jerusalem. [19] Then shalt thou be*

> *pleased with the sacrifices of righteousness, with burnt offering and whole burnt offering: then shall they offer bullocks upon thine altar."*
>
> --Psalm 51:1-19 *KJV*

Now, this is a Psalm that I read several times about David asking for God's forgiveness when he had an affair with Bathsheba. David's situation was different from mine. However, **I was at a place in my life where the Lord knew that I needed restoration from my broken and messed up life, even while I was on this writing assignment.** There are times when our spirit-man has that yearning desire to fast, but the physical flesh would sometimes distract us from making that sacrifice to surrender some time to fast and pray.

Have you ever been there? For me, it was a moment of confession, detoxing, and prayer for God's **pardon throughout every area of my life.** A time and phase of the known and the unknown seasons of brokenness, hurt, and pain that festered inside me. I needed a Spiritual circumcision of my heart, mind, body, and soul, and the Holy Spirit revealed it to me. No one can live without the Holy Spirit, who is the Spirit of Truth (*see* John 14:17) Therefore, without any hesitation, I followed the command of the Lord by applying this Psalm to my life. I had a self-searching examination which made things so real and clear that I need a spiritual detox from everything that would hinder my relationship with God.

The audible voice of God was so compassionate and clear to the depths of my heart! I wept for several days for this soul-searching disclosure that was so needed at that moment and time of my life. God is so awesome and powerful in searching our hearts and helping us to make things right. We just need to be in obedience to His commands, stay in His will, and REPENT when we are convicted to do so. I experienced peace, joy, and divine revelation to get me spiritually uplifted from one level to a higher level in Christ. All I could do was bow down and worship Him in tears, brokenness, and humility. Thanking God for not despising me but showing me the brokenness that was inside my heart.

Chapter 5: Humbling Myself in Fasting and Prayer

> *"The sacrifices of God are a broken spirit: a broken and a contrite heart, O God, thou will not despise"* (v17).

That day, I read Psalm 51 over and over. I sat down, and I wrote all nineteen verses down, planting every word in my heart and life in a searching manner. Even though this is a familiar scripture that I had read several times before, this brought forth a new revelation that inspired me to humble myself totally before God my Father. I realized every verse took on a new meaning, new thoughts, and new application, and I needed that direction so much. It is one thing to read God's Word, but it's another thing to meditate on it and apply it to your life! **You can only accomplish what God set before you by the direction and help of the Holy Spirit; He is your Teacher and Counselor. The Holy Spirit is perfect in everything, and He will complete whatever God assigns you to do by His grace and His power** (*see* John 14:25-26).

My mind transcended to an in-depth soul-searching while bowing down in humility. I said, Lord! Have mercy upon me; have Your way in me, so I can worship You in Spirit and Truth! Today, I confess that I am completely Yours, Lord! I am asking You to search me and make me clean inside and outside and deep within. Remove everything that will hinder me from fulfilling Your promise over my life. As I focused, prayed, and meditated on Your Word, I felt the Holy Spirit move within me, and I bowed down in praise and worship. I completely prostrated before the Almighty God, and I felt a surge of joy and peace like I never felt before as the Holy Spirit brought me to a higher place of worship. **My spiritual eyes shone within me like a 100/100 internal vision; just trying to apply every single word of Psalm 51 to my life was such a great revelation.**

The Holy Spirit is such a wonderful Teacher, and we should depend on Him to lead, teach, and guide us into the truth of the Sovereign God! Shortly after that, my spiritual eyes opened wider to a new dimension of God's amazing grace and vision to continue writing. I rejoice daily from the leading of the Holy Spirit, whose guidance has helped me tremendously along the way. It is a great step to come to repentance ground before the Lord, our Maker. Daily repentance is necessary because no sin can enter into the Kingdom of Heaven!

Friends, I went through a spiritual cleansing and washing of my inner soul that brought me such comfort and peace. I continued to read and seek God daily for spiritual purification and detoxing. **The Holy Spirit told me to continue fasting for three more days. This experience humbled me, so I praised Him and read and meditated on His words.** Our God is so amazing, and He is worthy to be praised in every situation. Three extra days with the Trinity were so sweet and refreshing to my soul! The Father knows our needs much more than we do and He knows just what to do to prepare us for His assignment and the journey ahead! How can I say thanks for His unfailing love, grace, and multitude of mercies?

During the next three days of fasting, the adversary tried to show up in different ways, but God will never leave us to fight our battles alone. He is the Great Shepherd who keeps on watching over us at all times. There was so much testing and a fight against principalities and powers. We know who we are serving, even when we are hardpressed, we will not stay in despair because God is fighting our battles (*see* 2 Corinthians 4:8-12). The enemy tried to distract me, but I covered myself in the name of Jesus, realizing that this was a sacrifice, so I had to focus on the Lord. I kept on reminding myself that I was not alone, but that Jesus was beside me every step of the way. I remember the compassionate love that Jesus showed me throughout my life and in my different dreams which brings me great assurance to depend on the Lord.

The Good Shepherd stayed beside me as the sweet Holy Spirit comforted and guided me. So, I kept on focusing on the goodness of the Lord, singing, and worshiping for the next three days, and the Lord brought me out victoriously. I was consistently feeding on His words and praying as I depended on the direction of the Holy Spirit. Oh, such a wonderful and sweet time with the Lord. Every time the enemy threw a device, I repeated, **Heavenly Father, You are in control of this battle in the name of Jesus.** My friend Jesus died on

Chapter 5: Humbling Myself in Fasting and Prayer

the cross for us, and it is through the shedding of His blood on Calvary that sets us free to put the enemy under our feet. For every stripe Jesus received, we can declare healing and deliverance. It was **the strength from Jesus' blood that pivoted me from my weakness to exercise the unflinching faith to carry on.** Oh, how I love Jesus' blood! His blood saved me, satisfied me, delivered me, and set me free so I can spend eternity with Him.

As I continued to apply Psalm 51 to my life, I felt a spiritual release deep inside. The Holy Spirit gave me more and more knowledge of revelation in the things of God concerning the writing of this book. Most of all, I started to get closer to and more dependent on the Holy Spirit for direction and revelation. I realized that I had suffered so much hurt, rejection, and brokenness along the way. God knows I needed to be free from the weight that easily beset me before I could continue with the writing. He knew that restoration was necessary, and I thanked God for the revealing Psalm 51 which rekindled the fire of the Holy Spirit in my Christian walk for the journey ahead. It was such an anointing that broke the yoke to set me free to walk into my destiny and purpose. **This walk with the Lord is a daily emptying and replenishing because this flesh continues to fight against the Spirit.** Therefore, we must walk in the Light, lest we fall into darkness and miss our way to salvation and eternal life.

Psalm 51:7 says, "Cleanse me with hyssop, and I will be clean; wash me and I will be whiter than snow." I was broken, even though I was not aware or maybe I was in denial, but I thank God for His revelation to repent. I needed God to mend and fix every broken piece of my life. Verse 17 says, "My sacrifice, O God, is a broken spirit; a broken and a contrite heart You, God, will not despise." God loves us and He will not despise us. I was rejoicing and thanking my Heavenly Father for fixing my broken pieces and giving me so much mental clarity. I said, "Thank You, Abba Father, for Your love and Your mercy toward me." I humbly lay down everything at my Savior's feet. Father, I want to live according to Your will and Your way and not my will. While I was waiting, He was pruning me, guiding me, and encouraging me. I will forever stand on His promises knowing that He will see me through, and He will do the same for you if you just wait on the Lord.

His Word declares, *"But they that wait upon the Lord shall renew their strength; they shall mount up with wings as eagle; they shall run, and not be weary; and they shall walk and not faint"* (Isaiah 40:31 KJV). We cannot faint when we wait upon the Lord, because He is always there leading us, guiding us, and renewing our strength. It is important to be obedient to the Holy Spirit, knowing that He lives within us as our Counselor, Teacher, and Advocate, as He guides us every step of the way. We must have faith and confidence in God as we believe and trust in Him, the one who will never fail us. God wants us to take time out of our busy schedule to fast and pray! Jesus also told us some things can only be answered through fasting and prayer. There were several victory testimonies in my life and also in the life of my family. I cannot explain it, but the presence of God's power within those three days brought so much joy and peace beyond my imagination.

I can assure you that you will experience a mighty move of God in your life as you set aside time for this sacrifice wholeheartedly and in humility. The Holy Spirit is such a wonderful Helper and a Mighty **Comforter to lead us on the path of righteousness. God's supernatural** and divine revelation empowered me to focus as I humble myself through fasting and prayer. God will do the same for you as you trust and believe in him to do the impossible. God did it for David and He will do the same for us. Keep on trusting and believing in the God of compassion. His love for us is unfathomable.

Prayer--Surrendering All to Jesus!

Our Dear Father, who art in Heaven. Holy be Your sweet and precious name. Thy Kingdom come, please let Your will be done in my life as I humbly depend on You. Father, I thank You for Your Word that I hid deep within my heart that I will not sin against Thee. Search me dear God, and free me from inward sins and all unrighteousness. Holy Spirit, thank You for Your divine revelation to apply Psalm 51 in my life. Today as I bow down in worship, I ask that You remove from me the weight and burden of sins that would hinder me from praising You. Let my mind be steadfast on You to deny the physical so I can receive more of You for the Spiritual. Remove every habit of the old flesh, so I can worship You in Spirit and Truth. Father, reveal to me the known and unknown secret sins that can hinder my breakthrough.

Today, I pray for added strength for my friend who will join me in this fasting. We are praying and believing for a revival to break out throughout all nations. Thank You Abba Father for the restoration of wisdom, knowledge, and understanding that you will do the impossible during this fasting phase. Dearest Father, please help us to apply Ezra 8:21-23, Psalms 35, 51, and 69, Jonah 3:5-9, Isaiah 58, Matthew 6:16-18, and Luke 18:1-12 over our lives as we sacrifice this time to spend with You. We thank You in advance for answering our requests, and also for the unanswered prayer. Thank You for Your anointing that will break the yoke of bondage and set us free to worship You. We give You thanks in Jesus' Holy Name. Amen!

Part 2: The Night of the Heavenly Dream

Chapter 6: Prayer and Intercession on a Cold Winter Night

Let us read together:

Apostle Paul tells young Timothy that, "Prayer is encouraged."

> *"I exhort therefore, that, first of all, supplications, prayers, intercessions, and giving of thanks, be made for all men. For Kings, and for all that are in authority; that we may lead a quiet and peaceable life in all godliness and honesty. For this is good and acceptable in the sight of God our Savior; Who will have all men to be saved, and to come unto the knowledge of the truth. For there is one God, and one mediator between God and men, the man Christ Jesus. Who gave himself a ransom for all, to be testified in due time. Whereunto I am ordained a preacher, and an apostle, (I speak the truth in Christ, and lie not;) a teacher of the Gentiles in faith and verity. I will therefore that men pray everywhere, lifting up holy hands without wrath and doubting."*
>
> --1 Timothy 2:1-8

Do you know that there is ONLY ONE MEDIATOR between God and man, and His name is Jesus, God's only son! With that being said, our daily prayer should be, thank You Jesus for standing in the gap for me. Even though Jesus died for us and paid the full price for our salvation, He continues to intercede for us daily because He knows that the adversary will try to use every opportunity to throw accusations against us. The above scripture is reminding us that Jesus is the one and ONLY mediator between God and man.

The Apostle Paul is encouraging young Timothy to keep on praying and give thanks, to encourage the people then and it is important to practice that same role now. The Apostle Paul was like a father figure to young Timothy, and he wanted him to tell the leader and others to pray and seek the true and living God not to listen to false prophets. That command is also relevant to us in our modern world because many false teachers in the world are trying to distract and derail God's people from the truth of God.

We, as believers, need to be in constant prayer with vigilant eyes so we can be alert and stay focused as we seek God's direction every day. God wants us to pray and intercede for people near and far. Therefore, we are encouraged to be in constant prayer because it is our main mode of communication to get to our Heavenly Father. Jesus is our number one role model who sacrifices so much time in praying to the Father for us. He encouraged His disciples to pray, leaving a great example for us to follow and practice. So, too, Apostle Paul is encouraging Timothy to intercede and pray that people will repent and turn to the Almighty God.

The enemy will never get tired of trying to kill, steal, and destroy us. We have to remember that the enemy knows the Bible and doesn't care if we know the Word of God or not. He aims to catch us at our weakest moment, so he can distract us and let us lose our way. But in the Mighty Name of Jesus, we are going to hit him with the Word so that he will flee from us. We are a big target to the enemy, especially if we are not applying the Word to our lives. That's why we should read and meditate on the Word. Most of all, apply it to our lives. This approach is necessary because it will help to prepare us to walk in the Spirit and not in the flesh, as we die daily. We should not hesitate to show love and appreciation to Jesus Christ for not only dying on the cross but for playing the role of a mediator and an intercessor for us. Jesus is our first and foremost role model in intercession, and He also wants us to pray for each other.

I know several family members, friends, and spiritual leaders prayed for me throughout the different seasons of my life. There comes a time when we need to focus our prayers on leaders from all over the world including people of all nations. The amazing thing about prayer is

Chapter 6: Prayer and Intercession on a Cold Winter Night

there is no distance, excuse, or limitation in prayer. The Bible tells us to "Pray without ceasing" (1Thess. 5:17). This means that we should be in constant prayer with God, always communicating with the Father, Son, and Holy Spirit. Praying anywhere, anytime, and for anyone, but not like hypocrites (*see* Matthew 6:5). Prayer is a wonderful way to communicate with the Supreme God, an act of fellowship that can bring unity to the body of Christ. It is a beautiful thing to adhere to the voice of the Holy Spirit as you humble yourself in prayer. I can never forget one particular night of prayer when the Holy Spirit instructed me to pray outside of my territory. A night when divine changes took place in my prayer life as the Holy Spirit commanded me to pray for my church family!

It was a frigid winter night in February of 2012 in Windsor, Connecticut, when I had the most phenomenal dream of my life. I was still in the recovery phase of a major abdominal surgery, which I had had four months before the dream. It was a time in my life when I was leaning on Jesus to rescue me from all the stressors blocking my breakthrough and my deliverance. I felt like my world was in turmoil, a devastating lump of frustration and confusion clouded my vision and breakthrough. However, I was holding on to the hands of my Savior! Deep within my heart, I knew this man, Jesus from Galilee, would never leave me or turn His back on me. Daily, He intercedes on our behalf. Through anguish and pain, the Holy Spirit will guide us into worship and prayer because He is always there, comforting us. That night, the Holy Spirit was cradling me in His loving arms as I reached out to God, my Father, for healing and deliverance!

I knew it was Jesus who was keeping me alive through all the attacks of the enemy coming at me from many angles. Jesus knows how to roll away our burden and cradle us in His big, loving arms. Sometimes, I had to stop amid the storm and give God praise for His kind and tender mercies, thanking Him for being my warrior in the time of war! He was always there, mending and fixing my broken and puzzled life. Thank You, Father, for Your never-ending love and warm protection over my life. Holy Spirit, thank You for residing in me! Let me never cease to acknowledge Your role and presence in my life. I pray I will always appreciate You and not be frustrated by the distraction of the enemy as You lead and guide me. I will stay focused on You only.

I can never forget that Sunday night when I was slowly walking up the stairs to my bedroom. I could hardly make it up the stairs, winded and out of breath for weeks. I intended to read for a while, pray, and go to bed. However, in the stillness and quiet moment of the night, I was having some sharp, lingering pain from my abdominal incision sites. So, I walked slowly up the stairs and down the hallway, holding on to the rails while balancing on the wall leading to my room. I called out, "Goodnight," to my daughter, whose bedroom was near my room. With gripping pain now all over my body, I reached out and opened the door, anxiously trying to get in bed before the pain got any worse!

After opening my bedroom door, I noticed the branches from one of my neighbor's trees swaying in different directions to the futile and gusty cold wind, brushing against the side of the house near the front window. Thinking aloud, "This is winter," I felt a chilly shiver trail down my spine. "This is going to be a very cold winter!" **At that moment, I didn't know that night was going to be one of the most beautiful and defining moments of my life. The night when my pain changed to healing and my sadness to gladness and I met Jesus face-to-face in my dream! Glory be to God!**

I struggled to make it into bed, but deep within my heart, I had already declared my healing, even though I didn't know what God had in store for me! So, as usual, I tried to settle in bed with a prayer book and my Bible ready to read, pray, and get some sleep. That night, I was also seeking the Lord in prayer for physical, psychological, spiritual, and mental healing, deliverance, and breakthrough. At first, I was praying for myself and all the problems and brokenness I was experiencing, mostly praying about my emotional well-being. I was crying out to my Healer, Jehovah Rapha, to deliver me and set me free from pain. I knew my Redeemer was always beside me, protecting, guiding, and healing me. So, I

Chapter 6: Prayer and Intercession on a Cold Winter Night

continued to pray and give God praise. Then suddenly, I felt the presence of the Holy Spirit moving in me, taking me to a secret place in prayer that I had never been before, a wonderful place of praise and thanksgiving. Everything felt so rich and wonderful in the presence of the Lord!

The Holy Spirit directed me to start praying for my family, friends, and church family. Most of the names I remembered, so I would call out their names in prayer and cry out to the Lord on behalf of my loved ones in whatever way the Holy Spirit directed me. This went on for approximately eighty to ninety minutes; I had never had this experience before while praying. After a while, I had a nauseating feeling and became sick to my stomach. I rushed to the bathroom and my daughter ran in to see me. I had spewed out a large amount of phlegm. Immediately after I rinsed my mouth, **I felt like all the organs in my body felt different, like an internal shift, resulting in added strength and power in my extremities. My pain and distraught body felt new and revived!**

Amazingly, I walked back to my room with so much strength, speed, and joy! Everything changed from feeling abnormal to feeling normal. There was an instant change in my entire body; a newness overcame me like a tsunami of peace and happiness. I was rejoicing and glorifying God while moving around with no pain. I was ambulating more steadily on my feet with no assistive device. Four months prior, I had had a ten-hour abdominal surgery. That surgery had me in so much pain. I was bent out of shape, having several recurring visits to the hospital for the past four months. So, this shift from pain to no pain was worth a praise dance and a shout glorifying God for healing me. I kept on repeating, "HALLELUJAH! HALLELUJAH!" Jehovah Rapha came to heal, deliver, and set me free! Glory HALLELUJAH!

So, I went back to my room, intending to get into bed. However, it was not to be. Not at all. The Holy Spirit inspired and commanded me to continue praying. So, I walked around in my room, praying and praising God. My entire being was lost in total worship. The Holy

Spirit took complete control! He was interceding for me in languages I had never heard before. It was powerful and amazing. The anointing was so rich, that my daughter came into the room and joined me in praising God. She was in disbelief when she saw me moving around and balancing on my own. I could not stop rejoicing and praising God, my Father, for His healing virtue and power that was making me feel so healthy and happy.

The Spirit made intercession for me, and I was praying in the Heavenly language for over one hour, not realizing that God was preparing me for the most beautiful dream of my life. The Holy Spirit is such an incredible Comforter, always interceding for us according to the will of God. *Romans 8:26-27 says, "Likewise, the Spirit also helpeth our infirmities: for we know not what we should pray for as we ought: but the Spirit itself maketh intercession for us with groanings which cannot be uttered. And He that searcheth the hearts knoweth what is the mind of the Spirit because He maketh intercession for the saints according to the will of God."*

It was a wonderful feeling and an awesome connection to be in the presence of the Lord late in the midnight hour, leading up to four or five o'clock a.m. That was my special private time with the King of my life! God wants us to be constant in prayer. Spending time with the Lord will lead to a divine intimacy with God, our Father. There is such a distinct feeling in the atmosphere when you set aside quality time with the Savior! The world seems quieter, and your ability to hear the Lord is so sharp. I love to seek Him late at night; I call it "my precious moment with King Jesus." The Bible tells us of several midnight encounters that some of the biblical characters experienced along their faith journey. For instance, Moses met with the Lord in the midnight hour: And Moses said, "Thus saith the Lord, about midnight will I go out into the midst of Egypt" (Exodus 11:4 *KJV*). We don't know when the Lord is going to turn up at our door. We must be ready to meet the Savior, day or night.

You may have a different preferred time to spend with the Lord, but any time you choose to spend with Him is just wonderful. Find a time when you can feel the breath of God whispering in your ears, telling you beautiful things like, "I am here with you; I will never leave you; I will love you forever and I will protect you from the schemes of the enemy." Jesus will whisper assurances to you when fear wants to hinder your peace. We all need that private place and time with Jesus. He is never tired of hearing our voices. Seek that special time and moment with your Savior, who is full of mercy, forgiveness, and love. It is so beautiful, sacred, and peaceful to receive His love and healing power even as you bow down before Him in humility!

Finally, after having such an awesome and glorious encounter with the Lord, I decided to go to bed. Laying in the semi-dark room, I was thinking, "We don't know why we sometimes experience affliction," but also remembering to give God glory for His healing power through it all. In my heart, I was rejoicing with praises coming from my lips as I crawled under the blanket, feeling completely healed, revived, restored, and refreshed in my mind, body, and soul! Glory to God!

Chapter 7: Hours Just Before the Dream

THOSE IN CHRIST WILL BE COMFORTED

> *"Blessed be God, even the Father of our Lord Jesus Christ, the Father of mercies, and the God of all comfort; Who comforteth us in all our tribulation, that we may be able to comfort them which are in any trouble, by the comfort wherewith we ourselves are comforted of God."*
>
> --2 Corinthians 1:3-4 *KJV*

The Apostle Paul is telling us in the above scripture that the Father of mercies, and the God of all comfort will comfort us in all our tribulation. This wonderful comfort that we receive from our Father of mercies we can extend to others who need to be comforted. In life, we will experience all kinds of difficulties in the physical and the spiritual realms. However, we have hope in God that He will never leave us comfortless. The Holy Spirit is our Comforter, and He is always there to give us the peace and assurance that He resides within us and is always interceding for us. Late in the midnight hour or early in the morning, the Comforter is working on our behalf and praying for us. It is a good feeling to be in a close relationship with our Lord Jesus Christ, the one who daily extends His grace and mercy towards us. My mind was fixed on the healing that took place in my body and I was feeling so relaxed in the presence of the Lord. The glory of the Lord filled my room and even in my bed as I lay down to sleep, I felt the tranquility of peace. The warm embrace of the spirit of the Lord within me and around me was glorious. The Omnipresent is here and I am confident that my sleep will be sweet because of the peace in my heart.

It was approximately five o'clock in the morning when I settled down

Chapter 7: Hours Just Before the Dream

in bed. I felt extremely happy, free, and overjoyed because the anointing of the Lord was so rich and powerful, and I felt healed and renewed after that encounter with the Lord. The Holy Ghost fire was so hot, rich, and powerful! It felt like a host of angels was there praising Jehovah Rapha with me. It is so amazing how the healing power of God can change your perception and attitude, leading you into a mode of praise, worship, and thanksgiving. The atmosphere was charged with the supernatural presence of the Lord. I could feel God my Father enfolding me in His arms of security and comfort! It was a place of comfort, peace, and serenity that could put anyone to sleep!

Soon after, I fell into a sweet sleep and a wonderful dream-- a dream that has changed my life tremendously over the years and encourages my family and friends in their Christian journey to be ready for the return of King Jesus. They told me it impacted their Christian life in many ways, drawing them closer to the Lord and deepening their curiosity about the supernatural encounter with Jesus. **I wish everyone could get a glimpse of the Heavenly bliss that I experienced in the beautiful dream. No words in any dictionary can describe the majestic beauty and the glory that surrounded Christ the Lord. It was far beyond my human comprehension to put into words, expression, or description.**

As Christians, we must stay in tune with the Holy Spirit at all times. We are in partnership with the Holy Spirit as He guides us into all truth. He is our Guide, our Strength, and our Comforter. Thank You, Holy Spirit, for leading me and guiding me throughout every season of my life. Thank You for the divine Heavenly revelation that You disclosed to me through this wonderful encounter, an epiphany that will stay with me forever. All praises to God Almighty!

Chapter 8: The Dream and Who I Saw in the Dream

"And they dreamed a dream both of them, each man his dream in one night, each man according to the interpretation of his dream, the butler and the baker of the king of Egypt, which were bound in the prison. And Joseph came in unto them in the morning, and looked upon them, and, behold, they were sad. And he asked Pharaoh's officers that were with him in the ward of his lord's house, saying, Wherefore look ye so sadly to day? And they said unto him, "We have dreamed a dream, and there is no interpreter of it. And Joseph said unto them, Do not interpretations belong to God? tell me them, I pray you." (Genesis 40:5-8)

Have you ever experienced a divine encounter with Jesus in a dream or a vision, one in which you are so baffled, that you can't contain your excitement? Deep within your heart, you know only God can give you the answers or the interpretation or He will send someone. As seen from the above scripture, the butler and the baker were anxious to tell their dreams and to get an answer. They needed an interpreter. Joseph turned up and he noticed that they were looking sad and asked them why they were sad. After responding to Joseph's question about their dreams. Joseph responded that interpretation belongs to God. Isn't it amazing how our God operated? He always has an answer coming straight from his breath through a mouthpiece, such as Joseph. The young man was bullied and rejected by his brothers. The one who was thrown in a pit and left to die! God will use the broken and rejected people to do his work if you make yourself available to be used by God.

Several years ago, I had a supernatural encounter of seeing Jesus descending from the right side of Heaven's Golden Gates. I can still remember every detail of that supernatural dream to this day. It's a

Chapter 8: The Dream and Who I Saw in the Dream

revelation that makes me freeze in shock waves of acute nostalgia, excitement, and awe every time I think about it, which is several times per day! This dream took me far away from the physical realms and into the Heavenly Spiritual realms with my Savior--a moment in time when I was trying to grasp and conceptualize the meaning, questions, and answers to this phenomenal dream. Soon after, I reflected on Joseph, who was called a dreamer and an interpreter of dreams, when he said, "Do not interpretations belong to God?" I knew then and now that it is only through the direction of the precious Holy Spirit that governs me that I have the supernatural recall to remember such a magnificent dream, especially the divine appearance of my Lord and my Savior that stays affixed in my mind forever! I know God is the only one who can give me an answer to some of the questions that arise from this phenomenal adventure in the Heavenly realms.

This exceptional dream took place on February 12, 2012, in Windsor, Connecticut, United States of America. I realized it was a divine appointment and a supernatural experience to see King Jesus descending from the Golden Gates of Heaven. There are several people in the Bible whom God communicates with through dreams and visions, and today God is still talking to His children in several different ways. The Bible tells us in Acts 2:17, *"And it shall come to pass in the last days, saith God, I will pour out of my Spirit upon all flesh: And your sons and your daughters shall prophesy, and your young men shall see visions, and your old men shall dream dreams."* This is the Word of the Lord from before time and space, and His Word stands forever. We don't know when the last days will be; however, God said He would pour out His spirit upon ALL flesh in whatever way He chooses. Therefore, we need to be spiritually alert and aware of such gifts and allow the Holy Spirit to direct us into the truth of God's will and plan after the pouring out of the Spirit of God.

Even though I had several extraordinary dreams of Heaven, which I would share with my family and friends over the years, this was the first dream that was so vivid and detailed, with so many Biblical characters, most of all, Jesus descending from Heaven in His fullness of glory! Furthermore, this dream has changed my life and relationship with the Lord for the better in so many ways. In addition, the Lord also directed me in another dream to write this book about the Heavenly dream and share it with the world.

In this encounter with the Messiah, I realized and understood even more that nothing in this world is more important than having a good relationship with the Lord. Jesus is coming back soon for a church without spots, blemishes, or wrinkles. Furthermore, the most important question that we should have at the center of our minds and the apex of our hearts daily is: *"Am I ready to meet the King who is the Ruler and Judge of the Universe?"* **Other questions are,** *"Am I living according to His will? Am I always seeking Him first and showing love to my sisters and brothers as He commands?* "These are some of the questions we should be asking ourselves as we await the return of the Lord. May your heart be blessed as you prepare to meet the One who chose to make you and me in His likeness and His image!

I desire that you will be blessed as you read about this amazing revelation I experienced with our Lord and King. Holy Spirit, I thank You for guiding me into all the truth as I penned all the information You directed me to record so it can be a source of help to empower everyone who reads this book or tells others. I trust and believe that this Heavenly experience will encourage you to fight the good fight of faith as you await the return of Jesus, the Messiah!

THE HEAVENLY DREAM

I dreamt that I was driving on Cottage Grove Road in Bloomfield, Connecticut on my way home from Sunday night service, which was after nine p.m. My daughter, Sivanaise, and one of her friends were sitting in the back seat of my car. In the dream, they both looked like age ten, even though, in reality, they were in their early twenties. As I approached the Commuter parking lot and was ready to take a left turn to Walcott Street, I looked up at the sky to the brightest light I had ever seen. **It looked exceptionally bright, so much brighter than**

Chapter 8: The Dream and Who I Saw in the Dream

daylight as if several suns were shining in the night coming straight through the car. I was so captivated by this array of shining light and brightness; remembering that this was after nine p.m. The beaming light flooded the Heavens above so brightly, illuminating the entire sky as far as I could see down to Earth! I stared so hard at the beaming light, which seemed as if it was coming from the farthest part of the sky towards me. Immediately, I felt my body lift from the car through the roof, swiftly going up into the clouds towards the bright light. Suddenly, I was in midair, locked in by the power of God Almighty! Everything within me and around me instantly changed for the better-- overwhelmingly transparent, bright, and clear! My body changed to total freedom of peace, tranquility, and joy! I had never felt like this before!

I kept looking straight at the light, and there through the ever-so-white cloud descending from the right side of Heaven's Golden Gates, was JESUS, MY LORD! I was in shock, and I was speechless, baffled by the glory and holiness of the King of Glory coming down out of Heaven! In awe, I stared in bewilderment and was rooted to a spot in the air where EVERYTHING felt new and beautiful! My eyes were fixed on the returning King of Kings! The Bible tells us in John 3:13, *"And no man hath ascended up to heaven, but he that came down from heaven, even the Son of man which is in heaven."*

There! My Lord and Savior was descending out from the Heavenly cloud in all His glory! JESUS, the Messiah, was looking straight at me with such illumination of bright lights! In those jaw-dropping moments, I couldn't explain my expression or excitement! Internally, I was screaming, "JESUS! JESUS!" He seemed so far up in the Heavens, yet He was close enough for me to see Him also standing in midair, looking down at me with **SO MUCH LOVE, OUTSTRETCHED HANDS, AND OPEN ARMS.** I kept on staring in astonishment and bewilderment! Then, while gazing, I began shouting so hard, "JESUS! JESUS! JESUS!" I felt as if I was going to burst with extreme excitement and astonishment.

Everything felt like waves of oceans of bubbling joy and happiness flowing through me, over me, and around me! Seeing King Jesus before my eyes, shining so gloriously bright and dazzlingly beautiful was beyond my imagination! **There is nothing to compare to the ultimate expression of God's love for us as seen and felt through His beloved Son Jesus. GOD IS LOVE!** The Bible tells us in 1 John 4:10-12, "*Herein is love, not that we loved God, but that he loved us, and sent his son to be the propitiation for our sins. Beloved, if God so loved us, we ought also to love one another. No man hath seen God at any time. If we love one another, God dwelleth in us, and his love is perfected in us.*"

Friends, I desire to have that divine encounter stay fresh within me forever, and I hope you are getting a picturesque image of this encounter! It was the most glorious experience I have ever had in my whole life. The entire atmosphere was Spirit-filled and supernaturally divine, extraordinarily gorgeous, and captivating! Seeing Jesus in the dream took me to Acts 7:54-60. Just before Steven was stoned, he spoke of seeing Jesus standing at the right hand of God! It was such a crucial and divine moment for him to see the glory of God! I am sure his joy of seeing God the Father and God the Son and having God the Holy Spirit with him led him into eternal rest and peace! Nothing else in the world matters when you are captivated and engrossed in the presence of God. So, in that Heavenly moment in Stephen's life, his physical body was stoned, but his Spirit was in the presence of the Lord! So too, I know that my Spirited body was in the presence of my Lord because everything felt amazingly different. I know my body has changed because of the feeling of purity and Holiness that was surrounding Jesus flows such extreme joy in my soul! My body was dead and transformed to total peace in the presence and glory of the Lord (*see* Colossians 3:3-4).

The anointing of the Holy Ghost helped Stephen to stay focused even as he was persecuted. The Bible tells us that Stephen, "*...looked up steadfastly into heaven, and saw the glory of God, and Jesus standing at the right hand of God*" (Acts 7:55). In this life, we too will suffer at the hands of those who do not believe in the True and Living God, but we can take a page from Stephen and stand firm and flat-footed for God, even through the trying circumstances, that this life is only

Chapter 8: The Dream and Who I Saw in the Dream

temporary. **There is a reward waiting for us in Heaven that cannot compare to the suffering we will experience on earth which will be eternal life with Christ our King. Most of all, living in the presence of the Lord forever should be the daily desire of our hearts!**

As I stood staring at Jesus, I was so eager and curious to run toward Him and to the Golden Gate, but I soon realized I could not move. I was held in that position in midair, looking at the most glorious scene one could behold! One of the amazing revelations was that Jesus seemed so far away in the cloud, yet He was so close as if I could feel and touch the powerful presence of His breath on me and through me! **My heart was on a marathon of its own! I can't say how many miles per minute! It was beating so loudly, pounding like a drum playing inside my head, even though I felt the pounding in my heart. I could almost feel the rhythmic thudding sound of extreme joy and happiness in my ear!**

I was in the presence of Jesus, the Messiah, the Son of the Almighty God, and He was looking straight at me with a floodgate of love and compassion! **Gazing at my Savior was staggeringly surreal! The sovereignty of the Great and Mighty King Jesus was breathtaking.** Seeing and experiencing the Holy Spirit that is living inside me was overwhelming. Sweeter than honey! **Jesus' shining eyes were piercing straight through me like a see-through mirror; He was looking at every atom, neuron, and fiber of my being!** This body He authentically made even the Spirit man was exposed to Him for criticism or rebuke; however, He was not reprimanding or condemning me. **His look spoke THE FRUIT OF THE SPIRIT with intense compassion and love in such a volume that I didn't want to be out of His sight!** I wanted to be in His presence, which captivated my attention to the point that I couldn't move. I was spellbound by the *Dunamis* power of the Almighty God, and it felt amazingly wonderful.

The atmosphere was different from anything I had ever experienced before. The tranquility of Holiness and Righteousness was beyond words or explanation! Even though I couldn't move, I was comfortable and relaxed just to be in the presence of my Lord. It felt like the clouds made a special cozy sofa for me so I could enjoy the picturesque scenery of Heaven as I kept looking at Jesus. The Bible tells us in (1 Chronicles 16:26-27 (*ESV*), *"For all the gods of the peoples are worthless idols, but the Lord made the heavens. Splendor and majesty are before him; strength and joy are in his place."* There is only one God that we are to worship, the One that can fill us with unspeakable joy. Only in Him can we feel and experience beauty, splendor, majesty, strength, and power. I can only feel unexplained delight in His presence, which rejuvenates every fiber of my being. The scripture also tells us, *"You make known to me the path of life; in your presence, there is fullness of joy; at your right hand are pleasures forevermore"* (Psalm 16:11). Hallelujah! I still cannot contain the elation of splendor and joy seeing my Savior bursting out from the cloud! **It was an extreme adrenaline rush of joy and happiness! Everything about Jesus is radiant, divine, sacred, holy, and righteous!** His light flooded the Heavens, and His holiness was full of sincere purity and truth!

During the dream, it felt like telepathic communication; Jesus was responding to everything I was thinking about, even before I could voice my thoughts. My thought process was severely stretched and extended to a different level of Heavenly wisdom of perfect happiness and delight in the presence of the Lord. His love was speaking to me without Him opening His mouth or making any gestures. **I could sense and feel the power coming forth from His presence as if He was injecting His compassionate love into me with passion and sincerity through the sharp, needle-piercing look coming from the eyes of such a bright light! His majestic aura filled the Heavens and saturated the entire world with unexplained LOVE--an unending love without boundaries, borders, or limits.**

Friends, I can't explain Jesus' love and compassion for us. There is nothing in the world to compare or match to the magnitude of endless LOVE coming from our Father above. Jesus loves us so much; you can't even measure it! David tells us, *"For as high as the heavens are above the earth, so great is his love for those who fear him"* (Psalm 103:11 *NIV*).

Chapter 8: The Dream and Who I Saw in the Dream

Jesus' love for us is unfailing, unconditional, unquestioning, and unlimited, from everlasting to everlasting. What a mighty and loving God He is, with so much love to generously share with everyone day after day! In return, Jesus wants us to love and worship Him in Spirit and Truth by following His commandments, statutes, and precepts. The Bible says, *"And thou shalt love the Lord thy God with all thy heart, and with all thy soul, and with all thy mind, and with all thy strength: this is the first commandment"* (Mark 12:30 KJV).

We don't deserve God's love; we walk away from God so many times and we don't warrant His new mercies and grace, but He continues to extend it toward us. The Bible tells us, "But after that the kindness and love of God our Savior toward man appeared, not by works of righteousness which we have done, but according to his mercy he saved us, by the washing of regeneration, and renewing of the Holy Ghost" (Titus 3:4-5). Our works and righteousness cannot save us. We are saved by Jesus' grace and washing of regeneration, which makes us new in the sight of God. **We have nothing to boast about, so we should not have so much pride that we cannot acknowledge that we are sinners and are only saved by God's grace.** Daily, we should seek the washing and purging of our sin-sick souls by being submissive to the will of God.

As the dream continued, I felt a newness come over me while I was in the presence of the Lord as if my new body was changing more and more, and I felt so much lighter! I knew I was in midair, standing before my Savior, but I had no idea what my body looked like; which I knew had changed! It may sound strange, but I did not check my body, nor did I have any desire to do so. Throughout the dream, my focus was to keep my eyes on Jesus and everything in front of me. There was so much glory and power coming from and around Jesus that I felt fixated to focus only on Him!

Friends, are you reaching out to Jesus? He has outstretched hands and open arms with nail-print palms to welcome you home! All He requires from us is a repentant heart to believe and surrender our life to Him. He is the only one who can save you from sin and give you salvation and eternal life! *Romans 6:23 says, "For the wages of sin is death; but the gift of God is eternal life through Jesus Christ our Lord."* Today I encourage you to choose eternal life through Jesus Christ, our Lord.

Chapter 9: Seeing Jesus in His Pearly White Robe

Transfiguration of Jesus Christ

> "And after six days Jesus taketh Peter, James, and John his brother, and bringeth them up into an high mountain apart and was transfigured before them: and his face did shine as the sun, and his raiment was white as the light. And behold, there appeared unto them Moses and Elias talking with him. Then answered Peter, and said unto Jesus, Lord, it is good for us to be here: if thou wilt, let us make here three tabernacles; one for thee, and one for Moses, and one for Elias. While he yet spake, behold, a bright cloud overshadowed them: and behold a voice out of the cloud, which said, This is my beloved Son, in whom I am well pleased; hear ye him. And when the disciples heard it, they fell on their face, and were sore afraid. And Jesus came and touched them, and said, Arise, and be not afraid. And when they had lifted their eyes, they saw no man, save Jesus only."
>
> --Matthew 17:1-8 *KJV*

As I continued to look up at Jesus shining through the cloud, I noticed He was dressed in an ever-so-beautiful pearly white robe with huge sleeves. The sleeves seemed as if they were folds floating endlessly within the cloud. I have never seen a robe so gloriously impressive to the naked eye. The sleeves were so magnificent, long, and wide; I did not see a hem, any borders, nor where the bottom of the robe ended. **This incredibly unique and distinctive robe seemed to cover the entire world! It was a robe of purity, holiness, supremacy, and endlessness.** Also, there was light with lively floating movements shining in the Heavens. It seemed to clothe the righteous and holy Savior, echoing the magnitude of His majesty, glory, and power that transcends to time and space.

I kept on staring in awe and bewilderment! Now, I can understand how the disciples felt on the Mount of Transfiguration! Before I had this encounter, it was unbelievably hard to comprehend what the disciples witnessed there in the presence of Jesus and hearing the powerful voice of God coming out of the cloud!

Breathlessly, I saw and beheld the divinity of the illumination of lights that filled the heavenly cloud around my Savior standing above and before me! *"His countenance was like lightning, and his raiment white as snow"* (Matthew 28:3). My senses were stretched to the next level, especially my vision. It felt like I had several pairs of eyes because of the magnitude of my ability to see everything crystal clear and in-depth. My vision was not 20/20 vision; it was so much brighter. However, I was too excited and in shock to ask any questions.

Our thoughts and focus should be more of Him and less of us, and that's exactly where my thoughts were, feeling such a yearning desire, passion, and hunger to be with Jesus that nothing else mattered. **One cannot get enough of sweet Jesus. The great Messiah can quench that thirst and longing because it is a spiritual thirst that can only be satisfied by Jesus!** Are you thirsting after His righteousness? Today, Jesus is calling you to come and draw from His well of living water! (*see* John 4:13-15).

Jesus will fill your spiritual water pot, and you will thirst no more; reach out and receive that living water from the fountain that shall never run dry! I admonish you not to refuse to drink the water of life from that free-running fountain! We get thirsty and sometimes dehydrated from not having enough physical or natural liquid. Likewise, **Jesus is that spiritual fountain that can hydrate your dehydrated soul with the supernatural water of life. We should not be running around with all kinds of sinful symptoms, being spiritually dehydrated, spiritually drained, spiritually malnourished, and spiritually handicapped because we are not drinking from the living well of Jesus.** Seek Jesus now; He is the Great Physician who can prescribe an invasive dosage of Holy Ghost water, infused with *Dunamis* power coming straight from His ever-

Chapter 9: Seeing Jesus in His Pearly White Robe

flowing WELL fully prescribed and paid for, to supply our daily needs. Jesus is the greatest scientist and the greatest physician ever to walk this Earth! Will you trust Him to physically, mentally, emotionally, and spiritually diagnose all your symptoms? Jesus can deliver you and save you from all unrighteousness (*see* 2 Kings 5:10, Daniel 4:34, Psalm 34:18, Psalm 103:2-3). **His BLOOD will heal, cleanse, purge, and make you whole. Jesus got ALL the remedy because He is the remedy! Jehovah Rapha—Our Healer!** (*see* **Matthew 4: 23-24). He will heal, deliver, and set you free.**

Continuing with the dream, I could not believe Christ my Lord was standing in midair looking straight at me! Yes, I was dumbfounded with curiosity, joy, and gladness, observing all the majestic beauty around me that kept appearing so swiftly, suddenly, and ever so fast. Jesus continued to look at me with so much love, gentleness, and compassion, with eyes full of grace and mercy. His gesture, along with His expression, spoke forgiveness and no condemnation. The words of Isaiah told us, *"I, even I am he that, blotteth out thy transgressions for mine own sake, and will not remember thy sins"* (Isaiah 43:25 *KJV).* Such a wonderful promise from our Savior! May we live according to the will of God by putting our complete and total focus on Jesus Christ our Lord, the One who can blot out our transgressions and remember our sins no more. Thank you, God, for being our forgiving Father!

We serve a God that is so big, a gigantic and enormous God that is without limit and measure. We can't help but fear this true and living God, the Supreme Author of the universe! This triune God reigns forever and controls the World, the galaxies, every atom, and every planet! He is an Omniscient God! He made everything perfect and put everything together with His blueprint in six days. Wow! My God! My God! Oh, how I love and adore You! You, Oh Lord, are excellent in all your works in Heaven, on Earth, and under the Earth! I join with David in Psalm 8:1,3,4, 9 when he says:

> *"O LORD our Lord, how excellent is thy name in all the earth! who has set thy glory above the heavens. v3 When I consider thy heavens,*

> the work of thy fingers, the moon, and the stars, which thou hast ordained; v4 What is man, that thou art mindful of him? and the son of man, that thou visitest him? v9 O LORD our Lord, how excellent is thy name in all the earth!"

Hallelujah! Seeing Jesus at Heaven's Golden Gates, I had so many questions, yet I dared not ask them. I can only imagine how the prophet Isaiah felt when he spoke about seeing the Lord and the beauty that surrounded Him—describing the appearance of the seraphim and how they cried to each other, "Holy, Holy, Holy is the Lord of hosts!" Can you imagine the atmosphere's beauty in the Lord's presence? He continued to say the house was filled with smoke. Even though it has been over two thousand years since the prophet Isaiah spoke those words, I am happy that the Word of God remains the same forever. Most of all, we are serving the same King, the Lord of hosts, the same Christ who lives forever more! Let Him be the ruler of your life!

I joined in with Isaiah when he said:

> *In the year that King Uzziah died I saw also the Lord sitting upon a throne, high and lifted, and his train filled the temple. Above it stood the seraphims: each one had six wings; with twain he covered his face, and with twain he covered his feet, and with twain he did fly. And one cried unto another, and said, Holy, holy, holy, is the LORD of hosts: the whole earth is full of his glory. And the posts of the door moved at the voice of him that cried, and the house was filled with smoke. Then said I, Woe is me! for I am undone; because I am a man of unclean lips, and I dwell in the midst of a people of unclean lips: for mine eyes have seen the King, the LORD of hosts. Then flew one of the seraphim unto me, having a live coal in his hand, which he had taken with the tongs from off the altar: And he laid it upon my mouth, and said, Lo, this hath touched thy lips; and thine iniquity is taken away, and thy sin purged. Also, I heard the voice of the Lord, saying, Whom shall I send, and who will go for us? Then said I,' Here am I; send me'* (Isaiah 6:1-8).

I am sure my eyes were popping out from my head in shock and

Chapter 9: Seeing Jesus in His Pearly White Robe

amazement looking at my Lord! Seeing Jesus on the right side of the Golden Gates of Heaven was beyond spectacular, it was so powerful and astonishing! Isaiah said, "Here am I; send me." Just like Isaiah, I am saying, **"Lord, send me; Lord, I am available to be used by You. Prepare and anoint my mouth only to speak and write what You assigned me to do. I said Lord, please burn out everything from my mouth and fill me with your Holy Ghost Fire! Use every area of my life for Your glory and to build Your kingdom!"**

There were times when I questioned myself, saying, "Lord, I am so unworthy to have seen all the beautiful things you set before my eyes." However, I look back and I earnestly thank God for this divine favor in allowing me to have a glimpse of this magnificent and **glorious paradise at Heaven's Gates. Sweet Jesus, I thank You for** preparing this home in glory for Your children and You promise that You will come back for those who live according to Your will and Your ways. Holy Spirit, I thank You for Your divine intervention and revelation as You gently walk and guide me through every word that is penned in the fabric of this book. Father, this is far beyond my imagination, but I will forever be grateful to You for Your kindness and blessings in every area of my life! Father God, You are so high and lifted! Lord, I want to bow down and worship You. You are the **King of all nations and there's none like you. Angels bow before You!** Jeremiah says:

> *"Forasmuch as there is none like unto thee, O LORD; thou art great, and thy name is great in might. Who would not fear thee, O King of nations? for to thee doth it appertain: forasmuch as among all the wise men of the nations, and in all their kingdoms, there is none like unto thee"* (Jeremiah 10:6-7).

In the dream, I noticed Jesus standing in an atmospheric glow of shining light traveling with and around Him. As I looked at this great King I saw and felt the magnitude of God's greatness, His awesome presence, and magnificent splendor! He appeared as if He was sitting or standing at the peak of the world with His skirt covering the entire universe. The Bible tells us in Isaiah 40:22, *"It is he that sitteth upon the circle of the earth, and inhabitants thereof are as grasshoppers; that stretcheth out the heavens as a curtain, and spreadeth them out as a tent to dwell in."* Looking from above, we appear small and powerless like grasshoppers, but God knows our names and numbers every hair on our head. We are precious in God's sight and His love for us goes far beyond our comprehension. It is only because of His love for us and extensive grace and mercies toward us that we have access to the kingdom of Heaven. Yet, the flesh would let us sometimes boast as if we are the ones who breathed life into our bodies! Living daily without acknowledging that God lends us His breath is pride trying to enter in to block our mind about the power and blessings of God over our life.

Never think you are going to wake up the next day because of your entitlement to have life without depending on God to breathe into you. We are nothing if we do not accept Jesus as the Lord of our lives! He is the only One that lends us His breath! Let us use His breath to adore and glorify Him as we prepare for His royal return! There comes a time when we must humble ourselves, repent of our sins, and live for Jesus. Jesus is the ONLY way! He is pure, and He is Holy!

The awesome and precious Lamb of God was so beautifully adorned in His pearly white robe spreading like a blanket over the world! Do you know Him as your personal Lord and Savior? God is commanding us to walk in His will and His way! Jeremiah tells us, *"But this thing commanded I them, saying, Obey my voice, and I will be your God, and ye shall be my people: and walk ye in all the ways that I have commanded you, that it may be well unto you"* (Jeremiah 7:23). The word of the prophet Jeremiah was to encourage people to serve the true God and stay away from false religion. The Word of God continues to be active and alive today, just like over two thousand years ago. Obey the voice of God, and it shall be well with thee. Obeying the word of God will bring blessings to us, our families, and our resources. If we disobey the Word, then cursed shall we be, and we will not flourish. Therefore, we need to walk in obedience to the Word of God. Live in obedience to His commands, precepts, and statutes. We want blessings to follow us and our lineage. The Word of God tells us about the blessings and curses of God if you do not obey God's holy words (*see* Deuteronomy 28).

Let God be your number one priority! His blessings will overtake you and your family. Jesus promised that He is coming back again to take us to the place He is preparing for His children. Are we preparing our hearts to meet the returning King of Kings? Friends, our Lord and Savior is coming back to take us to His eternal home in glory. Matthew tells us, *"And then shall appear the sign of the Son of man in heaven: and then shall all the tribes of the earth mourn, and they shall see the Son of man coming in the clouds of heaven with power and great glory. And he shall send his angels with a great sound of a trumpet, and they shall gather together his elect from the four winds, from one end of heaven to the other"* (Matthew 24:30-31). This is the word of God pertaining to the last days. Therefore, we need to be ready, watching, and eagerly awaiting the return of the Messiah! How will we react when we see our Savior face to face?

Jesus Descending From The Golden Gates Of Heaven

Poem: When I See My Savior's Face!

Hallelujah! Hallelujah! When I see my Savior's face!
Gazing at me with Love, Compassion, and Grace!
A face! Full of light, mercy, and endless Love!
This is JESUS, my Savior! Descending from above!

My body trembled and shook with numerous questions!
Yet! I'm so excited and happy. I dare not ask them!
This is God's son! He died on the cross just for me!
The great Messiah! He arose on the third day to set me free!

SWEET JESUS! With outstretched hands and open arms!
He is the only one who can calm my raging storms.
This is my Lord! Cloths in a majestic robe of pearly white.
His radiant appearance of such marvelous and stunning light.

A beam of his presence mirrors straight through my life!
There's nothing to screen, cover, conceal, or try to hide!
Lord! Please help me! This is a challenging race to fight!
As I face this journey day and night to make it right!

God loves us so much that he gave us his son Jesus Christ!

Poem: When I See My Savior's Face!

Jesus died on the cross for our sins, paying the full price!

Saints, will you believe in him for life eternal, He brings?

Do you know He is your Lord and Savior? He is the Royal King!

My friend, I can assure you that Heaven is beautiful, and it is so real.

Do not reject God our Father! His wrath, you will feel!

Choose JESUS now! And you will have Heaven Eternal Bliss.

If you don't, you will certainly fall into Satan's abyss!

Thank you, God! For the precious Lamb that was slain!

Because of His love, grace, and mercy, I am saved and free again!

JESUS! JESUS! O! Such a sweet and beautiful name!

He is the only One with Everlasting history and fame!

This beautiful Heaven is far beyond human comprehension.

Turn to God now! And make Heaven your final destination.

JESUS stands at the right side of Heaven's Golden Gate!

Daily Interceding for us Saints, so hold on to your faith!

Jesus is the ultimate sacrifice of unfailing LOVE; that's reality!

He is the One who bridged the gap dying on the cross for humanity!

The euphoric joy of seeing JESUS in the glorious clouds of Heaven!

And the atmosphere of love was sealing the promise God has given!

It is JESUS! The King that sitteth upon the circle of the Earth!

Pamalyn Lalor

Jesus Descending From The Golden Gates Of Heaven

Watching and protecting you, even before your mom gave birth.
Gracefully packed, woven, and sealed in His DNA!
Yes! God created man in His own image on the sixth day!

JESUS promised that He would prepare a place for you and me!
He is the PASSPORT to take us home, where we will be free!
Glory hallelujah! I am standing at Heaven's Golden Gate!
Basking in the glory of my Savior's endless love and grace!

Heaven! This wonderful PLACE, where I see my Savior face to face!
A beautiful place that we inherited through Jesus's love and grace!
Get ready my friend, The King of Kings is waiting, don't be late!
Jesus, our bridegroom will welcome you at Heaven's Golden Gates!

Chapter 10: The Golden Pearly Gates of Heaven

Jacob Dreams of a Ladder Reaching to Heaven

> *"And Jacob went out from Beersheba and went toward Haran. And he lighted upon a certain place, and tarried there all night, because the sun was set; and he took of the stones of that place, and put them for his pillows, and lay down in that place to sleep. And he dreamed, and behold a ladder set up on the earth, and the top of it reached to heaven: and behold the angels of God ascending and descending on it. And, behold, the LORD stood above it, and said, I am the LORD God of Abraham thy father, and the God of Isaac: the land whereon thou liest, to thee will I give it, and to thy seed; And thy seed shall be as the dust of the earth, and thou shalt spread abroad to the west, and to the east, and to the north, and to the south: and in thee and in thy seed shall all the families of the earth be blessed. And behold, I am with thee, and will keep thee in all places whither thou goest, and will bring thee again into this land; for I will not leave thee, until I have done that which I have spoken to thee of. And Jacob awaked out of his sleep, and he said, Surely the LORD is in this place; and I knew it not. And he was afraid, and said, How dreadful is this place! this is none other but the house of God, and this is the gate of heaven."*
>
> --Genesis 28:10-17 *KJV*

The above scripture gives us a vivid picture of Jacob's supernatural dream regarding a ladder reaching to Heaven–a dream still so profound to our lives about the promises of God not only to us but also to our seed. Surely, we realize that the same God that was with Abraham, Isaac, and Jacob is the same promise-keeping God who is still watching over us as we travel through this pilgrim's land. The journey set before us propels us through the different processes, stages, and seasons of our lives. Along this FAITH walk, our Heavenly Father continues to give us dreams and visions for various reasons, mostly to edify each other and to glorify Him. As I read and meditated on this scripture, I thanked God for the Holy Spirit for **giving me the spiritual discernment of the supremacy of God's power** and what He can show you through dreams and visions. Even as I think of Jacob when he said he dreamed, and beheld a ladder set up on the earth, and the top of it reaching heaven, I realized that there were some parallels of things I saw in my dream that stretched from Heaven to Earth such as the curtains, the robes, and David's harp, which I will talk about in the upcoming chapters.

In the dream of Heaven, as I continued to look at Jesus, I noticed the most captivating and fascinating Gates one could behold! **The Gates were golden with dazzling pearly designs of precious pearls so bright as if it was made out of bright golden lights that lit up the Heavens.** Even though the Gates were open at the entrance, all I could see were bright golden pearly lights embedded into the Gates that stretched far beyond the magnitude of my sight. Jesus was still in midair on the right side of the Gates with outstretched hands and open arms, standing in authority and power! Yet, He had one of the most radiant and breathtaking smiles of utter joy and gentleness one could ever imagine! His shining presence illuminated His glaring light to light up the entire world! The apostle John tells us, *"Then spake Jesus again unto them, saying, I am the light of the world: he that followeth me shall not walk in darkness, but shall have the light of life"* (John 8:12 KJV). Jesus' light will shine forever. Let Him be the light of your life. His light is everywhere and cannot be hidden because it illuminates the world!

The Golden Gates had the most beautiful architectural design to be seen with extreme brightness beyond our imagination. In my knowledge, I would do an injustice to the beautiful details if I tried to describe the magnificent decor on those marvelous Gates. However, with the help of the Holy Spirit, who brings my memory into the display, I am trying to give highlights of what I saw. I hope you can

Chapter 10: The Golden Pearly Gates of Heaven

use your imagination to capture the imagery of the Heavenly picture of the beautiful Golden Gates designed by the architectural hands of God.

The sparkling brightness and glare from the Gates were breathtaking and captivating. Still in shock, I could not believe I was at the Golden Gates of Heaven. **The formation of the Gates looked like gold rails between the spaces, coupled with magnificent pearls that were embedded within the spaces in a unique design. The gold on the rails was shining so bright that the height, width, and length were immeasurable because every section continued and went into the sky, which was so bright, that it went to infinity.** That authentic architectural design could only come from the Creator of the Universe. The color of the gold that made the framework and shape of the Gates was far beyond human perception. The brightness that illuminated so far and wide beyond what I could see, and measure was coming from the power and glory of God. Jesus knows all that information because He is perfect and complete in all His ways, and what He does stands forever.

My curiosity was running wild with excitement as I looked at Jesus and saw this awesomeness and beauty in front of me. I just wanted to run into His arms and go through those beautiful Gates, but I still could not move! My attention was fixed on Jesus, and at the same time, I was fascinated by the beautiful Gates of Heaven and all the Heavenly light that lit up the world. The Bible tells us there will be no night in Heaven, for the glory of God will give us light (*see* Revelation 21 & 22). Can you imagine? Oh, Hallelujah! I remained speechless, just trying to figure out if I could make out the decor, but I was too fascinated by all the beauty around me. I was trying to grasp this Heavenly decor of such radiant bliss and tranquility! I felt like an eager child who wanted to run wild because I was facing the King at the Golden Gates, and I was super excited and fascinated about everything before me. I wanted to satisfy my curious appetite for all the glorious inheritance that awaited me in that beautiful paradise called Heaven. That was one of my life-changing aha moments!

Jesus Descending From The Golden Gates Of Heaven

The Apostle John wrote about a new Heaven, a new Earth, and a new Jerusalem, the Holy City (*see* Revelation 21:1-5, 21-27). Saints of God, we must prepare our hearts as the Bride (**church**) adorned and waiting for the Bridegroom (**Christ**) as we look forward to that glorious day. This body will be changed, and everything will be new. We will not have or experience any more sin, sorrow, heartache, pain, or death because we will be with the holy and righteous God our Father. Glory Hallelujah! No more tears, no more worry, no more crying, no more heartache, no more death, no more BILLS, because Jesus paid it all on Calvary! Glory be to God! This is the Word of God, *"He that sat upon the throne said, 'Behold, I make all things new"(v5).*

The Apostle John describes the beauty and authenticity of this glorious mind-blowing Holy city of God which is full of splendor. **Thinking about a city of pure gold and transparent glass is enough for us to hold on to the promises of God.** Jesus promised us He is coming back to take us to a place that He is preparing for us, and we are standing on His promise. NOTHING IMPURE or DECEITFUL can enter this temple because our God and the precious Lamb are the temple, and they are righteous and holy. Jesus died to save us from our guilt and shame, but if we do not REPENT, live a clean life, and follow Christ, we cannot enter the Kingdom of Heaven. I can agree with John that **the Lamb is the lamp, for the glory of God gives light so that there will be no need for the sun or the moon to shine. Jesus, the Light, will illuminate Heaven and Earth, and there will not be any darkness.** Glory Hallelujah!

Saints, we need to die daily as we seek God for revelation and restoration in walking in the love of Jesus. That's one of the ways to grow is by killing this old flesh, my brother, and my sister! It is not easy, but by the grace and power of God, we can yield to the strength of God that lives in us to overcome the devil's temptation. The Word of God tells us that only those whose names are written in the Lamb's Book of Life will enter Heaven's Gates. I cannot forget the words my mother said to us ever so often, "You cannot have one foot in and one foot out; it must be Jesus all the way. Give your all to Jesus because when He died on the cross, He gave all of Himself for our sins." I can still hear my mother's voice saying those words and more. At times, I tremble because I know I need to kill some things in my life at that time. Oh! I thank God for praying mothers, not only our biological mothers but praying mothers of Zion who really can encourage and pray on our behalf and for children near and far. God wants us to love and care for each other at all times.

My friend, this is the Word of God! **We are serving a God who loves and cares for us, but if we reject Him down here, He will reject us too and say, "Depart from Me." Are you asking yourself, "Is my name written in the Lamb's Book of Life?** Today is the day of salvation; make Jesus your choice. Serving the Lord is not freeing us from challenges because we are living in a sinful world where we are continually fighting against the adversary who lives in darkness. Also, the Spirit and the flesh will always be at war, but we as Christians must put on **"The Whole Armor of God"** and let the Holy Spirit teach us how to fight in the Spirit and not in the flesh. We must remind ourselves that we are the children of light and not children of darkness. Therefore, we must try to model the Spirit of light as we represent the body of Christ by being Christlike in all our ways.

It is not easy, but with the strength and direction of the Holy Spirit, we can put the enemy to flight. Jesus is our Light in this dark world; He came to save us from the lies of the adversary and take us out of darkness into his marvelous light. We must remove ourselves from darkness and keep on seeking Jesus' light that will lead us into His path of righteousness. He will never leave us alone. He is our fortress, and He is our strength. He will fight your battle for you! We cannot give in or give up; there are some beautiful Golden pearly Gates to enter through! HOLD ON! There will be a new body and a new Jerusalem to behold; all things will be new to behold in the presence of the Lord! **The Word of God tells us that in Heaven Christ, "will transform our lowly body to be like his glorious body" (Philippians 3:21 *ESV*). That's a wonderful promise!**

Chapter 11: The Beautiful Swaying Curtains Above the Gates

> *"Bless the Lord, O my soul. O Lord my God, thou art very great; thou art clothed with honor and majesty. Who coverest thyself with light as with a garment, who stretchest out the heavens like a curtain."*
>
> --Psalm 104:1-2 *KJV*

This scripture tells us about the greatness of God, the only God clothed with honor and majesty. He is such a great and mighty God! As I continued to look beyond the Golden Gates in the dream, I noticed the most unique and rather beautiful curtains one could ever imagine that stretched from Heaven down to Earth. These curtains were rather rare in color, ambiance, and function. They were moving in a graceful and unified manner immediately behind Jesus and the Golden Gates. I was bubbling with curiosity to see what was behind the Gates and the flowing curtains that had this motion of unison about them. There was something amazingly attractive about the flowing curtains that looked so Heavenly and divine, which was locking my eyes to the supremacy of the Almighty God! The flowing curtains appeared as if they were making a graceful statement. I thought **this must be the heavenly musical drapes of many different, uniquely colored fine twined linen!** (*see* Exodus 26:1-14).

I was extremely excited and wanted to run and touch and feel the silkiness of these beautiful vivid and colorful curtains. The colors and materials were far richer and brighter than anything here on Earth. I could not tell if the materials were silk or satin, even though they looked like that from afar. These curtains appeared as if they had a personality of their own and were functioning by the direction of the

Chapter 11: The Beautiful Swaying Curtains Above the Gates

Father above as they floated throughout the Heavens! Again, I was spellbound with total admiration and excitement; I felt like I was there to view and admire some of the inheritances laid up in Heaven for us.

Everything God does is excellent and beautiful. For example, Exodus 26 gives us a description of His precise attention to the exquisite design of the curtains of the tabernacle. Every detail was precise and set in order. As I think about the curtains in my dream, I can't help but think of these curtains and the uniqueness of God's remarkable design in everything He made! He is the authentic author and designer of everything and everyone! There is no one like Him, and no one compares to Him! He is God all by Himself, and He reigns forever without any challenger or any competition because He is GOD!

As I continued to look at the beautiful curtains swaying as if to a melody behind Jesus and the Golden Gates, I was shocked to see the movement of the curtains. The curtains were moving in unison and harmony like a musical choir. You could sense and feel the powerful greatness of God in the movements of the curtains that stretched to infinity. **One of the other amazing revelations I noticed in the dream was how the uniqueness, vibrancy, honor, and majesty of God's presence covered the sublime atmosphere--even the curtains were moving in COMMAND in the presence of the King of Glory.** My mind was like a rushing whirlwind, trying to conceptualize the entire scenery; it was unbelievable, intriguing, and phenomenal.

I could not believe my eyes, trying to fathom the uniqueness of this scenic design in front of me. I had never seen any curtains this beautiful, with such big, bold, bright colors that looked like rainbow colors with indescribable shades. Unfortunately, I cannot describe all the colors to you because there were so many, and they were moving as if dancing to melodious soft, sweet, and beautiful music. **The lights from the Golden Gates sent glares of lights toward the exquisite curtains as they swayed in rhythmic locomotion.**

The beauty of Jesus is all around us. He has the power and authority to make a new Heaven, the Earth, and everything in it. Saints of God, get ready to behold and experience the Kingdom of Heaven, created by God's architectural hands of our Creator. I can only describe to you what I saw, but we know that Heaven is not a fairytale. Heaven is real; it is a place that Jesus is preparing for us. Heaven is God's dwelling place, and He granted us an open invitation to dwell with Him there. As I said before, **the word HEAVEN is mentioned over seven hundred times in the Bible. God wants us to know about His dwelling place. He wants us to think about it and desire to live there with Him.** Thank You, God, for extending Your love and Your amazing grace toward us and for granting us the privilege to live with You in Your kingdom. We thank You, Abba Father, that we are joint heirs with King Jesus, making us a part of this royal family.

My friend, let us live according to the Word of God and let our lives align with God so we, too, can live with Him and enjoy our Heavenly inheritance. The Bible tells us, *"He that overcometh shall inherit all things, and I will be his God and he shall be my son"* (Revelation 21:7 KJV). This is the promise of God. We are spiritually adopted into the family of God. Many scriptures describe different things in Heaven and speak of the inheritance in Heaven. It is our future home where we shall spend eternity with our Savior. Remember, our earthly home is TEMPORARY, but our Heavenly home is ETERNAL. Can you imagine there will be no rent, no mortgage no homelessness because we will be living in the Kingdom forever with our Redeemer, Christ the Lord? **Whatever you are going through here on Earth is nothing to compare to the glory awaiting us in Heaven, God's kingdom. Therefore, I am encouraging you, saints of God, to hold on to King Jesus.**

Nothing in this world surprises God, but for us, I am sure there will be some wonderful surprises and wonders in Heaven that will captivate our minds to the maximum. We are handpicked and chosen by the hand of God to partake in the Heavenly inheritance. Oh! What a glorious day that will be when we are ushered into paradise. Our Savior, we shall see! Just think of all the red-carpet celebrations and Oscar events, inaugurations of Presidents, Prime Ministers, Kings,

Chapter 11: The Beautiful Swaying Curtains Above the Gates

and Queens. Name all these wonderful functions that are taking place in the lives of dignitaries and other officials all over the world. Think of all the excitement, planning, and preparation for these earthly affairs. Of course, God wants us to enjoy our family, friends, and all these accomplishments that take place in our lives. However, we should not put anyone or anything before Him. God should be Number One in our lives as we prepare for His Royal return.

Think if you were invited to attend one of these events, which is only for a few hours. Wouldn't you look forward with great anticipation? I know I would be happy and also get prepared to attend looking lovely in some beautiful and expensive attire, even though the function is only for a couple of hours. We must remind ourselves that NONE of these functions put together can compare to what the Lord has laid up for us in Heaven.

Friends, let nothing nor anyone SEPARATE you from the LOVE of God. Let JESUS be Number One in your life and let Him remain Number One! **Jesus already paid for the ticket to our salvation which is priceless. It is all paid off in full with a zero balance. We do not need good or excellent CREDIT or be rich or famous to live with Jesus forever. All we need is clean hands and a pure heart.** Don't lose your soul to vanity. We can all receive blessings from God if we live a righteous life (*see* Psalm 24:3-6). We can live free from all the misery and frustration of this world when we surrender our all to Jesus.

Jesus made a total ransom when He died on the cross for our sins. All we are required to do is to believe in Him, obey His words, worship Him in Spirit and Truth, and live for Him! Can you believe that we will get an official invitation with our name signed with God's approval to say, "Well done, my child," having our name written in the Lamb's Book of Life? Consider it an official ceremonious welcome home to our eternal paradise made by the King of the Universe. It is a Hallelujah praise right there, to think about His love for us so we, too, can be called sons and daughters of God! The Bible tells us in 2 Corinthians 6:18, *"And will be a Father unto you, and ye shall be my sons and daughters, saith the Lord Almighty."* Father, we thank You for being the greatest Father of all to us. Please help us to be obedient to Your commands, precepts, and statutes. Jesus, please remember us when You enter into your Father's Kingdom.

We are only able to experience this access and rewards from God if we REPENT and live a life that is pleasing to God. **Do not be fooled by the lies of the adversary and lose your way from the Lord's direction of light and happiness to the devil's darkness and sadness. It is all right to put Jesus first, believe in Him, and trust Him with all your heart.** Are you ready to meet your true King? Get ready, my friend! He is coming soon! Will you be ready if the Lord should appear at this very moment? We don't get a warning when a thief comes to break in and steal; it is always an unexpected visit from an intruder. The Bible tells us, *"For yourselves know perfectly that the day of the Lord so cometh as a thief in the night"* (1 Thessalonians 5:2). Live every day of your life as the day of the Lord, so you will not be caught off guard! Make every moment a ready moment so you can see the returning King as He returns to fulfill His promise that He is coming back again. Daily, make your garment spotless, pure, clean, and white, ready to meet the bridegroom! Trim your lamp and keep it burning, for we know not the hour when Jesus cometh! One thing is for sure, Jesus is coming back as the Judge! God the Father gave His Son, Jesus Christ, the authority to come back to Rule and Judge the world (*see* John 5:26-29).

Chapter 12: Seeing Four Biblical Heroes

A Great Multitude Wearing White Robes

"And one of the Elders answered, saying unto me, what are these which are arrayed in white robes? and whence came they? And I said unto him, Sir, thou knowest. And he said to me, "These are they which came out of great tribulation, and have washed their robes, and made them white in the blood of the Lamb. Therefore, are they before the throne of God, and serve him day and night in his temple: and he that sitteth on the throne shall dwell among them. They shall hunger no more, neither thirst anymore; neither shall the sun light on them nor any heat. For the Lamb which is in the midst of the throne shall feed them and shall lead them unto living fountains of waters: and God shall wipe away all tears from their eyes."

--Revelation 7:13-17 *KJV*

"And after six days Jesus taketh Peter, James, and John his brother, and bringeth them up into an high mountain apart, And was transfigured before them: and his face did shine as the sun, and his raiment was white as the light. And, behold, there appeared unto them Moses and Elias talking with him. Then answered Peter, and said unto Jesus, Lord, it is good for us to be here: if thou wilt, let us make here three tabernacles; one for thee, and one for Moses, and one for Elias. While he yet spake, behold, a bright cloud overshadowed them: and behold a voice out of the cloud, which said, This is my beloved Son, in whom I am well pleased; hear ye him."

--Matthew 17:1-5 *KJV*

The above scriptures become so alive and active as you read and meditate upon the glory of God and the important role of several biblical heroes, as seen in the dream. These were heroes God used in different assignments that they could not accomplish without trusting and believing in God throughout their journey. They were committed even when faced with so many challenges and distractions from the adversary. Reading and learning from their testimonies assure us that if we put God first and do His will, we will end up victorious. The Word of God tells us that the Lamb of God is on the throne as He feeds those who came out of great tribulations. It is so reassuring and mind-blowing to think how God shall wipe away all tears from our eyes. We also note from the scripture the **appearance of Moses and Elias, two of God's generals who are now in their Heavenly home.**

These two powerful and divine scriptures took me back to the dream of seeing the Lamb of God standing right before me on the right side of Heaven. In the dream, while I was looking at Jesus and the Golden Gates and trying to comprehend all this Heavenly beauty around me, I wondered if it was time for me to enter through those beautiful Gates. I was so engrossed in this divine beauty, that I wanted to run into the arms of my Savior even though I could spiritually feel Him so close to me. **I tried to run towards the Gates, but I could not move. I was still in midair, I guess I was sitting on my Heavenly comfy sofa safe and at peace in the presence of the Lord.** My entire being felt completely different like I could move or fly without fear of falling. In my Heavenly body, I realized that I could see and feel things at a higher level of knowledge and understanding, like telepathic communication. Suddenly, a swift movement came out from the right side of the Heavenly cloud and stood beside Jesus. I **felt so much warmth of extreme joy and happiness as I recognized one of God's generals glowing beside Jesus! WOW!**

A: The Appearance of Father Abraham

Suddenly, I recognized that it was FATHER ABRAHAM, and I was excited and dumbfounded. He appeared from the right side of the Golden Gates with glowing light all around him. Still, in staggering shock and amazement, I noticed how he immediately landed on the left side of Jesus! I was so captivated by this interconnection of telepathic communication when straight away we recognized each other as I stared in astonishment! I started to scream, "Father Abraham! Father Abraham! DO YOU KNOW HOW MUCH I WANTED TO SEE YOU?" I never thought that would be the question I would ask Father Abraham when I met him face to face! He smiled at me with so much joy and happiness. Most of all, he knew who I was by his response through this awesome communication. I tried to run toward him, but my body still could not move. I was bursting with excitement and joy, realizing how immediately we both recognized each other, which was so surreal!

I know that this knowledge could only be the Heavenly knowledge given at that moment by God Himself. It was mind-blowing to know that Father Abraham died over four thousand years ago, yet we recognize each other like it was just yesterday we last saw each other. **Saints, the Second Coming of the Lord will be greater than we can comprehend! We need to BELIEVE that Jesus Himself shall descend from heaven with a shout with the voice of an archangel and with the trumpet of God, and all our loved ones that died in Christ shall come alive** (*see* 1 Thessalonians 4:13-18). **We will recognize our loved one who died in Christ thousands of years ago! God is so amazing! Thank you, God, for giving us wisdom.**

Jesus Descending From The Golden Gates Of Heaven

The Bible tells us, *"That the God of our Lord Jesus Christ, the Father of glory, may give unto you the spirit of wisdom and revelation in the knowledge of Him"* (Ephesians 1:17). This was a divine revelation and recognition that was taking place at the Golden Gates of Heaven in the presence of the Lord. Our Supreme God is so powerful, mighty, and amazing, that we can't understand Him, but for sure He understands us! We are talking about the Omniscient God of the Universe who causes us to wonder so many times because of His strength, awesomeness, and excellency! I saw so much more than I could imagine, comprehend, or explain in this unique enlightenment and encounter.

I was still in shock at the swift appearance, like a lightning flash, of Father Abraham standing on the left side of Jesus! The gesture he made to me, along with the welcoming smile, was so amazing and clairvoyant. I continued to look at him and Jesus in bewilderment and extreme joy! I could not believe I was looking at Jesus and Father Abraham; I felt my eyes popping out of my head with excitement and happiness! The presence of the Lord, Jehovah El Shaddai, The Lord God Almighty, was so rich, powerful, and holy.

I was spellbound and speechless by the brightness and glow of Jesus, the holy and righteous Messiah. Here, I was at Heaven's Golden Gates, surrounded by such tranquility, peace, love, and joy in the presence of the Lord and Father Abraham! I felt an abundance of love that surrounded me, which made me want to run, skip, and jump like an excited child lost in the Heavenly Ocean of tranquil love. I guess I was overwhelmed with a childlike spirit in the presence of my Lord and Savior! My urge to twirl my way around and go through those beautiful Golden Gates to the beautiful curtains and into that glorious paradise in front of me was super high! Now my mind goes to the scripture when Jesus says, *"Verily I say unto you, Except ye be converted, and become as little children, ye shall not enter into the kingdom of heaven. Whosoever therefore shall humble himself as this little child, the same is greatest in the kingdom of heaven. And whoso shall receive one such little child in my name receiveth me"* (Matthew 18:3-5).

A: The Appearance of Father Abraham

I felt completely like an excited child ready to explore all this blissful scenery before me. However, Jesus had me there for a different reason. Here, God is reminding us that we should humble ourselves as little children; then, they shall be the greatest in the kingdom of Heaven. **Our first role model is Jesus Christ, humbling Himself when He died on the cross for no sins of His own, but in obedience to His Father, He took and completed the assignment that was set before Him. Also, Father Abraham, a faithful hero of the Bible, exemplifies humility to God through his obedience, commitment, and tremendous faith in God and he was rewarded.**

This great biblical hero who obeyed God and left his father and his people to go to an unknown land was standing beside Jesus in front of me. He looked so young, like he was in his thirties, fully dressed in a magnificent white and gold robe. There was no doubt in my mind about his royal attire, as he exemplified the royalties of God standing confidently by King Jesus' side. Father Abraham looked bold, confident, and poised; bravery was written all over him. I could sense the unique bond and love they shared as they both looked at me with love beyond words. Abraham had many incredible encounters with God, and their relationship was interesting and rather unique. It is not surprising that God called Abraham righteous because he loved, trusted, and believed in God. He exercised extreme confidence in God and believed that God would always provide for him (*see* Romans 3 and 4). **He stood firm on the promises of God and stayed focused on the assignment God placed before him. Abraham knew that God would never break any of His promises because He is the God of truth.**

We are Abraham's seed and are encouraged to believe in the promises of God and seek to live a faithful life in the knowledge of God! Just like Abraham, we live in a world full of chaos, violence, and wars from every nation, a world where even our own family sometimes turns their back on us, leaving us to feel abandoned, lonely, and rejected. However, we are reminded to put our trust in the God of Abraham, who will never leave us alone nor will He forsake us! We must be committed and stand firm on the promises of our Abba

Father, knowing that He is our Jehovah Jireh, Our Great Provider. **God loves us so much that even when we don't merit His favor, He continues to save us and deliver us from the plan of the adversary.**

Father Abraham knew from experience that God always had a ram in the thicket, and that's what he told Isaac just before he offered up his beloved child to God. The Bible tells us in Genesis 22:13, *"And Abraham lifted his eyes, and looked, and behold behind him a ram caught in the thicket by his horns: and Abraham went and took the ram and offered him up for a burnt offering in the stead of his son."* Now, we see that this is a father of extreme faith in God and the things of God. He knew Jehovah would provide for him and that God was not slack concerning His promises, even when we can't see or understand them!

We ought to have complete confidence that our God cannot lie because He is the God of truth. Even though some days may be dark, gloomy, and uncertain, God promises us He will never leave us, and He will not! Our Abba Father is the God of the impossible and He will make a way out of every wilderness situation. He knows our minds and what we are thinking, bad or good, negative or positive. **Remember that He is the greatest neurosurgeon, who can dissect every neuron in our brain and put it back in order without any diagnostic tests, incisions, stitches, or scars. GOD IS THE GREATEST IN EVERYTHING!** He can fix and regulate every cell that is out of control and set it to function normally in the physical and the spiritual order anytime, just let Him into your heart. Hence, we are encouraged to set our minds on things above and stay in tune with the Omniscient God!

Father Abraham was called the friend of God more than once because he trusted, believed, and had complete confidence in God (*see* 2 Chronicles 20:7 and Isaiah 41:8). Abraham kept his eyes on the Almighty God and depended on Him in every area of his life. Moreover, he stayed close to God in prayer and built several altars along his journey, worshiping God in Spirit and in Truth.

Abraham obeyed God and was rewarded abundantly in many ways.

A: The Appearance of Father Abraham

God even changed his name from Abram to Abraham, making him the father of many nations. Also, his beautiful wife's name was changed by God from Sarai to Sarah (*see* Genesis 17). Abraham trusted God and exercised faith, confidence, and courage throughout his journey. Even though he was tested in many ways and faced several setbacks, he continued to be persistent in his faith walk with God. Seeing Father Abraham standing before me increased my hope much more that our God is a promise keeper, and He will reward us according to His riches in glory.

The Word of God continues to inspire us now, just like in the days of Abraham, Isaac, and Jacob, as seen in 1 Peter 1:2-9. It tells us of an inheritance kept in Heaven, *"an inheritance incorruptible, and undefiled, and that fadeth not away, reserved in heaven for you, Who are kept by the power of God through faith unto salvation ready to be revealed in the last time"* (vs. 4-5). Abraham's commitment and dedication to God set an ultimate example for us to follow through every season of our lives. We are motivated and encouraged to stay focused on sticking to the will of God for our lives, even if it takes many years. God's timing for our lives is not within our clock because He is God and knows best. We are the seed of Abraham, and he paved the way for us to trust and believe in God. Abraham was not perfect; but he stuck close to God, even though his father worshiped false gods (*see* Joshua 24:2). It is important to build your own personal relationship with God even if your family is not encouraging you to do so. At the same time, we must be committed to pray for them and encourage them to seek the Lord.

Everyone should be encouraged by Abraham's life and obedience to follow the pathway of righteousness to build a good relationship with our Abba Father! We should try to build a closer and stronger relationship with God in sincerity, faith, and truth every day. The apostle Paul reminds us, *"It is of faith, that it might be by grace; to the end, the promise might be sure to all the seed; not to that only which is of the law, but to that also which is of the faith of Abraham; who is the father of us all, (As it is written, I have made thee a father of many nations,) before him whom he believed, even God who quickeneth the dead, and calleth those things which be not as though they were"* (Romans 4:16-17).

As I continued to look at Jesus and Abraham, I couldn't help but see and feel the divine love and bond of what true friendship was like in the Heavenly atmosphere. God should be our first best friend because He is closer than anyone else to us. He knows everything about us and is compassionate about our daily lives. Jesus said to His disciples when He met with them in the upper room, *"Henceforth I call you not servants; for the servant knoweth not what his lord doeth: but I have called you friends; for all things that I have heard of my Father I have made known unto you"* (John 15:15). Jesus calls us His friend. It is such an honor to be called a friend of God. Father Abraham was called a friend of God, and because we are the seed of Abraham, we, too, are considered friends of God. God commands us to exercise that love for one another as much as He loves us. The Bible tells us in John 15:12-13, *"This is my commandment, That ye love one another, as I have loved you. Greater love hath no man than this, that a man lay down his life for his friends."* This love that God, our Abba Father, has for us is far beyond measures and any boundaries. That's the kind of love that flowed between Jesus and Abraham; it was a genuine and compassionate love of a godly friendship and relationship.

Let us too, like our great Father Abraham seek to have complete trust, belief, and faith in God our Father of all Fathers. Although his faith was tested to sacrifice his beloved son, Isaac, he believed in God and God did provide a lamb. Today, will you put your faith and trust in the God of Abraham, Isaac, and Jacob? Keep on praying and believing, He will come through for you and he will supply all your needs according to his riches in glory. Continue to rejoice in the Lord through the good days and the not-so-good days (*see* Philippians 4). **Abraham is called righteous because of his exuberant faith.** I can't believe that I see Father Abraham standing beside Jesus at Heaven's Golden Gates! The faithful Father of many nations.

Poem: Abraham, the Father of Faith at Heaven's Gate!

Father Abraham! Wow! Is this Father Abraham?
The great, righteous, and faithful Father of Many Nations!
Standing beside Jesus at The Golden Gates of Heaven!
The promise of inheritance and reward he has been given!

With confidence, belief, obedience, and extreme faith!
He put his trust in God, and for sure, he patiently waited!
He wore a beautiful robe, pearly white and shiny gold!
Looking so distinguished, young, charming, strong, and bold!

He answered God and took his wife and his nephew named Lot!
Traveling from Ur, tired and weary, resting at several spots!
Abraham was determined to fulfill God's purpose, will, and plan!
Even when Lot's servants quarrel over division and parcels of land!

He responded to his nephew with a peaceful and loving heart!
He told Lot, "Look, there is the land; go ahead and choose your part!
God told Abraham, "I will bless you with land as far as you can see!
Build nations, your children will outnumber the sands of the sea!"

At age ninety-nine, angels blessed him to have a promised son!
At age eighty-nine, Sarah laughed, thinking her days were done."
Trust God! One year later, Isaac-which means laughter was born!
Soon, Ishmael Abraham's first son and his mother Hagar were gone!

Abraham and Sarah were filled with love and so much thrill!
Until Abraham's faith was tested to sacrifice Isaac on Moriah's Hill!
He responded and trusted God's command in confidence and faith!
So, in faith he took Isaac, walked for three days, and didn't hesitate!

Jesus Descending From The Golden Gates Of Heaven

Upon reaching Moriah with Isaac, his beloved promised child!
The altar he built then with several pieces of wood he piled!
Isaac curiously turned and asked his father! Where is the lamb?
Abraham replied! My child, God will provide! He always has a plan!

Picking up Isaac and ready to sacrifice with a knife held high!
He heard a voice coming out of Heaven from the beautiful sky!
Saying loud and clear, Abraham! Lay not your hand upon the lad!
Now I know you would sacrifice your son because you trust in God!

He did not wait for God to provide a ram before he sacrificed Isaac!
He gave back the promised child because, in God, there's no lack!
Obeying God in faith, caught far in the ticket. God provided a ram!
God also gave us the ultimate sacrifice! JESUS, the precious Lamb!

Abraham is a great role model of faith, strength, and courage!
Reminding us to trust and believe in God and be not discouraged!
Even though Abraham stumbled and lied along the way!
He committed his life to prayer and believed in God every day!

He was called righteous because of his extraordinary faith!
Now, I see him smiling beside Jesus at Heaven's Golden Gates!
Seeing this patriarch of faith beside Jesus is such a divine revelation!
Abraham was faithful to God and got his ticket to eternal salvation!

He sojourned in a city and a foundation built by God's great hands!
A country where our Father made and ruled his promised land!
Will you stay faithful to God and live according to his divine plan?
God's plan is to prosper you, just like our great Father Abraham!

Poem: Abraham, the Father of Faith at Heaven's Gate!

The dream continues with Father Abraham looking exceptionally young, strong, brave, and handsome, standing at attention beside Jesus, our Lord! It was such a glorious and awesome moment to behold! The desire to run into their arms and embrace them was overwhelming and inviting. Though I still couldn't move, there was an interconnection of telepathic communication that was transmitting between us because I could feel their embrace, even though they were facing me from a distance. This feeling was so precious and glorious that I wanted to stay there forever. So, again, I tried to run toward them when suddenly my eyes shifted to the right side of the Golden Gates. I noticed another biblical hero suddenly burst out from the cloud and was standing beside Father Abraham's left side. Wow! Immediately, I recognized that it was…!

B: The Appearance of Moses

I was still in shock and captivated by the glowing light coming from the right side of the Golden Gates of Heaven when, lo and behold, I could not believe my eyes. Suddenly, I noticed MOSES bursting out from the glorious bright light as his body swiftly landed beside Father Abraham and Jesus. I could hardly hold my composure at this breathtaking moment as I looked at one of the most talked about prophets in the Bible! Moses had the most radiant and beaming smile on his face. Instantly we recognized each other, and I was screaming so loud, "MOSES! MOSES!" As I looked into his beautiful eyes, I said, "I DIDN'T KNOW THAT YOUR BEARD WAS SO WHITE!" Of all the questions I had, I never thought this would be my verbal expression to this powerful and patient biblical hero of all time! I was bubbling with the same childlike excitement and joy, basking in the surreal moment of seeing Jesus with these biblical heroes. They looked so radiant, bold, and handsome, standing beside King Jesus in their royal apparel! Moses, staring at me, had the warmest and most welcoming expression of endearing peace and love, with the same intense look of recognition on Father Abraham's face when he appeared.

Moses was wearing a long, beautiful robe of many royal colors, looking young, strong, and bold. He was not saying anything verbally, but the same interconnection of telepathic communication and love from the open-arm gesture held me captive to admire him even more. I wanted to run over and ask him several questions about his journey. I had so many questions about the different phases of his life, such as being in the Nile River and growing up in the palace, meeting with God with the burning bush, and meeting on the mountain for the commandments. I was always fascinated by the extreme faith and life of Moses, but ever since the dream, I have been so intrigued to do more research on this great prophet of God.

B: The Appearance of Moses

As I look over the life of Moses, this great prophet and lawgiver, I can't help but admire and appreciate his bravery, boldness, and courage through each season of his life. Exodus 3 tells us that Moses was born when there was a great depression and oppression in Egypt. The Israelites were unhappy because there was a new Pharaoh who was selfish and cruel. It was a time when the descendants of Jacob increased tremendously, which brought fear to the Pharaoh. He feared that the Hebrews would outnumber the Egyptians and become powerful, so he asked the midwives to kill every firstborn male child so they would decrease in number. However, those midwives were strong in their faith, and they feared God and refused to kill the babies. Even today, the adversary wants to kill us but God is keeping us alive for a reason and a season so He can fulfill His promise and purpose in us. We take authority in the Mighty name of Jesus and kill **every murdering spirit going around killing God's people right now in Jesus' name!**

Pharaoh was very angry and commanded his soldiers to go to the Hebrew homes to seek all the baby boys, kill them, and then throw them in the Nile River (*see* Exodus 1:15-22). Such a wicked and gruesome act against the Hebrew family! Pharaoh had no compassion or love in his heart for the Hebrew people he enslaved. The Bible tells us that the heart of man is desperately wicked (Jeremiah 17:9-10). We give thanks to our Heavenly Father, the Omnipresent God, who takes note of everything. This great and merciful God has a plan for all of us, and nothing nor no one can change nor kill the plan of God over our lives. He had a plan for Moses's life thousands of years ago, and He also has a plan for our lives.

It was during this time, at three months old, when Moses's parents, by faith, decided they would hide him in the river Nile. Wow! Can you imagine? This happened to be the same river Pharaoh told the soldiers to throw all the dead baby boys. I can't imagine the graphic picture of what that river looked and smelled like! However, **the eyes of God move everywhere; even when we are in a dead situation, Hallelujah! He is always there with His plan to save us.** Moses's life somewhat reflects several situations we are experiencing in our world today. Our God remains the same yesterday, today, and forever!

There was a time when Moses' mother feared for his life, so she hid him in the place where they would least expect to find him. His mother's intuition and faith in the knowledge of God's protection over this special child kept him safe from the murdering spirit that was lurking around everywhere! God was protecting baby Moses because He had a great plan for his life. So too, God is protecting and saving us from the adversary. Be encouraged, my friend, God's plan for our lives stands forever, and it is all for His glory. He promises that He will give His angels charge over us anywhere we are in this world so we can fulfill His will for His glory. We are hidden under the wings of the Almighty God. Therefore, I will not fear any plague around me because God will deliver us (*see* Psalm 91).

So, Moses was saved by the King's daughter when she went down by the Nile to get her bath. There in a floating basket was a beautiful Egyptian baby boy. **She fell in love with this baby and rescued him from the river. She decided to call him Moses, which means, "Because I drew him out of the water" (Exodus 2:10).** Moses's sister, Miriam, was watching from a little distance and came over and offered to get an Egyptian babysitter who just happened to be Jochebed, Moses's mother. How amazing! God has every missing piece of the puzzle for every one of us, no matter how complex we think our life looks. Our Heavenly Father is altogether wonderful, and He is in total control of every detail and fiber of our being.

Having Moses's biological mother as the babysitter gave her such a golden opportunity to teach him some wonderful truths about his culture and God. **It is so important to trust the wonderful work of God's hands in our lives. He holds us in the nail print palm of His great, big, mighty hands.** I am sure Moses's mother had some fear and was worried about her baby boy's life, but she believed in the God of the impossible. Moses's mother exercised faith and confidence in God that he was safe even though he was in the river where there were many dead bodies. **Psalm 23:4-5 reminds us, "Yea, though I walk through the valley of the shadow of death, I will fear no evil:**

B: The Appearance of Moses

for thou art with me; thy rod and thy staff they comfort me."

God commanded Moses to use his rod throughout the journey to perform several miracles. God's power is mighty, and it is everywhere! Even if you are tossed into the stormy sea and the raging river, His plan will never be extinguished by the hands of Pharaoh or any other devil or demon that rises against you. God will always rescue us from every dead and stagnant situation that is blocking our breakthrough. The Word of God is a sword to protect us daily. The God of Moses is the same promise-keeping God protecting us from behind and in front! Our Abba Father is the frontline Warrior who never gets weary, tired, or sleepy! Our Jehovah God reigns forever, and He lives forever more! The awesome God is Omnipresent; no matter where we are, He is always there fighting our battles and propelling us to our destiny.

For instance, Moses saw God at the most unexpected time of his life and in the most unusual place! It is important to make yourself available to the will of God in complete humility because He can visit you anywhere at any time. Even when we think we are incapable, God can use us to fulfill His assignment even when we doubt ourselves. **The exaltation and esteem from God in your spiritual growth is more important than the elevation you receive from man on earth.** Moses did not know that God would show up with such a big assignment for him to face the Pharaoh with a command to say, "Let my people go" (*see* Exodus 5:1-3). **Moses demoted himself for various reasons, but God promoted him for that season. God can use you even if you stutter! God can touch your tongue with the fire of tongs to purge you for His service just like He did with Isaiah (*see* Isaiah 6:6-8).**

Although Moses was hesitant, doubtful, and afraid to carry out the assignment, God reminded him that He was the One who made his mouth. The "I AM God" who sent him on the assignment would never leave him alone. It was a journey that lasted forty years, an assignment that happened thousands of years before Christ! Yet, it holds a magnitude of God's power, strength, and authority as He used Moses in such a supernatural and miraculous way to set the Israelites free from bondage.

This story gives us the courage to keep trusting in the God of the impossible. He is the way-maker God who opened the sea of deliverance for the children of Israel. He is still working miracles daily around the world today for you and me. Sometimes, we are so caught up in the distractions and the things of this world that we are unaware of the unseen destruction that the Lord saves us from. If we had a tiny glimpse of some of the principalities, powers, and rulers of darkness that the Lord saved us from, we would be shocked and more grateful for God's grace and mercies towards us.

Seeing Moses in this dream standing beside Father Abraham and Jesus was unexplainable and surreal, encouraging me to hold onto God Almighty. It was such a joyous moment; I felt like I was going through one of the most captivating phases of my life in this Heavenly Tour. Looking at Moses, who had several marvelous encounters with God on different occasions, was extremely exciting and encouraging! **Moses, the lawgiver whose life and faith were severely tested, had a rewarding relationship with God.** This fearless, brave, and powerful prayer warrior faced Pharaoh and stood on the promises of God even when the people murmured and complained. He continued to seek God in prayer for guidance and direction on his journey of faith, now I saw him standing at Heaven's Golden Gates, poised, young, and extremely happy.

As I stood, more questions flooded my mind. I wondered how Moses felt when he discovered himself as an Israelite who grew up in Pharaoh's palace. I also wondered about the role he played defending an Israelite when he killed an Egyptian, causing him to go into hiding. How did he feel being rejected by his people? (*see* Exodus 2:11-22). I was curious about his experience with the miracles God performed with the rod before he faced Pharaoh with the message from God. I thought about the patience he exercised during the period of the Ten Plagues and the parting of the Red Sea. I was curious about the writing of the Ten Commandments, his encounter with God on

Mount Horeb, and his reaction to his brother, Aaron, and the others who were worshiping false gods! (*see* the books of Exodus and Deuteronomy).

I was so anxious to know everything about his life as a biblical warrior, but none of those questions arose while I was there. I think God wanted me to enjoy that glorious moment basking in the presence of King Jesus with these biblical heroes at the Golden Gates of Heaven. This dream of such a supernatural revelation increased my faith, belief, and trust in God that He is not a man that He should lie (*see* Numbers 23:19). God's promise is sure, and He is real in action and deeds, which gives me the confidence to hold on to His unchanging hands.

I continued to look at Moses, the lawgiver who was a great and mighty warrior of God, one without fear. He faced Pharaoh, a ruthless political leader for the Egyptians. Even though Moses was brought up in Pharaoh's palace, he was determined to carry out the assignment that the Lord laid before him to go to Pharaoh to free God's people! Moses was faced with some challenging decisions because God hardened the heart of Pharaoh, but through faith and boldness, he was determined to carry out the plan. He believed in the God of the impossible to change the situation and the circumstances ahead of him.

As he journeyed along the way, he overheard so much grumbling and complaining from the children of Israel about the manna that God provided for them daily. They were ungrateful and wished to have meat and other food to eat, which frustrated him to the point that he asked God if these people were His children. Moses was overwhelmed and depressed, asking God to kill him because he was at a breaking point (*see* Numbers 11). Sometimes in our lives, we face similar circumstances as leaders, parents, supervisors, and managers serving in different capacities. It was during this time of anger and frustration that he disobeyed God by striking the rock instead of speaking to the rock (*see* Numbers 20:11). **Moses disobeyed God, and God has the right to discipline us even if you are Moses, the great**

lawgiver. The justice of the Lord stands for everyone and forever.

Although Moses didn't get to enter the promised Land, God allowed him to get a view. God always has a plan to deliver us from all wilderness situations because of His love, grace, and mercies toward us. Moses knew that he served a God of wonder that kept on doing the supernatural and was gracious toward the needs of His people. However, they kept on complaining and died before they got to enter the promised land (*see* Numbers 11). The natural man cannot understand the awesomeness of the El Shaddai God, The Lord God Almighty! However, when you build a spiritual relationship with God, you learn to keep trusting Him for the impossible by exercising and stretching your faith in the supreme God of the universe! Even though Moses was frustrated at times during his assignment, he always continued to seek God in prayer. He also went on fasting for forty days and forty nights more than once (*see* Exodus 34 and Deuteronomy 9). He depended on God to show him the way, even during the complaining from family, friends, and those under his leadership! He continued to seek God on behalf of the people.

Now I see Moses happy and glowing at Heaven's Golden Gates, standing beside Father Abraham and King Jesus! How awesome and great is our God to his children who love and obey him! **Today I am encouraging you to look past your impediments, avail yourself of God's assignment, and depend on him just like Moses. God is still appearing to his people all over the world and giving them a divine assignment. He will provide you with destiny angels to fulfill his purpose in you. God will work many miracles with the rod in your hands.** Will you put your faith to work in the assignment that God positions in your life? We remove fear and anxiety right now in the mighty name of Jesus. Step out in faith like Moses!

Poem: Moses! Moses! Take Off Your Shoes!

Moses! Moses! Take off your shoes from off your feet!
It was the powerful voice of God; No need to repeat!
This is Moses, the great Prophet with God's mighty rod!
He stepped out in faith and continued to believe in God!

Moses means–pull out of water; He was swaying in the Nile River!
Destined for the Queen to see the basket where he lay quivers!
In the bushes nearby watching was Miriam, Moses's sister!
Offering to help the Queen, she gets their mother as the babysitter!

In luxury, education, and wealth, Moses grew up in Pharaoh Palace!
Still, there came a time when there was quarrel, hatred, and malice!
He is an Israelite, slewing an Egyptian enemy, thinking, this is right!
Now exposed, he fled to the mountain because he feared for his life!

Forty years went by, married and a shepherd caring for the flock!
From the burning bush, God appeared and he was very shocked!
God instructed Moses to tell Pharaoh to; "Let my people go."
With a hardened heart, Pharaoh refused and said, "No!"

Moses continued to pray while using the great and mighty rod!
Encouraging the children of Israel to trust and believe in God!
Then the hand of death came and took away Pharaoh's son!
Pharaoh said to Moses take your people and go! Now, I am done!

So, the children of Israel packed and got ready to flee!
Led by Moses as they head toward the big Red Sea!
God directed him to stretch forth the mighty and powerful rod!
Then the sea parted, letting them through which made them glad!

Jesus Descending From The Golden Gates Of Heaven

The children of Israel are free on the next side of the land!
Looking back at Pharaoh as the sea closed on him and his gang!
Now they watch and see that their enemy is not only their footstool!
Swallowed by the raging waves, they became a sea of fish food!

Moses, this brave warrior with God's mighty and powerful rod!
Messed up a few times, but quickly prays and depends on God!
This Federal Official and Lawgiver went through life with a fight!
He fasted on Mount Sinai three times for forty days and forty nights!

God gave Moses the tablets with the Ten Commandments!
God set these moral laws for every man to obey and implement!
Returning to see the people worshiping idols for their god!
He threw the tablets, which broke into pieces because he was mad!

Moses reprimanded his brother Aaron for doing wrong!
He said, people "If you are on God's side, come along!
Today! Jesus is still asking the same question! Are you on my side?
My friend! Seek Jesus today; Don't delay. Get rid of pride!

With faith and confidence in God! Moses, hold on and travail!
Following the God of Abraham, Isaac, and Jacob, he prevailed!
This mighty warrior perseveres and sticks to God's master plan!
Fulfilling the vision, he only got a glance at the promised land!

I saw Moses the Prophet standing beside Jesus with exuberant faith!
Can you imagine? At Mount Sinai, he met with God face to face!
Are you ready to receive the promise from the book God has given?
You will see Prophet Moses when you enter this beautiful Heaven!

Moses! Accomplishing God's assignment with the miracle rod!
His mission was to follow, obey, and please the true and living God!
Caught sight of the promised Land, died at Moab at a good old age!
The only one buried by God is now at Heaven's Golden Gates!

Poem: Moses! Moses! Take Off Your Shoes!

The dream continued with me trying to run toward Jesus and these two biblical warriors, but I could not move, even though I felt like I was floating in midair. I was trying to comprehend all that was going on around me because everything seemed to be flashing so quickly and extremely fast. It was so amazing to witness the speed and swiftness of how things and people appear when you are in the heavenly realms! I was so intrigued and excited by what was happening before me in such a peculiar and unique manner. Then, in that quick and flashing instance again bursting out of the clouds from the right side of the Golden Gates came another biblical hero with such glowing bright light! My eyes felt like they were popping out of my head in shock and surprise as my gaze followed the light that swiftly landed someone else to Moses's left! There, he was…!

C: The Appearance of Elijah

My gaze was fixed on the glowing light, and to my amazement and joy, I recognized Elijah, another great prophet standing beside Moses. I was so thrilled to see ELIJAH, I screamed, "ELIJAH! ELIJAH! ELIJAH! I DID NOT KNOW THAT YOU WERE SO TALL!" Can you imagine that's the first thing that came to my lips? He also came out with the same welcoming gesture and a happy smiling face, with a bright twinkle in his eyes. He looked so tall, brave, young, and strong! Right then and there, we recognized each other, and I screamed so hard and loud with happiness, glee, and excitement, saying, "Elijah! Elijah!" Again, he responded in telepathic communication as if to say, "I am so happy to see you too, my dear child!"

His face was full of love and affection, and he had a welcoming gesture of open arms embrace. He, too, was wearing a magnificent robe of many beautiful colors, looking so poised and full of confidence! His appearance was of royal attire, just like King Jesus and the others. I could not comprehend or explain this mystical moment and time right before my eyes! It was far beyond explanation and was extremely holy, righteous, and glorious! I glared at the Prophet Elijah with a jaw-dropping stare of excitement, joy, and happiness! I stood in midair posture, looking, observing, and enjoying the most charming and intriguing scene of my life at the Golden Gates of Heaven!

I wanted to run and embrace him and ask him about the different situations he faced while he was on his assignment here on earth! There are so many interesting and powerful testimonies surrounding the life of Elijah. One of my favorites is Elijah meeting with the widow and all the miracles that took place in her life. She experienced an abundant increase in her flour and oil through prayer and obedience to the prophet sent from God. She also witnessed the power of God as her son came back to life when the prophet Elijah laid on him three

C: The Appearance of Elijah

times and prayed earnestly to God to restore life to him. God answered his prayer, and the widow was once again happy and truly believed in the God of Elijah, the Miracle-Working God! (*see* 1 Kings 17).

Elijah was a great warrior who, in his bravery, faced King Ahab and his wife Jezebel, the most savage and wicked ruler of Israel at that time (*see* 1 Kings 17). It was a perilous time when King Ahab and his evil wife **Jezebel were cruel to God's people that they were leading.** They worshiped idols and only believed in false gods, even though they were experiencing drought in the land because of their disobedience. Jezebel had several of God's prophets killed, and she brought in over eight hundred false prophets to worship the god Baal! However, Obadiah, governor of the house of Ahab, feared and believed in the true God. Obadiah hid one hundred of God's prophets by the fifties in a cave and fed them with water and bread. Although King Ahab was his master, Obadiah feared God and tried to protect some of God's prophets from these evil rulers.

It was during that time of drought that God gave prophet Elijah an assignment to go to King Ahab, who was looking for Elijah to kill him. Saints, **isn't God amazing? He will send you to the enemy's camp to fulfill His assignment and save His people from going down the dark road of hell. Most of all, He will protect you throughout the journey until the end.** After God gave Elijah his assignment, Elijah was not afraid to confront King Ahab and Jezebel about worshiping Baal, the false god. Elijah was brave and believed the true and living God would come through for him. He prayed fervently to God, and Jehovah answered his prayer in several miraculous ways as he stayed obedient to God!

Elijah, the prophet, was a great servant of God, and he challenged King Ahab and eight hundred and fifty false prophets on Mount Carmel to prove who was the real God to follow. Is it the Hebrew God or Baal? Elijah says, "And the God that answereth by fire, let him be God" (1 Kings 18:24 *KJV*). Imagine Elijah by himself; he knew the God he served and told them to go first. After they all agreed to the contest, four hundred and fifty of the false prophets prayed for hours, making a mockery of themselves by cutting into their flesh for several hours. There was no response from Baal because he was a false god who was powerless.

Elijah mocked them, telling them to call louder to their god, who would not answer them. Finally, they gave in after they lost their voices from begging and screaming to a false god. Elijah then called the people together, and following his instruction, they prepared an altar. Elijah prayed, and fire came down and destroyed the altar which was soaked with water, wood, stones, and a sacrificial bull, proving to the people who is the real God. They listened to the prophet Elijah and what he told them to do and which God to serve.

Even though there was a drought in the land, and it didn't rain for over three years, Elijah had faith in God and told King Ahab that it would rain! How can you not believe the prophet of God, who believed in the true God and prayed down fire from above, that the same God would send down rain? So, Elijah exercised his faith by earnestly praying and believing in God the Father that He would send rain, and it did rain (*see* 1 Kings 18).

Elijah had a wonderful relationship with God, whom he talked with often; he was faced with challenges just like we face in our daily lives. This great prophet felt abandoned and alone the day following the great miracle on Mount Carmel. Elijah was intimidated by Jezebel and her evil spirit, so he ran away into the mountain because he was depressed and feared for his life. He wanted God to kill him because he thought he was the only one still serving God and that the people were not obeying God. Saints, it is not good to assume that we are the only ones serving God. Many souls will not stain their garments, who are still walking with Jesus (*see* Revelation 3:4).

Even though Elijah was strong in his faith and had several miraculous prayers answered, he still experienced some doubts and anxiety after he was threatened by the Jezebel spirit. We, too, are faced with these demonic spirits that try to kill, steal, and destroy our breakthrough. We experience days when our faith is strong and

C: The Appearance of Elijah

days when we are fearful. However, we have a Father who loves us so much, and we take courage in His word that says, *"No weapon that is formed against thee shall prosper; and every tongue that shall rise against thee in judgment thou shalt condemn"* (Isaiah 54:17 KJV). We have the power and the authority to trample upon every Jezebel spirit that comes to steal our joy because we have a Father who is our mighty warrior. Seek to pray scriptures over your life when the enemy comes to derail and kill you. Scriptures such as Romans 16:20, Matthew 18:18, Luke 10:19, Zechariah 4:7. The Word of God is powerful; use it daily in reading, meditation, singing, praising, worshiping, and praying. The Lord appeared to Elijah in a gentle breeze to inform him that there were seven thousand people who continued to serve God wholeheartedly.

Then God gave him another assignment to anoint other future Kings and Elisha, his successor (*see* 1 Kings 19:16-21). God was with Elijah throughout all his testing, feeding him and protecting him from the enemy's hands, just like He is doing for us today. **The great prophet was caught up in a whirlwind of fire and was escorted in a chariot into Heaven. The same God that was with Elijah is the same God that is protecting us from the hands of the enemy.** We come against every Jezebel spirit that will try to hinder us from fulfilling our God-given assignment in Jesus's name. My friend, step out in faith and trust the God of Elijah. God will see you through to the end if you totally depend on him. We cast down every Jezebel spirit in the Mighty name of Jesus. Today, be encouraged in the word of God which said, *"There shall not any man be able to stand before thee all the days of thy life: as I was with Moses, so I will be with thee, nor forsake thee. Be strong and of good courage: for unto this people shalt thou divide for an inheritance the land, which I swear unto their fathers to give them"* (Joshua 1:5-6).

Jesus Descending From The Golden Gates Of Heaven

Poem: Elijah The Praying Prophet!

Prophet Elijah was brought up in Heaven in a Whirlwind of Fire!
Many looked as the chariots of horses lifted him higher and higher!
His Mantle with double anointing falls into Elisha's hands!
He too, started to preach, walking daily into God's perfect plan!

Prophet Elijah! A fearless, faithful, and obedient man of prayer!
Seek answers from God because he was a great prayer warrior!
He prayed to God to discipline Israel because of their disobedience!
This Tishbite prayed that they would obey God and be obedient!

Elijah "Yahweh is my God" faced Ahab with a message from God!
He stayed steadfast in prayer as he walked up to the mountaintop!
The false prophets failed in their battle against Baal, the false god!
But, Fire came on Elijah's altar, showing he serves the only true God!

The people repented and started to worship the Messiah!
Jezebel was angry, so sought to kill the Prophet, Elijah!
Elijah was depressed but obeyed God and went to the Brook!
Protected by God he was fed twice a day by Ravens at the Nook!

Sent by God to the Widow whose flour and oil were almost finished!
Elijah blessed the meal, which increased and never diminished!
Then her son died, and she blamed Elijah and couldn't stop crying!
The boy came back to life as Elijah lay on him three times praying!

Staying obedient to God, his Prayer life was full of miracles!
He depends on God, even in fear and through many obstacles!
He fervently prayed at Mount Carmel, face between his knees!
Saying to his servant seven times; Go back and look, please!

He believed in the Triune God and was not afraid to openly pray!
After all, God has all the answers, so in prayer, he constantly stays!
You may experience some Ahab or Jezebel in your daily life.
Keep on holding on to JESUS, He will save you from their strife!

The effective, fervent prayer of the righteous avails much!
Pray daily to your Father and experience his hands of gentle touch!
He removes the fear and gives us power, love, and a sound mind!
Elijah prays, seeks God, and receives the power of the Savior Divine!

God continues to provide, and he will send you your Raven!
Elijah didn't know that he would be caught up in Heaven!
The beautiful place that Jesus is preparing for you and me!
Friends, trust, and believe in God, for Prophet Elijah! We will see!

The dream continued with my excitement and happiness bursting through the cloud. I was so elated and thrilled to see the Prophet Elijah standing beside Moses, Father Abraham, and King Jesus. They were all looking so young, bold, and brave, just basking in the presence of the Lord! **I thought I could not have been more fascinated by this picturesque scene in front of me as I continued to look and admire Jesus and these Great Generals. I felt like I was seated in my Heavenly reclining chair relaxing in this glorious bliss of peacefulness!** Then, suddenly, I noticed another glow of bright light coming out from the right side of the Golden Gates! I just can't believe it! WOW! It was…!

D: King David Appeared with a Huge Golden Harp

I was gasping with an uncontrollable delight and emotion that had me spellbound looking as **David swiftly landed in front of the others! At this moment, I was dumbfounded, staring at David and how differently he was positioned from the others.** Still in midair, completely enfolded in the Heavenly atmospheric glow, surrounded by Jesus and all these veterans of the gospel. I can't help but give God praise, for this is "Heaven in Heaven" This experience is beyond my human comprehension; it was so divine, holy, and pure!

King David appeared sitting poised around a HUGE GOLDEN HARP which was stretching from Heaven down towards Earth. I was so excited and overwhelmed with jubilation, amazement, and curiosity that it shook my entire body! Still in shock with delight and elation of joy, I screamed, "DAVID! DAVID! I DIDN'T KNOW THAT YOUR HARP WAS SO BIG!" He, too, had the same look of recognition and interconnection by telepathic communication as he smiled at me with one of the most luminous smiles you can ever imagine. His eyes sparkled with a bright welcome stare of joy and happiness as he embraced the harp in such a graceful demeanor!

I quickly noticed that this unique instrument looked like it was built to stand in place from the Golden Gates of Heaven and continue down to Earth, where there was no end to this enormous and powerful harp. I held my hand up, feeling sure I would run or fly into his arms. I tried to reach out to touch him and the harp, but I could not move from my position. I felt as if I was in a Heavenly sitting room chair made to keep me focused on all the beautiful things happening in and around me. Although he appeared so close, he was far away, still on the right side of the Golden Gates, yet close enough for me to see the joy and happiness in his eyes. I was still in the same position bursting and bubbling with excitement, when I noticed David was in a sitting position across from the others. **He was so engrossed in playing the harp so skillfully and brilliantly in such a glorious and holy manner. It was surreal and mind-blowing; Heavenly HOLINESS filled the atmosphere with this unique music that I had never heard before!**

I knew the power of God kept me in that position so I could capture the picturesque moment of King Jesus and all these generals of the gospel. They all looked young, bold, beautiful, and courageous, with dazzling smiles of joy, peace, and happiness! So, I could join with David when he said, *"You make known to me the path of life; in your presence there is fullness of joy; at the right hand are pleasures forevermore"* (Psalm 16:11 *ESV*). All I could see and feel coming from them was the fullness of joy, sheer serenity, and divine tranquility. There was an everlasting pleasure of being in the holy and mighty presence of this divine God.

My friend, be encouraged about the Great Day that is coming when our Lord and Savior will return to take us home to the place He is preparing for His children. It's where we will experience the fullness of joy with our Messiah forever and ever around the throne of God! **We will join all these biblical heroes and will not have any more tears, pain, sorrows, or death! We shall rise and shine and God will restore everything that the adversary takes away from us because the King, who is the Son of God, is coming back with healing in his wings. Neither will there be any day or night because Jesus, "The Light of The World," will be shining all around us forever (***see*** Isaiah 60).**

As I continued to look at David as he skillfully played the most harmonious melodies coming from this awesome golden harp, I noticed that his head was bowed as if in worship as he moved his fingers so gracefully over the strings of this magnificent instrument. There are no words on Earth for me to express the ambient feeling of that moment; such peace and tranquility filled the atmosphere. **The presence of our Lord and Savior was so glorious, righteous, and**

holy, along with the beautiful glow of light that illuminated Jesus and these four generals. The Heavenly angelic music was marvelous, rich, and indescribable! HALLELUJAH!

It is David who said, *"O God, my heart is fixed; I will sing and give praise, even with my glory. Awake, psaltery and harp: I myself will awake early. I will praise thee, O LORD, among the people: and I will sing praises unto thee among the nations. For thy mercy is great above the heavens: and thy truth reacheth unto the clouds. Be thou exalted, O God, above the heavens: and thy glory above all the earth; That thy beloved may be delivered: save with thy right hand and answer me"* (Psalm 108:1-6 KJV).

David's eyes were closed, and he was so engrossed in what he did best; in his element, he praised and revered God. He was playing this awesome melody that was unique, melodious, and holy! **There was no singing; however, it sounded so amazing, like a Heavenly choir singing beautiful melodic songs with amazing, sweet, honey voices that you wanted to continue to listen to forever. The beautiful harmonious sounds felt as if they were stretching to all the nations around the world, from Heaven to Earth.** David said, *"My heart is fixed: I will sing and give praise. Awake up, my glory; awake, psaltery and harp"* (Psalm 57:7-8). David said he would wake early to praise God; he is known to be a worshiper who constantly praises God in different ways. Throughout his life on Earth, he used his harp to bring joy to others and King Saul benefited from the melody that comes from David's harp. King Saul's spirit was always restored and refreshed when David played his harp for him. David's music had a great impact on King Saul's spiritual well-being (*see* 1 Samuel 16:14-23).

King David was a born worshiper who found pleasure in writing beautiful poems and songs and he loved to play his harp as he basked in the mode of worship even as they brought the Ark of God. He found pleasure in dancing before the Lord with all his might. However, his wife Michal, daughter of Saul did not approve of David dancing in the street as he continued to worship God. Instead of encouraging him to praise and worship the true and living God, she despised him in her heart and confronted him. However, David,

D: King David Appeared with a Huge Golden Harp

unapologetic and unashamed, continued to praise God throughout the entire celebration (*see* 2 Samuel 6). Sadly, this led to her being childless. I think we can all learn several lessons from this scripture and apply them to our daily lives. The Bible tells us to rejoice in the Lord always (*see* Philippians 4:4-5). We should not despise anyone who wants to glorify God in holy worship, because our God is worthy of all praise. David's harp was a golden harp of praise, and he used it to honor and glorify God!

One of Merriam-Webster's meanings for the word harp is: *"a plucked stringed instrument consisting of a resonator, an arched or angled neck that may be supported by a post, and strings of graded length that are perpendicular to the soundboard."* In all my life, I never sought to know what King David's harp looks like or what it sounds like. However, in the dream, **I was totally engrossed and fully mesmerized by the beautiful golden shiny color and the enormity of this unique harp!** The outline and shape were not visible for me to compare with Merriam's description because the golden color looks like shining light fused in the formation of a harp that David sat around in mid-air. Even though I could see his fingers moving, they moved as if they were glares of light coming from the light of our Savior and the glorious illumination from the Heavenly atmosphere down to Earth. Most of all, the melodious sound coming from this great instrument was such a piece of captivating music, one that my heart and soul were so engrossed in as I centered my attention on the splendor and glory that filled the Heavens.

This moment was really fascinating and brilliantly illustrious! The aura around Jesus and these biblical heroes was surreal, peaceful, and sanctified! King David was so focused as he skillfully played the most harmonious and holiest music one has ever heard. His music echoed throughout the Universe as he moved his gifted fingers over every string of his magnificent harp. **My body felt like every fiber within me was melting from the music, and the glory of God that filled the Heavens was so rich, magnificent, and powerful, bringing reverence to God in praise and worship!** The above scripture tells us how David's heart was fixed on God, and he sang and praised early in the morning. He did not hold back on his praise to God the King. **He praised God among people, anytime, anywhere, and among all nations. Do not hold back on your heart of worship and praise. God is seeking for true worshippers!**

One of David's Psalms of praise says God is worthy of praise and he will exalt God the King. It says, *"I will exalt you, my God, the king. I will praise your name forever and ever. Every day I will praise you and extol your name forever and ever. Great is the Lord and most worthy of praise; his greatness no one can fathom"*(Psalm 145:1-3). David! A man of praise and worship! A mighty man of valor! A man after God's own heart! A great poet! A great musician and songwriter!

Now, I was looking at David at the Golden Gates of Heaven, so happy and engrossed in playing his harp in the presence of the Lord. David never failed to express to God how he felt about everything, seeking God's forgiveness on several occasions. No wonder God said he was a man after His heart *(see 1 Samuel 13:13-14)*. When he wrote that song, he was singing a petition for God's help. It's a song to remind us that even when we have difficulties, we should still have our hearts fixed on the Lord. David said, *"Be thou exalted, O God, above the heavens; let thy glory be above all the earth" (v5)*. He sang of God's mercy, which is above the Heavens, and his Truth unto the clouds. Our God is so Mighty, Powerful, and Great; He is worthy of all our praises. He is a Great God who merits our undivided attention when we worship and praise Him, fixing our mind, soul, and body on Him only, because He is worthy of our praise.

I was still stunned at all the different kinds of melodies coming from this spectacular and amazing instrument. To this day, I am still in shock and amazement as to the size and beauty of his harp! That breathtaking moment of a lifetime gave me joy and hope that one day I will see Jesus again along with these heroes of the gospel of Jesus Christ! It was so hard to fathom and digest the midair scenery before me. It was Jesus the Messiah! The King of all Kings! The Lord of Lords! It was our Prince of Peace with David sitting across from Him in humility and Heavenly worship. David is the greatest musician in the Bible; seeing him in this atmosphere of humility, posture, and holiness before Christ our Lord was surreal and glorious. These phenomenal feelings could only be felt in the Heavenly presence of the Lord. It was really, Heaven in Heavenly atmosphere! There were unimaginable and unexplainable Heavenly sensations coming from the Father above in this divine and holy paradise in this glorious moment!

I was still looking at King David and was captivated by the beautiful and fascinating instrument of such shining gold. Its unique design could only be made by the authentic builder of the world, God Almighty. I wanted to run to him and ask him questions about the harp and the music, his encounters with Goliath and King Saul, his conquering Jerusalem, and his days as the King of Israel. There are so many amazing chapters about the life of David that I would have liked to ask about. However, the Heavenly atmosphere was so awesome, sweet, and holy that I did not think about anything but just being in the presence of my Savior and these biblical heroes.

I was held in this midair position, just looking at King Jesus and these four biblical heroes who were so beautifully dressed in kingly attire. They were all looking so young, strong, and brave, ready to be used by God for whatever service He wanted them to perform. They did not communicate with me physically, but they were all communicating with me in an interconnected telepathic manner, which was so precious and fascinating. I was so intrigued and excited by all the Heavenly scenes happening so swiftly before me I didn't want it to end. **To say I was in shock and super happy would be an understatement. I was totally intrigued by this atmosphere of holy tranquility! There are no words in the dictionary to describe this moment of nobility, an extremely happy and fulfilling peace and joy in the presence of the Lord.** Friends let us, like David, find time for God by staying in His presence. God inhabits our praise, and we should do so with joy and gladness!

David said the Lord reveals the path of life (*see* Psalm 16:9-11). David expressed that the Lord would not leave his soul in hell but would show him the path of life. David stayed in the presence of God as he continued to build a relationship that was loving and close to God. Even when he messed up several times, he repented and, in humility, he sought God's forgiveness, asking God to wash, cleanse, and purge him with hyssop (*see* Psalm 51). David humbled himself before God, acknowledging that he had sinned and was seeking his forgiveness. We can learn some wonderful lessons of faith from the lives and testimonies of these biblical characters. We are serving a God full of grace and mercy who never ceases to forgive us and extend His love to us if we diligently seek Him in repentance.

We should be motivated to spend more time with God, seeking to know more about Him as we build our relationship with our Lord and Savior. David explained the fullness of joy he found by being in the presence of the Creator. I was looking with eyes popped open to the widest extent, and my jaws almost dropped to my knees in sheer surprise after surprise! I was lost in a world of extreme peace and unspeakable happiness, praying that this would never end.

However, still in shock and bewilderment, I was thinking about how these great biblical warriors burst out of the cloud and stood beside Jesus' left. It was so surreal, breathtaking, and amazing! They all appeared one after the other as if Jesus beckoned them to come to His left, ready to be at His command. I was to the far right of Jesus so I could see each one's face and the beautiful welcoming smile that stayed on their faces. I stood there gazing! Bursting with curiosity and all kinds of questions that I had not thought of asking because everything happened so fast, and God had me there for different reasons.

Every time I read a Psalm or think of David as I saw him in the dream, it encourages my heart even more and increases my faith to hold on to the hands of God. Even though David fell short of the glory of God several times, his main focus was to please God! His love for God was pure and unimaginable through his expression, action, praise, and worship! God wants us to seek Him first and to give Him our hearts so we can do His will. In doing that, He can use us for His glory, and that's the most important thing that we should desire in life! We should have a yearning desire to do the Master's will by denying ourselves and following Jesus (*see* Luke 9:23). We too like David can seek after the things of God and serve Him in Spirit and in Truth. God is seeking TRUE WORSHIPPERS! Will you give him full worship today? Will you worship Him in Spirit and in Truth? He is depending on you!

Poem: David! The Musician After God's Own Heart!

David! --"Beloved! "The Shepherd and the youngest of Jesse's sons!
He was busy taking care of the flocks here and there under the sun!
God anointed and appointed him to be one of Israel's Kings!
This great news from Samuel the Prophet sent by God he brings!

I saw David at Heaven's Gate sitting around his giant golden Harp!
Skillfully playing delightful music, looking poised, and sharp!
This amazing instrument stretches from Heaven down to Earth!
Given the thrilling sounds of unrecognized music, I was fully alert!

King David was facing Jesus and these Biblical Heroes of long ago!
He brilliantly played great music from the enormous Harp of gold!
There was no choir singing in this glorious Heavenly atmosphere!
Just sounds of sweet melodies that bring peace and joyous cheers!

I could not find words to express my excitement, joy, and glee!
Oh! Lord, this is so awesome! This must be Heaven's jubilee!
Sitting in mid-air, relaxing, and enjoying this breathtaking moment!
As I watched his fingers move up and down this vast component!

Yes! This is David the King, who has done so many wrongs!
He asked God's forgiveness while praising him in music and song!
Humbly, he bowed to God, fasted, and prayed, and never departed.
God said! This man, David, is a man who is after my own HEART!

Joyously, he played his harp and was so engrossed in his element!
I can hardly contain myself as I listen to this beautiful instrument!
The fearless King dances up and down the street, as the music rings!
Now, he is at Heaven's Gate entertaining Jesus, the returning King!

Poem: David! The Musician After God's Own Heart!

Hallelujah! Hallelujah! For eternal joy, the great Messiah brings!
Hosanna! To the Lord of Lords and praises to the King of Kings!
Singing as he cares for his sheep, even on the mountain he climbed
Trying to live a guilt-free life while experiencing hatred and crime!

Glory be to God! He is sitting across from Jesus at the Golden Gates!
Enjoying each moment playing sweet melodies to Jesus, face to face!
David seemed poised, happy, and relaxed playing his Golden Harp!
The melody of joy, peace, and happiness echoes deep in my heart!

Even though he was mocked, teased, and bullied by his brothers!
With confidence in God, not even by Saul, he was bothered!
Behind the scenes, he built a relationship with God the Father!
So, he faced Goliath, with a sling in hand, five stones, he gathered!

David slew Goliath, one steady sling and a flat stone in his hand!
Many were singing, "David killed Goliath! It was a bang!"
So much jealousy consumed Saul–he grew extremely mad!
He went Searching to kill David, which made some people sad!

Saul tried to kill David, but God showed up with his deliverance!
David cut a piece of Saul's skirt to show the proof and evidence!
That the God of David is still setting us free from every Goliath!
The adversary! comes to kill, steal, and destroy, but he is a liar!

God's anointing was on David, one of the greatest Kings of Israel!
You may be facing the evil spirit of Saul! Trust God, He is real!
If you are going through the storm or get swallowed by a great fish!
Remember! Jesus will come and He will pull you from the ditch!

David experienced failures with several tests of ups and downs!
But God protected and anointed him to wear the crown!
His confidence in God gave him the strength and courage to cope!
While abounding in humility, gratitude, joy, and hope!
Now! I see King David playing his Harp with so much happiness!

Jesus Descending From The Golden Gates Of Heaven

In an atmosphere of tranquility, and sweet Heavenly bliss!
Friends, Salvation is free if in Jesus you confess, and believe!
Jesus is our Passport to Heaven, so eternal life we can freely receive!

Chapter 13: Changes in my Thought Process

"Call unto me, and I will answer thee, and shew thee great and mighty things, which thou knowest not."

--Jeremiah 33:3 *KJV*

"Such knowledge is too wonderful for me; it is high, I cannot attain unto it."

--Psalm 139:6 *KJV*

"For now, we see through a glass, darkly; but then face to face: now I know in part; but then shall I know even as also I am known."

1 Corinthians 13:12 *KJV*

The dream continued with another amazing discovery of my thought process, which was more enlightened and in-depth of greater understanding. The above scriptures express the great and mighty things that God has in store for us that we are not aware of in our natural body and this present world. Our knowledge will be expanded because we will be face-to-face with Jesus! Hallelujah! God changed my thought process to such a dimension in the dream that was far beyond my human comprehension. It was mind-blowing! Things that our earthly mind cannot contain we can only envision these great things in the supernatural presence of the Lord. The Spirit of the Lord sent such a magnitude of wisdom, knowledge, and understanding during that moment revealing light in the presence of the Lord. The kind of revelation I was experiencing during that extraordinary and profound dream was astounding. The magnitude of my vision was far beyond eagle's eyes in that which I could see and imagine beyond my natural perception. Everything seemed so close, very sharp, and more real as if I could use my eyes to touch and capture things close to my face.

Being in God's presence changed everything for the better. God allowed the eyes and understanding of my heart to open to a deeper level of knowledge and sensitivity to the people and the things happening so swiftly before me. **I felt like all of my senses were at an expansion of a unique and deeper level of knowledge of the things of God.** It felt almost like I had a seventy-five-voltage bulb (75V) that blew, and Jesus replaced it with a two-hundred-voltage bulb (200V) which was extremely astonishing because Jesus' glow of light and brightness filled the atmosphere with such a Heavenly radiance and saturating glow!

The awesomeness of what I was experiencing was incomprehensible. Discovering that everything around me was crystal clear and felt near was awesome and surreal! Everything in the presence of God is so new and beautiful with an exceptional, unexplainable brightness. **This was far more than I thought I could take in, but Jesus allowed all this exquisite creativity to penetrate and stay in my mind! The clarity of things was amazingly captivating!**

Friends, I am encouraging you to have Heavenly thoughts and desires because it will be worth it after all when we get to the glory land. That's how marvelous and real everything felt and seemed. There was so much to conceptualize at that moment, with Jesus and the others looking at me with warm, welcoming, loving stares! I hope that as you continue to read, you will feel the presence of the Holy Spirit, drawing you closer to Emanuel. Please, allow yourself to be in the atmospheric presence of Jesus on this Heavenly journey as Jesus leads and guides you through this marvelous tour. He is the infinite God who never ceases to love and care for us. He is always with us through every walk of life and He is the only way to Heaven.

Another amazing discovery was that during the dream, **I realized that I was having so many heavenly thoughts and emotions which flooded me with oceans of cheerful delight. Joyfulness was all around me! There was nothing to distract me or worry my mind.** Again, when you are in the presence of the Lord, there is unspeakable

Chapter 13: Changes in my Thought Process

joy. It was unexplainable! The Bible tells us in *Psalm 16:11, "Thou wilt shew me the path of life: in thy presence is fullness of joy; at thy right hand there are pleasures for evermore."* It is a wonderful feeling to be in the presence of the Lord and the generals of the Bible. Throughout the dream, everything felt like a new page that needed to go on to infinity. I just wanted to stay in that moment of belonging with Jesus on this heavenly journey! It was so alarming that I had no recollection of the past hurt, pain, or difficulties. All I could focus on was that moment as I continued to look at Jesus and enjoy all the heavenly bliss around me.

Everything that comes into view looks so fresh, new, and extremely beautiful! I had never experienced so much peace and tranquility. The serenity of this awesomeness seemed so unreal, but it was the reality of the Heavenly glory of Jesus's presence right in front of me. It is difficult to describe the atmosphere because of the intensity of God's power around the Golden Gates! Oh! Hallelujah! Saints, we cannot fathom all the marvelous things our Savior is preparing for us in the New Jerusalem. The Merriam-Webster dictionary describes New Jerusalem as *"the final abode of souls redeemed by Christ."* The Bible tells us about the Holy City of God. *"And I John saw the holy city, new Jerusalem, coming down out of heaven, prepared as a bride adorned for her husband"* (Revelation 21:2). **As a bride, we should be ready to meet our bridegroom, who is Christ the Lord.**

Children of God, make ready your hearts to meet your King; He is coming to escort us to the marriage supper. I humbly thank the Holy Spirit, my leader and guide, for helping me to capture this glorious moment with the Messiah. I hope that you are getting a glimpse of the majestic and glowing moment in the presence of Yahweh, the Great and Mighty God with everlasting history and fame! No one can ever measure up to Jesus Christ's supremacy! He is our Lord of Hosts!

During the dream, that special and sacred feeling was magnificent and authentic; it felt like I was hugging love, peace, joy, and happiness in an ocean of tranquility with waves of calm and restfulness from my Lord! A great sensation of the euphoric tenderness of God's love was all around me, embracing me with so much security and assurance. Jesus' love transcends all the love you can ever think of or imagine, a love that surpasses and covers all the hurts, pain, depression, oppression, abuse, rejection, or doubts you have ever experienced. **The awesomeness and joy of feeling serenity and ultimate peace are worth much more than the daily trials we face here on Earth.** I just wanted to be there, in the presence of the Lord, I did not want to come back. But God has a different plan for my life, so here I am telling the story. Thank you, God, for Your favor and blessings on me. Our Father will do it for you too. I also wanted to explore and enjoy whatever was beyond Heaven's Golden Gates and those beautiful curtains, but I must wait for the timing of God's plans for my life.

I am looking forward to the return of King Jesus when I shall behold Him; then, I shall see beyond the Golden Gates and much more. Jesus held me in that posture until He decided to move me, and that's what He is doing to us daily. He keeps His eyes on us in every move we make because He ordains it that way, and we should also focus on Him and less on the things of this world. At that moment, I became aware of so many things at a higher and deeper level of the supremacy of the Omniscient God! Surely, God is God all by Himself. I can say my wisdom, knowledge, and understanding were enlightened by the inspiration of the Holy Spirit. The Bible tells us that the eyes of our understanding will be enlightened (*see* Ephesians 1:18). The Apostle Paul spoke about the sealing of believers by the Holy Spirit (*see* Ephesians 1:13-21).

Jesus was still standing at the right side of Heaven's Golden Gates, looking at me with eyes that were full of compassion, grace, and mercy. Yet, He was ruling the world with authority, wisdom, and power in such a masterful way. This is the Omniscient God who rules Heaven and the Earth! Oh! The Supremacy of Christ is expansive and holy throughout the world! He's so powerful, amazing, and unique. There was so much revelation around me; I could not believe I had an understanding far beyond my imagination with no worry about anything. I was experiencing sweet, holy, and righteous thoughts.

Chapter 13: Changes in my Thought Process

Heavenly thoughts throughout the dream. This was surely the greatness of God's mighty power and the Holy Spirit, which was operating through me in such a manner to heighten and enlighten my spiritual eyes to all these heavenly delights.

I am sure I looked shocked, surprised, and bewildered! But Jesus was looking at me with such stillness and quietness because He knew everything about my thoughts and emotions. Also, nothing surprises or shocks Him about us! King Jesus was so calm and in total command and control of the entire Universe while observing everything about me and, at the same time ruling and controlling the world! God knew about our unformed body even before conception took place in our mother's womb! (*see* Psalm 139:14-16).

God is our Master Scientist who genetically formed every chromosome that connected us in such a marvelous masterpiece. **God's predominance supersedes the wisdom and knowledge of man,** no matter how great a scientist you are, you are still second; Compared to God! Why? Because He is the one who made us in His image and blew breath in us so we could become a living soul! No one else has the power or knowledge to form man. There is no other God like our Jehovah! (*see* 1 Chronicles 17:20). Moses told us in Genesis 2:7, *"And the Lord God formed man from the dust of the ground and breathed into his nostrils the breath of life; and man became a living soul."* What if God did not blow his breath into us? We would just be a form shaped out of dust without any life. But God loves us so much that He lends us His breath, and so often, we take it for granted without acknowledging that He is the Creator, the only giver of life.

God did not withhold His love from us when He chose to sacrifice His son to save us from our sins. Are we daily showing and sharing God's love the way He deserves to be loved? He is the only God; there's no other God but Me, He said (*see* Exodus 29:2). Are we putting others before God? Are we **stingy** in giving God the praises and worship that belong to him? The great and mighty God has all the power to change our daily thinking and shift our minds to think and do things in such a unique way. God our Father who can regulate our thoughts about the past and to process things in the present is above all gods! The Omniscient God never sleeps but allows us to sleep and have dreams, visions, and beautiful memories. This great God is the one who gives us wisdom to put our five senses into action and he can change the function of our brain in the twinkle of an eye. Let us show love and appreciation to our Heavenly Father. Let the mind of Christ be a part of our daily lives so we can center our thoughts on the things of God.

God is the only one who can blow breath into man! Yet, we walk around proud like any peacock with feathers of pride on the top of our heads as if we are the ones to blow breath into each other. Oh no, my friends, think again! God wants us to show LOVE and have godly thoughts and ideas for each other, just like He has good plans and good thoughts about us. **We need to share God's love because our size, strength, and power are like grasshoppers. We are powerless without God in our lives, but more POWERFUL when God is in control.** God is the only one that sits on the circle of the Earth and He has all the power and authority to govern His universe as He places clean thoughts and ideas in our mind. Don't let the devil corrupt your mind to think evil and do evil to God's children. Let the mind of Christ fill your hearts with peace and love to share. Christ is the one who has the power to stretch out the Heavens as curtains (*see* Isaiah 40:21-24) He is such a great and mighty God and He loves us unconditionally and He expects us to show love to each other every day.

God wants us to love Him with all our heart, mind, soul, and strength (See Mark 12:30). When we love and appreciate God then we will have a stable relationship with Him, which will strengthen our walk with him so we can have holy thinking. We will be more empowered to fight against temptation from the enemy when we think Christlike. Can you imagine the plans that God has for us in Heaven? Such as increasing our knowledge and understanding so we won't worry or think about the things of the past. Now is not the time to accommodate the lies of the adversary, instead we need to focus our eyes on the return of the Savior and live in peace with each other.

Chapter 13: Changes in my Thought Process

God is making a note of every deed, good and bad, so stay focused, wise, and alert in the knowledge of God! We are living in a world with people who are harboring evil thoughts and wicked ideas; So many murdering spirits are busy killing people all around the world. Friends, remember, the adversary comes to kill, steal, and destroy, but Jesus comes to give us abundant life. The Bible tells us that we must not kill; if we do, we shall be in danger of judgment (*see* Matthew 5:17). Today, let us kill the spirit of pride and burn it out from the root in the name of Jesus so we can fellowship with the Lord in humility. It was pride that caused a war in Heaven, and Satan was cast out (*see* Revelation 12:7-9). Let us bury the pride of life and live in humility as we look into the interests of others who need our help. Jesus is the model of humility! Let us not think of ourselves as better or higher than others (*see* Philippians 2:1-3). **We are all God's children walking in the ministry of servitude.**

There are times when we become blind because we allow sins to enter our hearts by listening to the lies of the devil! I encourage you today to wake up from your slumber of complacency and pride. Let us give our all to the Supreme God, who lends us His breath because of His endless love for us. Do not be deceived by the devil and his tricks. He aims to distract and derail you from your Heavenly desire and destination. His mission is to destroy our families and us. Jesus is the only way to Salvation, His love for us is without limit He came to save us. God never hesitated to show His love towards us, nor did He withhold His precious gift, His only Son, Jesus Christ, from us. Instead, He gave up His beloved Son to die for our sins so we could gain eternal salvation through His resurrected power.

Throughout the dream, Jesus was so near to me that I could feel His presence around me. He is Omnipresent. Jesus is closer than your next breath. Why? Because He is the breath of life. You cannot live without Him. The Bible tells us, "For in Him, we live, move, and have our being..." (Acts 17:28). God wants us to live for Him. He is happy when we honor, worship, and praise Him. He gave us breath so we can praise Him at all times. What if God said, "Today, I am going to **take My breath away from everyone!** "Then you and I would not be here. Let the mind of Christ reside in you at all times so you can have holy thinking with Heavenly thoughts and desires.

Chapter 14: I Had No Memory of The Past, No Sadness or Pain

"A New Heaven, A New Earth, and A New Jerusalem"

"And I heard a great voice out of heaven saying, Behold, the tabernacle of God is with men, and he will dwell with them, and they shall be his people, and God himself shall be with them, and be their God. And God shall wipe away all tears from their eyes; and there shall be no more death, neither sorrow, nor crying, neither shall there be any more pain: for the former things are passed away. And he that sat upon the throne said, Behold, I make all things new. And he said unto me, Write: for these words are true and faithful."

--Revelation 21:3-5

The above scripture reminds us of some of the promises of God and some of the amazing discoveries He has in store for us in glory. The presence of the Lord was so phenomenal and divine throughout the dream, I cannot explain it, but it was unimaginable and unbelievable of the majesty of this great God of the Universe. We serve an awesome and gracious God! I had no kind of physical pain or discomfort while I was with Jesus. How can you feel pain in the presence of the Lord? Knowing that He is Jehovah Rapha, I was healed even before falling asleep that night, but during the dream, my complete body felt cured and free from all aches and pains. Glory hallelujah! The above scripture reminds us of the promises of God and the benefits that we will reap. Now, I can say I experienced and reaped some of those benefits and promises of God's divine healing during the dream because this old body was transformed into a new spiritual body in the presence of the Lord.

I also felt like half my age (thirties) with so much vitality, energy, and strength that was full of the glory of God. Several times I tried to run toward Jesus and the Golden Gates, but my body could not move, and I did not feel any regrets or sadness! Instead, I had a feeling of contentment and real joy and happiness as Jesus chose to keep me in that position until He was ready to release me, or I would see another shift of something, or someone appear before my eyes.

There are also some special times in our everyday lives when God wants us to keep our eyes focused on Him so He can demonstrate His fullness for our next agenda. A time to be still and set your mind on God and have Heavenly thoughts and desires to seek things that are above. **There was such a special peace and calmness that one can only find and feel when in the presence of God. We are encouraged to set our affection on things above which are eternal; things on earth are temporal.** Therefore, we should not put our focus on the temporal things of this world. Do not get distracted by the attractions of the worldly things that the adversary will steer in our daily lives (**see** Colossians 3).

As the dream continued, I realized I had no recollection of anyone or anything behind me. It felt like it was the beginning of all the newness of life without experience. My mind was so captivated by the power and presence of Jesus that all I wanted was to be there with Him. There were no feelings of missing anyone or longing to see anyone or anything except what was happening in front of me. Can you imagine? My daughter and her friend were in the car with me before my body left the car! Still, I had no recollection of them during the entire dream. I didn't think about them or worry about how they were going to get home or what had happened to the car. Everything in my past was BLANK and I was now experiencing absolute newness in the presence of the Lord. Everything was beautiful, new, and holy, super awesome!

Jesus' POWER captivated me with such intensity that I only wanted to keep my eyes focused and cued to His precious face. My mind was fixated on Him! I didn't worry about anything in that Heavenly dream, I stayed focused on Jesus, and what was ahead of me! I felt a

Chapter 14: I Had No Memory of The Past, No Sadness or Pain

sense of security and belonging in His presence that kept my eyes engaged and fixed on Him at all times. Even though I admired all the beautiful things around me, my center of attention was on Jesus, my Lord! In life that's what we should do, **keep our eyes focused on the Lord.** There was nothing to worry or think about except the events of that moment with my Lord and Savior.

Everything was unique, exceedingly great, glorious, divine, and marvelous! It was a great pleasure to experience this magnitude of Heavenly elation, unspeakable happiness captivated in a fountain of love from Christ, my Redeemer! Jesus has the most unthinkable and unimaginable things prepared for us! We must believe in Him and live for Him as we look forward to spending eternity with Him in glory! The Bible tells us, *"But as it is written, Eye hath not seen, nor ear heard, neither have entered into the heart of man, the things which God hath prepared for them that love him"* (1 Corinthians 2:9 *KJV*). Our natural eyes haven't seen it, but the Holy Spirit shall inspire us to discern through the Spirit of God what He wants us to see through faith, believing in the impossibilities of God's glory. The Apostle Paul tells us, *"But the natural man receiveth not the things of the Spirit of God: for they are foolishness unto him: neither can he know them, because they are spiritually discerned" (1 Corinthians 2:14 KJV).* We need to be alert discerners and keen listeners to the voice of God and try not to become prey to the schemes of the adversary.

Friends, I am encouraging you to stay focused so we can spiritually discern and be wise in the things of God. We will face all kinds of adversities living in this sinful world, but nothing can compare to the paradise that Jesus went to prepare for us. God promises to those who overcome, *"...I will give to eat of the tree of life, which is in the midst of the paradise of God"* (Revelation 2:7).

Another discovery in the dream was that all my senses were so alert and on point at a higher and newer level. My understanding and knowledge of what I was seeing, feeling, and thinking around me were far beyond what I have ever experienced in my life. **Things seemed crystal clear as if my sensory-motor system was running on**

a speedometer far beyond any human radar. Also, my confidence in the presence of Jesus was totally in His control--nothing could ever go wrong because I was in the presence of my Savior.

Even though I was still held up in midair, I did not feel like I was going to fall, nor was I feeling any fear of heights. I had no form of pain or discomfort to confine or discourage me from being free. There were no physical, psychological, or mental worries or pain: total calmness and tranquility of peace. My mind, body, spirit, and soul felt super new, free, calm, and alert. All fears, worries, and anxiety were gone; everything changed for the better while I was with Jesus. That's the feeling that the Lord will grant us when we get to Heaven. We cannot feel and experience those emotions in this world that is full of sorrows because the enemy is always stabbing us with all kinds of suffering. The father of lies is always trying to distract us with his lies and fears but in the new Earth and new Jerusalem, there will be total peace and joy with our Savior.

The adversary wants us to always feel timid and afraid, but we must remember that God did not give us the spirit of fear, doubt, or anxiety, so we will have those feelings when we are here on Earth but not in Heaven. In the Kingdom of Heaven, we will only experience peace and joy. Jesus came to give us peace and a sound mind (*see* John 14:27). Therefore, when we are in the presence of the Lord, no sin can be present. **Nothing negative can exist in God's presence because He is completely PURE and HOLY.** We must stand on the promises of God that He lives within us, so fear cannot reside where God lives. We overcome fear by exercising our faith in God and depending on the Holy Spirit to guide us. We must remind ourselves that we are more than conquerors; we are survivors and overcomers, feeling and experiencing total confidence of safety and protection by the great and mighty God who watches over us! We should thank the Holy Spirit daily for the spirit of wisdom, knowledge, and understanding! We just need to believe and remember that the risen Christ is sitting in Heaven, guarding and protecting our Heavenly inheritance!

Just imagine yourself working so hard to purchase your dream home

Chapter 14: I Had No Memory of The Past, No Sadness or Pain

and looking forward to relaxing and spending some sweet time with your family, a time in your life when you will experience joy and happiness because of your achievement, even as you pay your bills to sustain your basic human needs. This is so important, but these accomplishments only last for a short while because earthly possessions are temporary. Solomon reminds us that everything was meaningless; he gained nothing, and all was vanity upon vanity. He says, *"Yet when I surveyed all that my hands had done and what I had toiled to achieve, everything was meaningless, a chasing after the wind; nothing was gained under the sun"* (Ecclesiastes 2:11 *NIV*) Everyone looked forward to their earthly home to live in peace and happiness but they are times when we losses our homes through different tragedies which can be so sad and devastating. However, when we compare it to our home in Heaven, nothing will corrupt or demolish it because it was built by the perfect hands of God. We should also look forward to our Heavenly home with Jesus which is our future home, and it is eternal. So too should we prepare our Spirit body to prepare for God's Kingdom. Everything done in the flesh is temporary (*see* 2 Corinthians 5:1-5). Are you looking forward to your Heavenly home? **Heaven is a beautiful place made by the mighty and powerful hands of God our Father! A beautiful paradise, a glorious mansion that Jesus went to prepare for us, our eternal home fully paid for in glory.**

Standing there with Jesus in front of me and looking straight through me with so much love and compassion is far beyond human perception. Even though He looked like He was thousands of miles away, I could still feel His powerful presence like a gentle breeze around me and beside me; and at the same time, I could feel with the intense pounding of my heart that He lived within me! Super amazing! What a mighty God! Shocking, yet astonishing and so real! Nothing or no one in this world can compare to this divine Omniscient, Omnipotent, Omnipresent God. We don't need to believe in evolution or false gods when we have a great big, wonderful God like this! The Creator of ALL living, breathing, and moving things. His attributes and characteristics are seen and felt everywhere!

As Jesus continued to look at me and through me, yes! I felt the power and piercing of light from His eyes going through me. I felt like a mirror, which was transparent to Jesus. As I think about that moment, I often say to myself; O Lord, there is nothing to cover or hide from you! God knows our complete genetic composition! We are woven from His image and His DNA. How I trembled at His piercing look but felt relaxed and at peace because of the compassion I felt from His grace and His mercies! I felt no rebuke or condemnation! Surely, He is a gentle and meek God who looks at us with sincere admiration as if to remind us that He made us in His image and cares for us in every situation. **I was so mesmerized by His power, strength and might that be in great control. I felt glued to all this supernatural glory and Heavenly beauty and glow that I was thinking, this is it! I am here to stay forever with my Lord!** However, Jesus had different plans for me.

My friend, all the brains put together in this world cannot understand this great and Mighty God who is watching over the entire Universe with a master plan which includes you and me. He is the Creator of the visible and invisible who can present us holy, unblameable, and unreproveable in His sight! He is our El Shaddai! He is the Alpha and Omega, the Beginning and the End, the Sovereign God who owns and rules this Universe forever! He is the Governor and CEO of Our Souls. The Great Mind Regulator. He is your God and He is my God too! OH! HOW I LOVE HIM! The King who brings newness to everything because of His Holy RIGHTEOUSNESS! HOLY! HOLY! HIS NAME IS HOLY!

Chapter 15: Jesus Walking Beside Me and He Gave Me a Unicorn

"Yea, though I walk through the valley of the shadow of death, I will fear no evil: for thou art with me; thy rod and thy staff they comfort me."

--Psalm 23:4

"The Lord Jesus Christ be with thy spirit. Grace be with you. Amen."

--2 Timothy 4:22

"The Righteous Shall Flourish"

(See Psalm 92 for Scriptural References)

The above scripture tells us that Jesus is always walking with us, even when we are walking through the valley of death filled with dead bones. He is always present because His Holy Spirit lives within us. As I continued to look at the whole scene before me, I could not help feeling the unexplainable joy that this is where I am going to be with my Lord. Where I shall be to sing praises unto thy name, the Lord most High! I thought, "I am here at Heaven's Gate with Jesus and these Biblical Heroes, and they are ready to usher me in and give me a tour of this fantastic Paradise. I was so happy and excited; I was beyond words! Psalm 92:4 says, "For thou, Lord, hast made me glad through thy work: I will triumph in the works of thy hands." I felt safe and secure in that atmosphere of glorious comfort and divine rest. Everything felt so sweet and peaceful, and I was super ready to see what else was behind those Golden Gates and those beautiful Swaying Curtains.

Then, just before I could utter my thoughts, they were all looking at me with so much compassion and love. Suddenly, I felt a powerful, but sweet electrifying shift in my body, and I was back on Earth still in the dream with Jesus to my left. Furthermore, I was at the same intersection where the dream began, and Jesus was walking close beside me as if heading towards my home. (This intersection was about three miles from my house, and everything looked pretty much the same in the dream.) It was at that moment that I realized I was in familiar surroundings. Jesus was physically right beside me, even though it looked as if He was far from Earth. I could almost feel His hands and eyes guiding me on the road that leads toward my house. **I also realized that time, space, and action changed so suddenly and extremely swiftly! I felt like a butterfly ready to pop from my cocoon flying around in the wonderful presence of my Lord**! His presence and power were so Mighty and vastly tremendous! **It felt like He used His eyes to move us around, as things were moving so swiftly but in DIVINE ORDER. EVERYTHING was extraordinary and graceful!**

I noticed all the biblical characters were not with us anymore. Just like they swiftly appeared, they suddenly disappeared without a trace. I didn't see when they left or where they headed to. It was so amazing to realize how things happened so swiftly while in the presence of the Lord. Even though Jesus was walking beside me, He was facing me and operating in the fullness of His glory. He was still up in midair but was so close to my side, walking beside me, leading, and guiding me as He continued walking on the road with me. I could feel and sense His Omnipresence, strength, and arms of protection as He comforted me on this journey to my home in telepathic communication. **It was majestic, holy, and surreal! All these wonderful feelings were flowing around me, before me, and deep within my heart. I felt the feelings of adrenaline rush going through me from being up at Heaven's Gate and then back to Earth with my Savior leading the way.** I could still feel the compassion, gentleness, calmness, and sweetness of my Savior floating both around and inside me. *The magnitude of the Holy Spirit FIRE was so powerful*

Chapter 15: Jesus Walking Beside Me and He Gave Me a Unicorn

and amazing; at the same time, it was beyond unique, astounding, and breathtaking! Talking about the fullness of joy, peace, and happiness as He walked beside me was INDESCRIBABLE, INCREDIBLE, and UNEXPLAINABLE!

The magnitude of God's amazing power and supremacy is ready to pull us into His unconditional LOVE and POWER! Just let Him in! He was not talking, but the communication with the Holy Spirit was so divine, the atmosphere held so much glory and power of the Almighty God! It felt like something you wanted to touch, embrace, and cling to until eternity came. My friend, God is still pouring out His spirit upon all flesh. All He wants us to do is to be obedient and live faithfully for Him as we serve Him in Spirit and Truth! Without Jesus, our life has no meaning nor an eternal future to live with Him forever. So today, make Jesus your choice! He will never leave you or forsake you! Isaiah 41:10 tells us, *"Fear thou not; for I am with thee: be not dismayed; for I am thy God: I will strengthen thee; yea, I will uphold thee with the right hand of my righteousness."* This is the promise of God for us to put our faith and confidence in Him. **There is no need to be afraid or worry because He will uphold us with His Mighty Right Hand of Righteousness!**

Saints, we have a friend in Jesus, walking beside us day and night. It is such a privilege to have the HOLY SPIRIT living inside us, a mentor who is always present to lead and comfort us. HALLELUJAH! Jesus is our Shepherd, always protecting us. It doesn't matter where you are in life; **Jesus cares for the broken-hearted, forgotten, rejected, educated, uneducated, kings, queens, handmaids, rich, poor, black, white, and every color from all nations who are held captive by the lies of the accuser.** If you let Jesus into your heart, He will set you free and walk beside you all the days of your life. He will keep you safe and secure in His warm, loving, and powerful arms of LOVE and COMFORT. Glory to God!

Even at this moment, Jesus is beside you, loving you and protecting you from all harm and danger. Right now, you may be grieving, sad, lonely, worried, or depressed about a situation that is out of your control or someone who broke your heart or your trust. Don't worry; Jesus is right there beside you wiping all your tears away. Your tears won't fall to the ground because Jesus bottles all our tears and puts them away. He keeps records of our sorrows and our tears in His book (*see* Psalm 56). Jesus is always a present help. The Bible tells us in *Psalm 46:1-3, "God is our refuge and strength, an ever-present help in trouble. Therefore, we will not fear, though the earth gives way and the mountains fall into the heart of the sea, though its waters roar and foam and the mountains quake with their surging" (NIV).* This is the promise of the Lord that He is our refuge and strength through the midst of all the storms in our lives.

God is so much bigger than all our problems put together; even as you are reading and holding this book, He is protecting you and watching over you. Jesus knows your name and is calling you to come unto Him. Jesus is saying, "My child, even when you are walking through the valley of death, decisions, obstacles, trials, tribulations, or sickness, do not fear. I can save you, heal you, deliver you, and set you free. I have my rod and staff to find and deliver the lost sheep." The first person that I saw in the dream was Jesus with outstretched hands and with open arms. It was so overwhelming and amazingly inviting to see the welcoming arms of my Savior. Even though I did not physically run into His arms, I could still sense and feel His love, embrace, and sincere compassion around me and through me! I want so much to be continually in the Heavenly presence which is unspeakable.

> *"But my horn shalt thou exalt like the horn of an unicorn: I shall be anointed with fresh oil."*
> –Psalm 92:10

As Jesus continued to walk with me, we came to another intersection, and He took a left turn which led us closer to my home. I know Jesus is the All-Knowing God, but it was still amazing to see all the turns He would make even before I turned. He was always ahead of me,

Chapter 15: Jesus Walking Beside Me and He Gave Me a Unicorn

leading me toward my home, and I still felt Him at my side! All of this was through telepathic communication. Immediately after Jesus made that left turn, **I was surprised and amazed by the most beautiful baby creature I had ever seen! It was lying in a little cuddle in the corner of a beautiful lawn at the first house on my left, very close to Jesus' right.**

Still in shock, I kept on staring in disbelief and bewilderment! Although I was still in the dream, I had never seen such an animal at that home before! So, I kept looking in astonishment, realizing it was **a golden-bronze baby unicorn.** It looked like a newborn baby with such soft, delicate brown bronze-colored skin without hair. His skin was smooth and silky, with the cutest face I have ever seen on an animal! As I looked closer, I saw the unicorn lying on a soft-looking velvet blanket on the beautiful lawn! I was so fascinated and in shock because Jesus was looking at my response, and I was wondering in shock and amazement, "Where did this beautiful creature come from, and why wasn't it with his mother?" All kinds of questions were running through my mind as I stared in admiration and curiosity at this unique UNICORN! Instantly, I felt so much love and compassion for this beautiful creature! I was so excited, surprised, and curious, I was about to burst with bubbles of love flowing inside of me as I looked at this baby unicorn and Jesus at the same time. The passion of love that flowed from me towards this little creature was unbelievable and sweet as if I had met him before!

The entire scene felt like oceans of love flowing and infusing around us. It was divine and sublime to have such an awesome experience with Jesus standing beside me, looking at me with so much amusement in His eyes as if to say around me is the pleasure of joy! I could not take my eyes off this perfectly beautiful creature. I was looking at Jesus with so many questions that I did not need to ask because He was responding in actions by telephonic communications and body language. Then He gestured to the unicorn and said," Pick it up!"

It was surreal when Jesus told me to pick up the unicorn, He still appeared calm and gentle. Even though it felt like thunder vibrating in the Universe coming from the power that expels through His sweet authoritative voice (See Psalm 29). **Which speaks about, "The majesty of the voice of the Lord." For sure Jesus's voice makes such a difference in our daily lives. We need to be keen listeners to the loving and compassionate voice of our Savior.** Meekness is also one of the attributes of our Savior, yet He showed His divine strength, boldness, and authority throughout the dream in such a commanding way. He is the greatest Commander and Chief of the Universe. Jesus continued to exercise The Fruit of the Spirit, as seen in Galatians 5:22-23.

This was the first time throughout the dream that Jesus spoke to me. I heard His voice while His eyes were fixed on me while gesturing towards the unicorn. I took one step toward the beautiful bronze baby unicorn, but just before I could pick it up, I saw a red car drive up next to my right. **Out of the car came this man, about seven to eight feet tall, and of a distinctive GIANT Size. He got out of his car so quickly, rushing towards me and the baby unicorn. He stepped past me with such forceful power and was trying to pick up the unicorn. However, after two attempts, he was unable to pick up this beautiful baby unicorn.**

Jesus then said to me a second time, "THAT IS YOUR UNICORN; PICK IT UP! I GAVE IT TO YOU! IT WILL TAKE YOU ANYWHERE YOU ARE GOING." **Without further hesitation, I reached over, and the beautiful baby unicorn immediately sprang into my arms. We were cuddling each other as if we had known each other for a long time and were anticipating this moment of divine meeting. It felt almost like a reunification between a mother and a baby!** Except, there was no sign of a mother or any other animal, and I had no thought of asking. It was wonderful and breathtaking just to be a mother, grandmother, or whoever God wanted me to be to this precious creature at that moment! It felt like a ceremonial moment of connection with this adorable unicorn that was affixed in my arms so quickly, just like a newborn baby clinging to its mother through a

Chapter 15: Jesus Walking Beside Me and He Gave Me a Unicorn

passionate bonding phase. In the meantime, Jesus was looking on with so much love and admiration on His face! **It was one of the most joyous moments that I have ever experienced. It was a dream within a dream!**

I gently caressed his soft and delicate body as he snuggled closer to me! The connection between us was phenomenal and surreal; we were responding to each other through the Supreme Power of Jesus, looking at us in joy and fullness of authority and command. I didn't see when the intruder disappeared, and I was enjoying my new and precious gift. The interrelationship between us was unique and extraordinary, to say the least. It was such a sweet and magical moment trying to discover all the beautiful features of this unique creature that was moving so joyfully in my arms. I could feel shivers of joy, glee, and excitement as I cuddled this fascinating creature that was so full of strength and vitality!

The unicorn started to snuggle and move more vigorously in my arms, just like a newborn baby but so much stronger and he was growing so rapidly. During that time, I thought, "This is just a baby; I don't think it can carry me!" Jesus, the All-Knowing God, knew what I was thinking and was looking at me calmly. Then suddenly, the unicorn sprang from my arms and jumped, danced, and frolicked in front of me with so much vigor, energy, and excitement. Still in shock and awe, I couldn't believe what was happening before my eyes! ***Psalm 29 spoke about "The majesty of the voice of the Lord." Verse 6 says, "He maketh them also to skip like a calf; Lebanon and Sirion like a young unicorn."*** I guess, I was experiencing a skipping baby unicorn, and I was too happy and excited to ask any questions.

In the meantime, there was telepathic communication taking place between my Lord, the unicorn, and me and it was beyond my imagination. Amazingly, this unique creature was skipping right in front of me as if to say, "Do you want to play? I have a surprise for you, my daughter in a playful **manner!"** I felt like a little child with my new-found pet having all the amusement while Jesus watched us having all the fun in the world. It was so fascinating that I just wanted to continue to play but there was much more surprise coming my way!

To say, I was astonished is an understatement! Right before my eyes, a miracle took place that changed the size of my skipping unicorn to a larger figure! It was no longer a baby unicorn! This mythical creature started growing right in front of me and now appeared to be about three feet tall. Still in shock, excitement, and bewilderment to see how fast this creature was growing, I was still wondering if he could take me to places. At this time, we were about two miles away from my house. I thought it was still too small to carry me! I must have thought out loud about the strength and ability of the unicorn. Jesus kept looking at me, still following and protecting me, staying to my left. It is so amazing to see and observe the Omnipresent God watching me with so much joy and admiration!

Jesus did not respond to all my questions; He just kept showing me the answers through His marvelous work. He is Great and Mighty! He is the "I AM God." He is the God that said, "Let there be light." He is the God that said, "Peace be still." Oh Hallelujah! What a mighty God we serve, and He was walking beside me in this beautiful dream on my street! My eyes beheld the beauty of the Lord and His handiworks right before my eyes! HALLELUJAH! The unicorn, to my amazement, began to grow even faster than I could imagine!

I was trying to conceptualize the growth of the unicorn that was taking place super-fast with Jesus looking on! I was dumbfounded and stood there staring and startled at this miraculous moment! **In a moment, this cuddling baby unicorn changed in different sizes and stages to this big, bold, and super strong animal that I had to look up to see his ever-so-beautiful face!** This amazing creature changed rapidly to the size of an enormous stallion. **It was a BEAUTY! So unique and fascinating! Most of all, it belonged to me, this precious UNICORN (gift) that Jesus said would take me anywhere!** Jesus, in the stillness of that moment, was showing me His Majestic Power, and without a word, the rapid growth of the baby unicorn surprised and startled me, but I was beyond excited, happy, and content. It was

Chapter 15: Jesus Walking Beside Me and He Gave Me a Unicorn

the most beautiful golden bronze creature I had ever seen in all my life. In shock and disbelief, I was looking at Jesus and the beautiful giant stallion UNICORN in front of me!

Jesus looked at me as if to say, my child, remember I am All-Powerful and All-Knowing God; I can do anything and change everything! The Bible tells us in Jeremiah 32:17, *"Ah Lord God! behold, thou hast made the heaven and the earth by thy great power and stretched out arm, and there is nothing too hard for thee."* I looked at Jesus, still in shock and bewilderment, thinking, "Can this beautiful gigantic creature be mine?" This beautiful unicorn was so much bigger than me and was now standing so alert and powerful in front of me as if to say, "I am ready to take you anywhere you want to go." Yet, he was graceful and gentle, still with a bright bronze color and now with lots of golden hair all over his body, especially on his head and his tail. His bronze-looking horn in the middle of his forehead pointed proudly and strongly. All I wanted to do was pet and caress his beautiful body! However, Jesus has other plans for me.

I was still in shock, admiring this remarkable creature and looking at Jesus in wonder, joy, and excitement! I was so intrigued and fascinated by this creature that I couldn't stop admiring it while so many questions raced through my mind. Just as I was about to ask a question, suddenly and swiftly, I felt my body shift, and I was sitting on the back of the beautiful unicorn. Amazingly, no one picked me up, but I felt my body swiftly shift from off the ground and I was sitting on the back of my unicorn. I did not see Jesus anymore, but I could still feel His presence beside me. I felt so secure on the back of my unicorn, as if my body were made to fit in a socket seated comfortably for a flight of a lifetime. **This action happened so quickly, almost as if I was snatched away with one deep breath! I realized I was sweetly relaxed on the back of this ever-so-strong unicorn as he flew high up in the air. I was enjoying this Heavenly flight of a lifetime! I hoped it would not end!** We swiftly flew over mountains, hills, roofs, and walls of several houses. This must be the Heavenly flying ride of this miraculous bronze unicorn sent by Jesus to finalize my tour into Heaven. A Heavenly ride indeed!

Then suddenly, I landed so gently and smoothly straight to the entrance of my home in seemingly a flash of a second. That's what it felt like! My body moved so gently and swiftly, and it felt like someone instantly got me off the back of the unicorn without any struggle or difficulties! Suddenly, I was standing on my front porch staring at the door and I had no idea where the unicorn had gone so fast. It was amazing to feel my body swiftly go on and off this ever-so-tall unicorn! I could sense that the unicorn was responding to the command of Jesus by doing precisely what he was told to do, then was gone within seconds. Still in the dream and in shock, I realized that I was standing at my front door, looking around for Jesus and the unicorn, but they were not there.

Reluctantly, as I reached for the lock, I started to experience a multitude of Earthly emotions like sadness and despair, especially when I didn't see Jesus or the unicorn. In my soul, I yearned to walk through the Heavenly realms back to the Golden Gates of Heaven! Sadly, I opened the door, walked through, and woke up from my sleep crying because I didn't want the dream to end, and I was crying because of such a marvelous encounter with the Christ! I was also praising and worshiping God for His divine intervention in this Heavenly dream. I could feel the sweet presence of the Holy Spirit rejoicing with me as I reflected on the beauty and HOLINESS of our Savior! It felt like the Holy Ghost Fire was shut up within every atom of my body! The Heavenly encounter was so glorious, Holy, and sweet.

I looked over at the clock and realized it was only seven a.m. I could not believe I had only slept for approximately two hours and had such a wonderful revelation of seeing Jesus in Heaven. Now, I could not stop crying because I did not want the dream to end, nor did I want to come back to Earth. So, I started to praise and glorify God for His grace and His mercies and most of all, for favoring me with this beautiful dream. I acknowledged that even though I had such a lovely dream, deep within my heart, I wished it was not a dream; I wanted to be there with Jesus and all those Biblical Heroes. I also realized that the Lord wanted me to have that encounter to comfort me and others,

Chapter 15: Jesus Walking Beside Me and He Gave Me a Unicorn

especially after the healing phase I experienced before the dream. I was still in the Heavenly mode of praise, and worship, while still trying to comprehend this glorious encounter.

I was crying uncontrollably and praising God when my daughter came into my room to check on me. I was so overwhelmed with joy and happiness that it took a while before I could tell her the dream. After I told her the dream, she, too, was rejoicing, and we were both just thanking God for His divine visitation. After so many years, I still get a euphoric sensation thinking about that supernatural encounter with the Kings of Kings and the Lord of Lords! Jesus is coming back for His prepared people to take to His prepared place in the kingdom of Heaven.

It is still surreal, and I just cannot describe the atmospheric changes of that awesome encounter in seeing King Jesus. During the dream, I had no recollection of things in the past, only what was taking place in that beautiful moment with Christ, my Lord. **Everything was so pure, holy, new, and beautiful. It seemed like a new beginning of eternal life, and I was ready to go through those Golden Gates.** However, Jesus had a different plan for my life, and who am I to question the plan of God over my life?

We cannot and should not underestimate what the Lord entrusts to us so we can do His will while we depend on Him. God is still allowing His spirit to fall on all flesh from every corner of the world. He wants us to avail ourselves of His will and His way so He can use us. We may not know how, when, or where He is calling us from to service, but we are all servants of God, so be ready to yield to His voice. Jesus came down from Heaven to serve us wholeheartedly by fulfilling the assignment from His Heavenly Father. So too, God wants us to serve Him in spirit and truth by serving each other in love and unity! Jesus is our primary role model in the function of servitude. All He wants us to do is to pick up the cross and follow Him. *The Bible tells us that Jesus looked at His disciples and told them, "Whoever wants to be my disciple must deny themselves and take up their cross daily and follow me. For whoever wants to save their life will lose it, but whoever loses their life for me will save it"* (Luke 9:23-24 *NIV).* Following Jesus's model will lead us to eternity with Him forever, but we must deny ourselves of the things of this world. Our lives can only be saved through TRUE repentance and having a Christ-like relationship with Jesus Christ our Lord!

God is so awesome, and He never leaves us alone. He wants us to trust and believe in Him with all our hearts, mind, and soul. My thought process was racing on a supernatural radar of electricity during the dream! It was so amazing and extremely real! It is humanly difficult to comprehend or explain the divineness of Jesus' presence, even though He was watching and guiding me in the dream. I could still sense His love, authority, and power as He ruled the Universe. It is unimaginable to think His love for us is so sincere, pure, and forgiving. Yet, we do not realize how much He is protecting us from so many dangers that come our way every day.

He is so awesome in controlling and ruling the entire Universe. Most of all, He uniquely controls our minds to function distinctively and gloriously. Our Heavenly Father is the CEO of all authority in the Heavens and the Earth. Hallelujah to our Abba Father! In Matthew 28:18, Jesus told his disciples, *"All authority in heaven and on earth has been given to me."* He is the All-knowing God; you cannot run from Him or hide from Him. Just imagine, He numbered the hairs on your head, not just counted but numbered them. We are more valuable than many sparrows (*see* Luke 12:7).

He takes care of us in such a special and majestic way, yet we often turn our backs on Him, and we should not. We are serving a Supreme God who is the Chief Inventor. He alone rules from the beginning to the end. Romans 13:1 tells us, *"Let every soul be subject unto the higher powers. For there is no power but of God: the powers that be are ordained of God."* How can we not serve such a mighty God? There is none like Him; no one can ever match up to Him. So why not love him and serve Him in Spirit and in Truth? He knew your name even before conception was initiated in your mother's womb!

Chapter 15: Jesus Walking Beside Me and He Gave Me a Unicorn

I am so IN LOVE with my Strong Tower as I depend on Him daily to embrace me in His sweet loving arms of divine love. **I depend on Him to navigate me through all the hurdles and chaos of this jumbled and puzzled world by His Power and His Strength. I cannot afford to ever fall out of love with the Word of God because when I stay in the Word, I know I am secure in the bosom of my Lord.** Jesus is so sweet; He is sweeter THAN the honeycomb. Psalm 119:103 tells us, *"How sweet are the words unto my taste! yea, sweeter than honey to my mouth!"* The Bible also says, "The angel of the Lord encampeth round about them that fear him, and delivereth them. O taste and see that the Lord is good: blessed is the man that trusted in him" (Psalm 34: 7-8 *KJV*). God is our present help at all times. Be encouraged that the unseen eyes of the Lord are everywhere watching and protecting us from the wiles of the enemy.

Every so often when I think about the dream and remember how the Lord gave me that beautiful unicorn and how much He stayed beside me and was protecting me from the enemy, I am encouraged that Jesus is always walking beside me and I will not be afraid. I am also encouraged by the Word of God in Acts 18:9-10 where the Lord spoke to Paul in a night vision saying, *"Be not afraid, but speak, and hold not thy peace: For I am with thee, and no man shall set on thee to hurt thee: for I have much people in this city."* There is no situation too big or too hard for God; He will deliver us from every fear that the enemy wants to throw at us.

As I think about the intruder who made two attempts to take the unicorn (gift) that belongs to me, I can't help but think how the adversary tries to stand in our way and put fear in us to block our vision. **However, Jesus, our blessed Savior is right there to give us the strength and faith to PICK IT UP AND TAKE BACK EVERYTHING THE ENEMY STOLE FROM US!** The following scripture referred to the strength and vitality of a unicorn which is a non-domesticated animal. Unicorn appeared nine times in the KJV following scriptures, as seen in, Numbers 23:22, 24:8, Deuteronomy 33:17, Job 39:9-12, Psalm 22:21, 29:6, 92:10 and Isaiah 34:7. Here, we see from these scriptures that unicorns are as REAL as the Word of God is REAL.

This same kind of VIGOR, POWER, STRENGTH, and VITALITY that Jesus showed me as I witnessed the miraculous transformation that took place with the Unicorn. My friend, Jesus encouraged Paul that he should not be afraid, and He is right there beside you telling you the same thing too. He wants us to speak and hold not thy peace because He is with us, so no one can hurt us or harm us. Reach out in Faith and crush the head of the serpent that is standing in your way and killing your success and your dreams.

Jesus came to heal, deliver, and set us free from the bondage of sin that is crippling His children. Jesus said to the man at Bethesda pool: *"...Rise, take up thy bed and walk. And immediately the man was made whole, and took up his bed and walked"* (John 5:8-9). Jesus has the same power and authority then as now. When Jesus tells you to pick it up, don't let anyone stop you or delay you from your progress. God wants us to exercise our faith and believe that He is the Mighty Warrior and He can break the neck of the adversary. One of the amazing things that Jesus did was to tell me to pick up the unicorn in a commanding voice. He did not look, talk, or beckon to the intruder. Soon after, I realized that the intruder retreated out of sight! The enemy must flee when you resist him (*see* James 4:7). Jesus wants you to reach out and pick up whatever He gives you to excel in life and He will see you through to the finished end. We have to stay focused and keep our eyes on Jesus, so we won't be distracted by the enemy when he turns up on the scene to steal what the Lord has in store for us. Today is the day to put FAITH over fear and take back EVERYTHING that the enemy stole from you and your family. Retrieve everything that the enemy steals from you and your family in the name of Jesus.

I am happy and humbled to write about this strong beautiful UNICORN that took me on the most awesome flight of a lifetime. A **supernatural experience of God's divine authenticity even in the** demonstration of this non-domesticated unicorn that He gave to me.

Chapter 15: Jesus Walking Beside Me and He Gave Me a Unicorn

During the time I was with the unicorn, I had a divine sense of peace, comfort, and protection. Now, I joined with Job who says, The Lord uses animals to illustrate His majesty and the unicorn is among these animals. Unicorns are real animals made by God as seen in the above scriptures. The Webster dictionary defines UNICORN as *1 (a) "a mythical, usually white animal generally depicted with the body and head of a horse with long flowing mane and tail and a single often single spiraled horn in the middle of the forehead." (b) an animal mentioned in the Bible that is usually considered an aurochs, a one-horn rhinoceros, or an antelope." 2: something unusual, rare, or unique."* So far, we can see by the dictionary's definition along with the above scripture that a unicorn is a very rare, unique, and strong animal, one that God used to illustrate His Wisdom, Power, and His Majesty.

It is my special gift from my Lord and Savior, a reminder that Jesus is always walking beside me, guiding, and protecting me from the hands of the enemy. Jesus stayed close to Paul, and He is still staying close to us and our loved ones. He is our Good Shepherd, and He will always lead us to the green pasture, and He will restore our soul so we can bloom.

Also, Psalm 92 says, "The righteous shall flourish." This Psalm is a book of giving glory, honor, thanks, and praise to God for all His wonderful gifts and promises that He continues to flourish to His children day and night. During the dream, I was in a mode of praise because I could feel my body moving in the Spirit of happiness and worship even though I was in midair. Sometimes in life, we feel bombarded with all the trials and distractions that the enemy will throw at us, a time in our lives when we wonder how some people are flourishing (*see* v 7). However, verse eight reminds us, "But thou, Lord, art most high for evermore." A very encouraging promise for us to keep faith alive. Verse 10 says, "But my horn shalt thou exalt like the horn of a unicorn: I shall be anointed with fresh oil." HALLELUJAH! During that moment, I had my eyes fixed on the unicorn that Jesus gave me. Friends, I want to encourage you that no matter your age or stage of life, the word of God says, "The righteous shall flourish..." (*see* v 12). "They shall still bring forth fruit in old age;

they shall be fat and flourishing" (*see* v 14). "To show that the Lord is upright: he is my rock, and there is no unrighteousness in him" (see v 15).

Glory be to God; because He is our rock, we shall not be afraid, and we shall not be moved. The strength of God was shown to me through the strength of the unicorn which He gave to me in this mind-blowing dream. My experience with the flying unicorn, which exhibits such strength and vitality was beyond my imagination, one that I wished everyone could experience. We are encouraged to fear the Lord and trust Him in everything. Trust the Lord in all your endeavors and taste His goodness as we experience His grace and mercies daily. Keep on falling in love with the King of Kings; He brings love, peace, happiness, and joy to the world. Most of all, He brought free salvation for all who trust and believe in Him. Are you looking forward to all the beautiful and amazing gifts, treasures, and inheritance that God has stored for us in Heaven? I am looking forward to seeing my **BEAUTIFUL BRONZE UNICORN** again! **My friend, whatever the Lord places before you, reach out in FAITH and, "PICK IT UP."**

Chapter 16: The Lord Uses Animals to Illustrate His Majesty
-EVEN A UNICORN-

"Will the unicorn be willing to serve thee, or abide by thy crib? Canst thou bind the unicorn with his hand in the furrow? or will he harrow the valleys after thee? Wilt thou trust him because his strength is great? or wilt thou leave thy labor to him? Wilt thou believe him that he will bring home thy seed and gather it into thy barn?"

--Job 39:9-12 KJV

(See the book of Job for scriptural references, including Introduction to Job)

In the Content: "Why do the righteous suffer? This is the question raised after Job loses his family, his wealth and his health. Job's 3 friends—Eliphaz, Bildad and Zophar— come to comfort him and to discuss his crushing series of tragedies. They insist his suffering is punishment for sin in his life. Job, though, remains devoted to God through all of this and contends that his life has not been one of sin. A fourth man, Elihu, tells Job he needs to humble himself and submit to God's use of trials to purify his life. Finally, Job questioned God and learned valuable lessons about the sovereignty of God and his need to totally trust in the Lord. Job is then restored to health, happiness and prosperity...even beyond his earlier state."

In the above content, the question is asked: "Why do the righteous suffer?" The answer to this question was puzzling and disturbing to Job then and it is still a question that no one can give a solid answer to, because only God knows the answer. The Omniscience God is the

ONLY ONE who has the ultimate POWER to discern and search the heart, mind, body, spirit, soul, action, and attitude of man. This UNIVERSAL God is the Father and CHIEF of all creation who has the infinite wisdom and knowledge to create man in His image and have a plan for everyone (See Genesis 1 & 2). Our great and Mighty God is not an evolutionist! He is the TRUE and LIVING GOD who is the author and perfecter of our faith, who endured the cross for our shame (See Hebrews 12:2-3). **He is the Supreme God that DECREES Heavens and the Earth and everything underneath the Earth and all things therein.**

He is the one with all the authority of His divine laws and orders for man to live by and obey. Also, He is the answer to man's day-to-day questions for over two thousand years ago and He remains the same until eternity comes. God has the UNIVERSAL MASTER KEYS to all the questions and answers that we wrestle with or are baffled about daily in our human minds! **With that being said, will you let GOD be the Master OF YOUR MIND?**

The Apostle Paul tells us, *"God that made the world and all things therein, seeing that he is Lord of heaven and earth, dwelleth not in temples made with hands; Neither is worshipped with men's hands, as though he needed anything, seeing he giveth to all life, and breath, and all things; And hath made of one blood all nations of men for to dwell on all the face of the earth, and hath determined the times before appointed, and the bonds of their habitations"(Acts 17:24-26);*

God is the one who forms the foundation and border of this complex and beautiful Universe. He alone has the power, wisdom, and strength to put things and people in order whenever He chooses to do so because He, "... reveals Himself in His creation" (See Romans 1:18-20). **He didn't ask for any help, nor did he need an assistant to establish the equator of the world with these unique details that show the creativity of His Mighty Hands. It is God who has the original copy authentically designed for every living and nonliving thing He created which included MAN.** The greatness of God is everywhere, and He is the one who chose to fill the world with different kinds of species which are billions in number. He is The Ancient of Days with ALL authority to rule and govern the world by Himself because His POWER is UNLIMITED and UNQUESTIONABLE. Who can understand or dispute the thunder of God's powerful voice? His majesty and power supersede everyone put together! (see Job 26).

Therefore, no one has the authority to question God about his plans for even our lives or the plans for His Universe even though He gave us free will (*see* John 3:14-21). God can choose to try us by assigning the adversary to test our faith just like He did in the life of Job. That doesn't mean that God is unjust or that He doesn't love and cares for us (*see* Job 1 & 2). God is greater than any human and He is not unfair in anything He does because He is full of Wisdom, Knowledge, Understanding, Power, and Forcefulness (*see* Job 12). He has the final say in our lives as to WHO, WHAT, WHEN, WHERE, and WHY certain things happen to us. No matter what we are going through, God wants us to TRUST, BELIEVE, and OBEY Him in everything. God is the one who makes the ultimate decision in our lives as we see in the life of Job, who God says is a perfect and upright man. Yet, Job experienced severe losses of everything including his health, and his children but he did not blame God, nor did he sin (*see* Job 1).

Despite all the sufferings we are experiencing God can carry us through because we are never alone, and He is faithful. The Bible tells us, *"There hath no temptation taken you but such as is common to man: but God is faithful, who will not suffer you to be tempted above that ye are able; but will with the temptation also make a way to escape, that ye may able to bear it"* (1 Corinthians 10:13). God's promises are sure and He will never go back on His Word because He is not slack concerning any of His promises. God will ALWAYS make a way out of the wilderness because He is Omnipresent! He will rescue us and lead us away from the danger zone day and night. There are times when we become tired and weak, but when we are at our weakest God is at His strongest.

Serving God doesn't mean that we will be free from problems or testing of our faith like in the life of Job. Sometimes, God wants to test our faith for different reasons that we don't seem to understand during the testing phase. Job realized that he was going through a test, and he still needed to trust and believe in God, so he placed his hope in the God who would deliver him (*see* Job 13:15).

Have you ever been in a rut of disarray, confusion, and questioning? A time in your life when everything seems like they are going in the wrong direction, and it seems like no one cares? A trying time when we would get into self-pity and doubt and question God. wondering, does Jesus care? I am here to tell you, yes, He does care! Without a doubt, I can say Jesus cares because His love for us is unfailing, and His heart is touched with our grief. Psalm 147:3 says, *"He healeth the broken in heart, and bindeth up their wounds."* Jesus is blessing and comforting everyone that mourns all over the world.

Friends, Jesus is right there in the middle of your storms. Just like Job, we have to remind ourselves that we are serving a Sovereign God who is full of divine wisdom, that is far beyond our human understanding. God has the supreme power and authority to do whatever He wants to do in our lives. Even to permit Satan to touch us, but not to kill us (*see* Job 1 & 2). He is God and we are not aware of the conversation that He is having with the adversary to test us (*see* Job 1).

There are some wonderful lessons that we can adhere to from the dialogue between God, Satan, Job, his family, his servants, his friends, and Elihu in the life of Job. God says that Job was perfect and upright, and one that feared God and eschewed evil. Yet, the Lord allowed Satan to test Job and afflict him with boils. A time in his life when he felt alone and hopeless because he lost everything including his children. Despite it all, Job did not turn his back on God, instead, he bowed down and worshiped God even through the "crushing series of tragedies."

Job questioned God if He was a just God, why did this happen to righteous people and not to the unrighteous. Job kept on lamenting to a point in his life that he said, "The day of my birth is cursed." He

Chapter 16: The Lord Uses Animals to Illustrate His Majesty

even desired to die because of what he was going through (*see* Job 3 & 7). He was experiencing a crucial time of physical and psychological dilemma, more like his world was upside down. He was also grieving and mourning, questioning why God destroys the perfect and the wicked. Job was devastated so he cried out to the God of wisdom and strength, asking God to show him his sins even as he thinks about the shortness of life. Job was at a point of hopelessness, confusion, and despondency (*see* Job 6,9,10,13,14&17). Man cannot explain nor understand God's mysterious ways because we are not God and He wants us to put our trust in Him.

Can you imagine not only losing your health and wealth but ALL your children and his wife showing no empathy? She was not comforting him nor encouraging him. She wanted him to curse God and die. Rather harsh and cruel coming from his wife! (*see* Job 2:9). **However, she responded out of sadness, pain, and suffering, because she too was broken and grieving about the whole ordeal. Can you picture yourself losing so many things along with your ten children, and seeing your husband in such a state of misery with draining skin sores all over his body? She was sad, hurting, and mourning deep within because she was experiencing losses of TEN children that she gave birth to out of love and affection.** Yes, it was a crucial time in her life when she should seek God in faith alongside her husband and try to give each other comfort and hope.

However, it seems as if she was not much help and support to her husband, but she was still in the picture. We know that his wife was still around because he mentions her in Chapter 19:17, Job says, "My breath is strange to his wife..." Also, in Chapter 31:10 Job said, "Then let my wife grind unto another, and let others bow down upon her. "Job was experiencing mental anguish with everything that he was going through. It was affecting his physical and personal appearance to the point that he thought his wife was no longer attracted to him. Also, it must have been devastating for her as a mother and a wife to experience such great losses. She was seeing things in the physical and not in the spiritual like we often do when we are at our weakest point. Nevertheless, her response to her husband was not a reason to curse God and tell her husband to curse God and die. At that moment, neither she nor Job knew what plan God had for Job. God reminds us in Matthew 5:4, "Blessed are they that mourn: for they shall be comforted." We thank you, God, for being our Comforter even as we see in the life of Job.

Our Friends and family may mean us well, but most of the time, they don't have the answer or the solution to our problems. We can see that Job's three friends came and sat with him for seven days and seven nights and were silent, which is what we need at times. The sound of silence when we can't figure out things and we are kneeling around the seeking station of God! Soon after, they opened their mouths and began to talk, and one by one they started to accuse him wrongfully to which Job continued to defend his relationship with God (see Job 3-32). Then Elihu, who was the youngest, came into the picture and told Job to humble himself before God. Stating that God is great, and He is a just God and sometimes He allows things to happen to us to draw us closer to Him (see Job 33-37). This dialog went on for a long time and Job did not respond to them; he did not seek answers from friends or family. Job wanted God to answer him, and God did surprisingly answer him (see Job 38-42).

Amazingly, the Lord answered Job out of a whirlwind, asking Job several questions to which Job had no answers (see Job 38-39). God **did not address or respond to any of Job's questions about his illness or his losses.** Instead, God asked, *"Shall he that contendeth with the Almighty instruct him? he that reproveth God, let him answer it. Then Job answered the Lord, and said, Behold, I am vile; what shall I answer thee? I will lay my hand upon my mouth (see* Job 40:2-4). Job realized that he was wrong because he was no match to ask the Almighty God questions about the order and operations of the World. Job soon saw the immensity of the Power of this sovereign God of the universe. God also took Job on a great virtual tour of the Universe by asking him over seventy rhetorical questions about the foundation and the details of the cosmos world and everything therein.

He questioned Job about the formation and operations of the

Chapter 16: The Lord Uses Animals to Illustrate His Majesty

firmament of the Heavens and Earth. Questions such as, *"Who is this that darkeneth counsel by words without knowledge? Gird up thy loins like a man; for I will demand of thee, and answer thou me* (Job 38:2-3). I trembled as I read through these questions trying to comprehend the WISDOM, POWER, and EXTENT to these questions to which ONLY God himself knows the answers. These are questions that we often don't even consider or give any thought to as we travel through this complex and unique world that is created by the Omniscient hands of God. We are so caught up with our problems just like Job that we don't give a second thought to God's Majesty as he rules and operates this wonderful Universe.

God also asked Job about the immensity of the animal kingdoms and the order of it all, to which Job did not have a clue or ONE answer. Here, we see God's power and His covenantal relationship with even the animal kingdom is far beyond human understanding. For instance, in Job 40-41 God gave Job a detailed description of the **Behemoth** and **Leviathan** which are the two largest and strongest wild animals that He created on the fifth day. These animals cannot be tamed by man and are fierce enough to cause chaos in the Universe; Because of their exuberant strength and framework, only God can conquer them!

God spoke to Job about the Behemoth which I made along with you, as being a powerful grass-eating animal. He is "the chief of the Ways of God. "He is one of the first largest and strongest animals God created to live on Earth (*see* Job 40:15-24). God wants Job to know that He can protect him from the Behemoth even though he is such a strong and dangerous creature, that He is mightier than this monster. God wants Job to trust Him in every area of his life.

God described the Leviathan as, "King over the Children of pride." Which is another large and fearless sea monster, one that shows God's power of creation (*see* Job 41). Leviathan is mentioned a couple of times in the Bible, to which I will mention a few. Psalm 74:13-14 says the Leviathan are multi-headed sea dragons that were killed by God and their pieces were given to the people in the

Wilderness. Psalm 104:25-26 speaks about the manifold wisdom of God's creation on Earth and the great sea with numerous beasts great and small. In Isaiah 27:1, The Prophet speaks of Leviathan the piercing crooked serpent who was slain by God. Also, in Genesis 1:20-21 God spoke about the great sea monster. The above scriptures describe Leviathan as a multi-headed dragon, a great beast, and a serpent which was made by God, but He is not more powerful than God.

Here, we see where God demonstrates His authenticity of His powers and His Supremacy even in the illustration of the Behemoth and Leviathan that Job can relate to through the description given by God. We know that Job has a wonderful relationship with God and God said Job was a just man. However, now that he has seen the Lord and talked with the Lord out of the whirlwind has opened his spiritual eyes to appreciate God on a newer and higher level. Job said my ears have heard of you but now my eyes have seen you (*see* Job 40).

In the end, Job humbled himself and he was sorry for asking God so many questions and he repented. God called Job His servant, cleared him of all his wrongs, and blessed him abundantly (*see* Job 42:7-12). However, God's wrath was kindled against Job's three friends and they had to offer burnt offerings and Job prayed for them as the Lord commanded (*see* Job 42:7-9). "The Lord restores and doubles Job's possessions." God did not only restore his health and wealth but he gave him seven more sons and three more beautiful daughters. Job lived to see even his fourth generation and died, being old and full of days (*see* Job 42).

God wants Job and us to be cognizant that He is the Supreme God who holds the Universe in His Mighty and Powerful Hands. He is in control of us as much as He is in command and control of these two great creatures that were created by Him. God extends His grace to us not to condemn us but for us to know that He is more than ENOUGH, and we should Keep on trusting Him to do the impossible in our lives. He spoke to Job about these animals to give him an extensive explanation of their strength and even their framework; yet

Chapter 16: The Lord Uses Animals to Illustrate His Majesty

they are no match to the Omniscient God of the Universe. God in His authority and His Mighty force can call things that are in disorder back into order whether through suffering or blessing. God is excellent and He is perfect in all His ways, even as we think about his divine creation in making man in His image which is unbelievable and pretty awesome.

The Book of Job is so unique and fascinating in so many ways. It reveals some of the characteristics and majesty of God's power throughout the entire dialog with all the characters, with God being the Judge of all Judges. Going through these chapters is like preparing us for King Jesus's return sitting in a courtroom with God our Father who committed His Son Jesus Christ to Judge the world. **Can you imagine having Jesus who is the Judge of all Judges telling us to sit up and answer Him like a man? Pretty serious court cases that we cannot avoid or have a "Failure to Appear" (FTA) beside our names when Jesus returns. Neither can we provide any witnesses or get an attorney even if we are a quadrillionaire! WOW! We will ALL be in attendance when we MUST rise to the King of Kings and the Lord of Lords! Oh! What a day that will be, when our Savior we shall see sitting on His Judgment Throne! MY GOD! MY GOD!**

The Apostle John says, *"Jesus is declared the Son of God.' God committed all Judgement to His Son Jesus Christ"* (see John 5:16-47). Are you ready for the court case with Jesus Christ? The difference is that God already says that Job was," ...perfect and upright, and one that feared God, and eschewed evil (Job 1:1). Are we trying to live a Christlike life that is pleasing to God? Jesus is the answer, and He is the ONLY Way! Deep within our hearts, we don't have the answers to our day-to-day problems and situations that we are facing in life! Neither do we have the answers about God's creation or how He should rule and govern His world. No one can compare to God's wisdom, nor can you compete with him or against Him. Furthermore, some secret things belong to God alone and there are other things that He will reveal to us (*see* Deuteronomy 29:29).

We need to remind ourselves that silence from God doesn't mean that

God is not listening to us or that He is not in control. Remember, it was God who had a conversation with Satan about Job and permitted Satan to test Job (*see* Job 2). God is aware of what we are unable to understand, visualize, or comprehend because we are limited but He is the LIMITLESS God of the Universe. **His wisdom, knowledge, and resources NEVER run dry or empty. Neither is there any shortage or bankruptcy in God's Bank. Our Heavenly Father is SUPER RICH in EVERYTHING because He owns EVERYTHING!** He is the great and Mighty God who can change our lives from rags to riches or riches to rags. God wants us to believe that He is in control, and He is more than enough.

In Job Chapter 39, we read that, "The Lord uses animals to illustrate His majesty." **This is one of the main chapters that caught my attention in such a mighty way regarding my Heavenly dream. It was during that supernatural dream when Jesus gave me a BRONZE BABY UNICORN (foal or sparkle) which miraculously grew into a strong majestic seven to eight feet UNICORN.** This is one of the amazing creatures God asked Job about in Job 39:9-12, to which Job still did not have an answer, nor do we. Unicorns are REAL animals that are unique, and strong and they are mentioned NINE times in the King James Bible. All creatures are important to God, they are a part of His beautiful creation. (*see* Genesis 9:1-17). *"The rainbow confirms God's covenant"* It is God who said, *"And I will remember my covenant, which is between me and you and every living creature of all flesh; and the waters shall no more become a flood to destroy all flesh"* (v15). The Lord is majestic in everything He makes, He sets His glory above the Heavens and His work is excellent upon the Earth (*see* Psalm 8:6-9).

He is God and He can make ANYTHING just the way it pleases Him, even the beautiful UNICORN with one horn in the middle of their forehead, to illustrate the creativity of our Sovereign God. He made all these wonderful animals and birds that have different appearances in looks, shapes, and sizes just the way He wants them to be. He explains some of the work of these animals, by delegating different chores and power to them individually to which Job had no concept

Chapter 16: The Lord Uses Animals to Illustrate His Majesty

about their ability to function or perform. The scripture illustrates the manifold wisdom of God through the demonstration of strength and the unique build of these animals.

In Isaiah 34, the Prophet spoke about "JUDGMENT AGAINST THE NATION." God referred to several animals including the unicorn as He demonstrates what will happen because of man's disobedience on the day of the Lord. Isaiah warned that God will pour out His wrath against the nations if they don't listen to the voice of God and turn from their wicked ways. If you continue to be rebellious and live in sin, then you shall fall in God's fury where He will destroy all nations until they stink from their carcasses. This is very graphic, but this is the Word of God as spoken by the Prophet Isaiah. Everything in Heaven and Earth that people put before God will lose its shape and size because Judgment is on the land.

Here, we see where Isaiah mentioned several animals including the unicorn to be in action on the Lord's Day. In (v7) he says, *"And the unicorn shall come down with them, and the bullocks with the bulls; and their land shall be soaked with blood, and their dust made fat with fatness."* Now, we see where the Lord has delegated work for even the unicorn. Jesus is coming back as the Judge of the world, and He is very detailed in all the events that will take place on the Lord's Day. In (V8), Isaiah says, "For it is the day of the LORD'S vengeance, and the year of recompense for the controversy of Zion." There will be vengeance on all generations including rich and poor, black, brown and white, the high and the low. If they don't repent and turn to the Lord, then no one will escape this day. Like Job, we all need to wake up, repent, stop being rebellious, and turn to God who has all the answers to man's questions.

I have so many questions in life's journey, and I am sure you have some questions about our trials, tribulations, and the test of time. Regardless of the situation, whether we get an answer or not, God wants us to remember that He is enough and He will deliver us. No matter what we are experiencing in this present life; Our Dearest Father is so much BIGGER than what we are going through. The

Word of God is so comforting as we see in the Introduction that restoration took place in Job's life. Also, in the Key Words, God will comfort us if we turn to Him.

Key Words: It says, *"Christians today are not exempt from broken hearts or "suffering," but through it all we, like Job, can rest in the fact that God is fair, omnipotent, omniscient and sovereign. He will "comfort" us if we will turn to Him."* That's what God requires from us, He wants us to turn to Him because He judges us fairly and He will never leave us alone. The following theme will give us background knowledge that the adversary cannot attack us unless God permits him. It also explains why we sometimes suffer, and that God will deliver and He remains enough through life's challenging times.

(See the Themes: In the Introduction of Job)

It clearly states that *"Satan cannot bring financial and physical destruction upon us unless it is God's permissive will, and God will set the limit. It is beyond our human ability to understand the "why's" behind all the suffering in the world. Rest assured...the wicked will receive their just dues. We cannot blame all sufferings on the sin in a sufferer's life. Suffering may sometimes be allowed in our lives to purify, to test, to teach or to strengthen the soul by showing us that when we have lost all, and only God remains...God remains enough. God deserves and requests our love and praise regardless of our lot in life. God will deliver all suffering believers either in this life or in that which is to come."*

There are times when we will experience all types of losses because we are living in a sinful world that is full of chaos. However, our great God can give us quadruple and even more, because He is the God of abundance (*see* Deuteronomy 28:1-14, Ephesians 3:20, Exodus 34:6, Proverb 3:10). We don't know why the righteous suffer, but we know who to put our TRUST in and who to BELIEVE at all times. I am sure we all feel like Job in different seasons of our lives. However, we are encouraged by the life of Job that God loves us and He cares for us. God will restore and revive us to much more than we have before. He promised that He will never leave us nor forsake us (*see* Deuteronomy 31:8).

Chapter 16: The Lord Uses Animals to Illustrate His Majesty

Are you feeling like Job as you go through the different phases of life, even though we may not be wealthy or perfect and upright like Job. There are times when we feel like we are at the crossroads of adversities, pain, anxiety, sadness, loneliness, depression, worry, and confusion. We might not have a fourth person like Elihu to say, "Great men are not always wise: neither do the aged understand judgment." He continued to say, "For I know not to give flattering titles; in so doing my maker would soon take me away" (Job 32:9 & 22). Elihu responded that "God sometimes uses affliction to turn men back to Him, " and "It is unthinkable that God would do wrong, nor should we be self-righteous. We should remember that we serve a God who is great beyond human understanding, and He continues to work wonders" (*see* Job 33 to 37). God is always in perfect control of the Universe and He is in control of you because He loves you with an everlasting love.

I experienced some trying times in my life when my world felt as if nothing was going in the right direction, there was chaos everywhere I turned. Through it all, I had to hold on to the hands of my Savior. I had several questions for God to which I still don't know the answers, but just like with Job, God did not answer any of my questions. **Instead, he responded by still giving me the gift of life and I am so grateful to be alive and not looking like what I have been through. God provided me with so much comfort and joy in different areas of my life. Joy unspeakable**! Oh! I thank you, Abba Father, for the many blessings that you bestowed upon me throughout EVERY phase of my life. I have learned to TRUST in God and believe in his PROMISES, most of all to SEEK Him in everything. I am sure you have your testing and your testimony! Take a moment to thank God that you are still here to tell the story! To God be the glory!

I do remember after my fourth miscarriage, which included an ectopic pregnancy, I was extremely sad and depressed for a while because I desired to have more children. However, I had to get up and get out of that place of worry and thank God for blessing me with my one daughter. I had to align God's words to my heart and say, "I will not be anxious, but I will rejoice in the Lord always" (*see*

Philippians 4:4-7). Jesus is the only one who has your inner thoughts, emotions and desires and I am so glad he searcheth our heart and He knows the desires of our hearts. God kept me in his big loving arms and cradled my heart with so much love during that time!

After about a decade, I experienced so much joyfulness from being a foster mother to several children as I reunited some with their biological parents. The Lord blesses our family with several new births, including twins, my three granddaughters, and many other children within my community. **Thank You, God, for unspeakable joy and happiness that I am now having which outweigh the pain, depression, and sadness that I experienced years ago. Now, I can say without a doubt that the joy of the Lord is my strength and I thank Him for His love and His compassion that failed not (***see*** Nehemiah 8:10).**

We all have difficulties throughout our journey with different phases of trouble and triumph. Through it all God wants us to stay committed and believe that He is always ENOUGH. Your experience for breakthrough may be different from others but one thing is for sure, God has the answer to your situation. Just like Job, keep your faith and your confidence in God strong. Don't turn your back on God because you don't know the reason why you are going through a transitional season of testing. Put your TRUST in Jesus who wash and purge you with HIS BLOOD and fill you with HIS HOLY SPIRIT. **He is not just enough but He is more than enough, and He will come through for you. God knows how to heal our broken hearts and gives us peace and assurance in the midst of the storm (***see*** John 14:27).**

God fixed my troubled heart, and He will do the same for you. No matter what you are going through, remember that He is the Potter, and we are the clay (*see* Isaiah 64:8). He came through for Job and He will do the same for you. I experienced His greatness so many times throughout my life BUT the miracle that He showed me in the dream with the UNICORN is beyond my comprehension, one that I will hold dear to my heart until He returns. I have so many questions

Chapter 16: The Lord Uses Animals to Illustrate His Majesty

about this unicorn, and I am sure Jesus will give me all the answers someday if He chooses to do so.

Our God is great, and his power is dynamite! Look to God FIRST because He is our Father and His love for us is unfadable! God is always watching over us, and He is listening to all our cries and lamenting. He sees the pureness and impurity of everyone's heart, and He knows and feels our sadness and pains. This light affliction that we are going through is only but for a moment (*see* 1 Corinthians 4:17-18). He is our Father and He will let you ask all these questions as you listen to friends and family to see whose advice you will take and who you will turn to just like Job. Will you depend on him and seek him in praise, worship, and prayer and less complaining during the trials? No one can understand God's power from on high, but He understands us and He cares and He is listening. The wonderful thing about God is that He will always answer us with a yes, or no, or wait on Him. Because He is the author who penned every piece of information about our life and our existence. He can also lovingly discipline us anytime He chooses to do so.

It is important to keep the faith alive because we are serving a God who can change the impossible into possible at any time. Through it all Job was trying to be humble and not wanting to upset God by repenting in dust and ashes (see Job 42:1-6). We don't know God's plan for our lives, we just have to look to Him in faith and believe that He will come through for us in His own time. Even if we fall on our faces and lose everything, God can, and He will restore and replenish us to much more than what we lost because He is Sovereign.

Even with modern technology, man can calculate and compute various things about the Heavens, Earth, planets, species, and more. However, you cannot give the answers or an explanation to all these questions that God asked Job. Do we have the answers to all the questions that God asked Job? God asked Job to save himself if he was able. Such an impossible question for anyone, to which Job had NO answer (*see* Job 40 and 41). Now, that same question is pointing toward us today! Can you save yourself? The answer is NO! We are all saved by God's grace because Jesus loves us unconditionally (*see* Ephesians 2: 1-10, Romans 5, 2 Timothy 1:9, Titus 3:1-8).

Even though man feels as if they are so smart, wise, rich, and famous, we should not forget who allows His abundance of blessings to fall on us and give us life. We cannot diminish the POWER, STRENGTH, MAJESTY, and EXCELLENCY of our Supreme God of the Universe. We are faced with all kinds of dilemmas in this troubled world, but God has the master key to all our questions and concerns. He is the wheel in the middle of the wheel (*see* Ezekiel 10:10). God will never abandon us because He is the Good Shepherd, who is always searching for His lost sheep. You may have several questions too but just like Job let us repent and cover our mouth and believe that God is always more than ENOUGH.

Poem: The Mystical Bronze Unicorn!

There on the evergreen grass in the corner of my street!
A beautiful golden baby unicorn lay cuddled, cute, and sweet.
Looking at me with piercing, bright, shining, and loving eyes!
Dainty little body, chubby feet! unique and not a bit shy!

Jesus told me to pick up this beautiful creature of golden brown!
Just then, an intruder reached for my baby unicorn, and I frowned!
This intruder tried twice to pick up the unicorn that belonged to me!
But the unicorn stayed cuddled, and the intruder then retreated!

In a commanding voice, Jesus said, it belongs to you! PICK IT UP! It will take you where you want to go! My unicorn sweet buttercup!
He sprang into my arms, which made me very happy and surprised!
Slumbering closer to my embrace, as he keeps looking up to the sky!

To my amazement, this majestic unicorn of bronze color!
Start moving strongly in my arms, as his body grew fast, and fuller!
He sprang quickly to the ground, dancing, jumping, and frolicking!
I felt so much power, and energy, next to him as I kept skipping!

The Bible tells us that, "God brought him forth out of Egypt;
He hath as it were the strength of a unicorn: he shall eat up
the nations his enemies, and shall break their bones, and pierce
them through with his arrows." (Numbers 24:8) KJV

"Will the unicorn be willing to serve thee or abide by thy crib? Canst thou bind the unicorn with his band in the furrow? or will he horror the valley after thee? Wilt thou trust him because his strength is great?

or wilt thou leave thy labor to him? Will thou believe him, that he will bring home thy seed, and gather it into thy barn? (Job 39:9-12) KJV.

God will always show His handiwork to all His sons and daughters!
Is there ANYTHING too hard for our loving and caring Father?
He who holds this cosmos world in the palm of His mighty hands!
Makes and describes the strength of Behemoth and the Leviathan!

God gave me this unicorn to express his power and his love for me!
A special gift from Jesus Christ, the greatest King, is *He*!
This unicorn (my buttercup) stood tall, proud, and very strong!
I am so happy and fascinated because, to me, he belongs!

Suddenly and swiftly, my body was sitting on his broad hairy back!
To my surprise, I felt a smooth flying movement as I totally relaxed!
Within seconds we were flying over houses, mountains, and plains!
I felt so much joy, happiness, and excitement I could hardly contain!

I relaxed on my unicorn with his graceful body and signature horn!
Suddenly and sadly, I was home, and my unicorn was gone!
Deep in my heart, I miss my buttercup; at times, I feel like crying!
Missing the thrill and excitement of my unicorn as we were flying!

I am looking forward to seeing Jesus at Heaven's Jubilee!
I am sure I will see my unicorn, waiting there to welcome me!
Are you looking forward to seeing the HOLY LAMB of GOD?
He is the returning King of Kings and He is the Lord of Lords!

END OF THE HEAVENLY DREAM

Part 3: Second Dream: Seeing Jesus With A Book in His Hand

Chapter 17: Yes! To the Call of God's Assignment After the Second Dream

"Blessed is he whose transgression is forgiven, whose sin is covered. Blessed is the man unto whom the Lord imputeth not iniquity, and in whose spirit there is no guile. I will instruct thee and teach thee in the way which thou shalt go I will guide thee with mine eye. Be ye not as the horse, or as the mule, which have no understanding: whose mouth must be held in with bit and bridle, lest they come near unto thee."

--Psalm 32:1-2 & 8-9 *KJV*

In the above scripture, David is explaining that only God can remove our transgression and iniquity and replace it with blessings. When we are washed and free from our burden of sins then God can use us to carry out His assignment. We need to repent so we can be free from our transgressions so the Holy Spirit can take total residence in us. Jesus promised that the Holy Spirit would teach us, instruct us, and guide us into truth and testify of Him Jesus. God wants us to be wise in Him and not stubborn like a wild horse that has no understanding of when to be still or when to attack. We cannot be wise in our own eyes; we need to acknowledge who God is and the amazing things that He can do in our lives. He is the number one teacher, counselor, leader, and guide with the Mighty power to help us fulfill His assignment.

Are we eager to respond to the call of the Lord, whether we think it is a small or big assignment? Are we being faithful and trustworthy in obeying the God who anoints and calls you to do His assignment?

Chapter 17: Yes! To the Call of God's Assignment After the Second Dream

We may come up with different answers, especially when we are so lost in the trials and chaos of this world. It may just be a time in our lives when we think our world is spinning so fast that we don't want to stop or be interrupted in the middle of the spinning wheel of struggle and limitation! I think those are the times when the Lord chooses to meet us at the most unexpected moment so He can use us to concentrate on Him and not the world. There comes a time in our lives when we realize that it is not about us, but it is all about serving JESUS, the Master! We need to wake up from our slumber and say Yes! Lord Yes! I am available to be used by You to do Your will. Please come in and have Your way, dear Lord! I will follow You and I will serve You!

The scripture tells us that we cannot serve God and mammon (Matthew 6:24). We should not live or act like the Pharisees. Instead, we should focus our full attention on the things of God and follow in our calling and assignment. In moments of uncertainty, we would rather say, "No!" But who would want to say no to God? We need to stay faithful to God in anything He assigns us to do. By doing so, He will increase our assignment to bigger tasks, knowing that we will depend on Him to carry us through the process. We cannot depend on our strength and might but only on the strength, power, and Spirit of the Lord. It could be the most crucial time in our lives when God wants our attention to focus on Him and not to be distracted by the things of the world. His Word encourages us, saying, *"He that is faithful in that which is least is faithful also in much"* (Luke 16:10).

So many biblical Heroes were called at the most unexpected time of their lives to answer the Call of God! They followed through even when they were unsure and afraid. They knew that God would never fail them nor leave them alone. We must remind ourselves that life is not always about us and what we want. It is all about fulfilling the will of God and walking in His plan and purpose for our life. For example, Noah was called to build an ark. Even though people mocked and criticized him, he was determined to keep building the ark.

He was committed to obeying God and exercised faith in God's plan for him and his family (*see* Genesis 7). God also called Abraham to leave his father's house and go to an unknown land (*see* Genesis 12). It was not an easy transition, but he had faith in God and was called righteous because he exercised faith in God (*see* Genesis 15:6). Also, Moses was busy taking care of the flock when God called him to set the Israelites free! Moses was hesitant and worried that his speech impediment was a problem, but God chose and used him as the leader for the Exodus assignment (*see* Exodus 3).

In my situation, I thought I was not spiritually ready because I had so much going on in my life and in my family's life! I was a bit fearful and in doubt, and I knew it was the plan of the enemy trying to put fear and doubt in me. Therefore, **I had to seek God in prayer and fasting for His will and purpose over my life so I could walk into my destiny. Are you at that crossroads of decision regarding the call of God over your life? Pull forth a grain of mustard seed faith and step into the footprint of God's righteousness and His plan for your life.** Take a transitional leap, jump out with confidence, and trust God that He will lead and guide you through every turn and corner of your decision. Keep praying and believing, knowing that He did it for many others and He will do it for you too.

YOU ARE NOT ALONE! The Holy Spirit, our darling Counselor, Teacher, and Guide, is always interceding for us every second because the accuser is always trying to accuse us of doing wrong. Jesus is beside you, protecting and propelling you as you travel through the process of hope with divine determination. God has good plans for His children, leading and guiding you into His plan of peace to prosper you for His glory. God will come to us in many ways and through various people to alert us to get out of complacency and into His assignment of integrity and satisfaction!

It was October of 2013, exactly twenty months, after the Heavenly dream that the Lord appeared to me again in another dream. In this dream, **I saw Jesus with His hands outstretched, showing me a BOOK, and telling me to write about the dream of Heaven. It was**

Chapter 17: Yes! To the Call of God's Assignment After the Second Dream

King Jesus! This, again, was mind-blowing and somewhat frightening. I was looking at Jesus in shock and I was puzzled with many questions that I did not open my mouth to ask because Jesus already knew what I was thinking. Jesus looked at me with a look that spoke straight to my mind, and I was still in disbelief, in a dream that was so real.

I kept looking at Jesus with the BOOK in His hands, still in bewilderment about this assignment that seemed unattainable. Jesus knew what I was thinking about aloud, "If I am telling many people about the dream, do I need to write a book?" I was caught up in my flesh even in the dream! Here, I was still wondering, *do I need to write a book?* This was more like telepathic communication! Finally, my Savior's audible voice responded, "BECAUSE I TOLD YOU TO WRITE THIS BOOK." **Suddenly, He was gone, just as swiftly as He came into my room in the early morning hours. That's exactly how quickly He disappeared out of sight, even though I could still sense His presence around me.** I was thinking aloud, "Did I say yes to this assignment? I know I cannot say no, because this was a command from God, and I dare not question His command, not even in my dream!" So, I said, "Use me, Lord, for your service!"

I jumped out of my sleep as if I was holding the book in my hands, still in shock, while trying to comprehend what had just happened. All kinds of thoughts were running through my mind; I was trembling somewhat as I made a note of the dream! My heart felt like it was pumping out of my chest, and my hands were shaking! I was wide awake, alert, and oriented, yet in disbelief at seeing the book held out in the hands of my Savior. Soon after, I began to pray and could not go back to sleep even though it was about five o'clock in the morning. **I was trying to process the encounter of my Lord and Savior, not just showing me a book, but commanding me to fulfill an assignment about the Heavenly dream!**

I was astounded, puzzled, and perplexed! I think all my nerves were running on an automatic charge, with my heart palpitating out of the normal range! I said, "Oh, Lord! Have mercy on me," because I was still in shock mode, feeling inadequate! So, I called on Jesus for help and support. The Holy Spirit began to comfort and encourage me that He was there to guide me throughout the journey! **I needed to trust Him and believe that Jesus is the All-Knowing God who knows what is best for us and is always there to lead and direct us even when we are faced with doubts and fear.**

The Prophet Isaiah wrote in a part of his theme that *"God is our eternal Comforter, Redeemer, and Savior. God will pardon us of our sins if we will forsake our past and trust in Him."* He continued to say, *"Deliverance is of God, not of man. The greatest success in the world is being obedient to the will of God."* This is the Word of God to all nations then and now. I said to God my Father, ***just like you did for Cyrus, please put your hand over my right hand.*** I know this is the way that you can help us to subdue nations as you go before us to make the crooked places straight (*see* Isaiah 45:1-6). God is calling us by name, and He will even change our names at times, just like he did with Jacob and renamed him Israel and it is all for his glory because He is God Almighty (*see* Genesis 35:10-11). **Father, please help me to exercise the greatest success in the world by being obedient to your will and your way.**

Immediately, I said, "Father, I am available to be used by You. Not my will but let Your will be done in me." Thank You, Father, that You called me by my name for this special assignment. Such favor, I will not take for granted; all glory belongs to You, God, my Father. Even though I have yet to understand Your plan for my life, my thoughts and will are totally in Your hands. As You lead, let me humbly follow after Your will and Your way! The way and the path may seem so crooked and unpaved, but Your words remind me that You will make the crooked places straight. Father, just like You did for Jacob, Your servant, I know You will do the same for me.

God, my Father, I thank You for preparing me and equipping me for a time and season as now. Holy Spirit, I thank You for taking complete control of every step I take to venture into the unknown, and for reminding me that I am not alone but that You are with me.

Chapter 17: Yes! To the Call of God's Assignment After the Second Dream

You are the same God that gave comfort and protection to Jacob; I know that Your power, strength, and might continue to be the same. Thank you, Emanuel, for all Your love and for keeping me in Your tender care and multitude of mercies. I know that Your grace is sufficient to keep me as I take one moment at a time through this process. Have Your way, Father, Son, and Holy Spirit in my life so that I will have attentive ears to Your call, acknowledging that You are Lord, and there is none other like You. I worship and praise You for who You are in my life! You are Majesty, King of the Universe. Dearest Father, please take the lead as I take one moment at a time to accomplish what You set out for me to do! Your direction and Your will and Your way only must I obey!

We are encouraged to obey the voice and command of God! He wants us to be humble and quick to respond to Him, not hesitate or make any room for the adversary to put fear in us. No one is above the authority and command of God. We need to be always subjected to His Majesty and let Him have the first and final say in our lives! At that moment everything seemed so hard and insurmountable with different challenges surrounding me and my family. The flesh was trying to discourage and derail me from God's plan and purpose in my life. BUT GOD! We must remember that God will not give us an assignment bigger than the plan He has for our lives. We just have to believe in His plan and exercise FAITH over fear. Deep within my heart, I knew I needed to fast and pray against the fear and doubt because I felt I was not ready. Nevertheless, I knew the God I serve would guide me all the way and He will do the same for you. **Our God knows exactly how to get us out of our comfort zones as we face difficulties and challenges, pushing us out of complacency to fulfill His purpose in us—a time in our lives when we depend on His strength and power.**

Even though we know we are saved and are children of God, sometimes fear and doubt creep in to haunt us and block our faith. That's the time to dig deep into the word of God, I guarantee you that you will find strength and wisdom from the breath of God. Friends, don't be fooled; the adversary is after you every moment he can get to distract and derail you twenty-four-seven. The enemy is a liar and he is patiently waiting for a moment when we are at our most vulnerable time to attack, trick, and deceive us. **We MUST be steadfast in our relationship with the Lord, so we are not easily persuaded by the cunningness of the enemy. We must crucify ourselves daily so we can walk in the spirit of God and not in the flesh that will easily deceive us! We dare not leave any loophole for the accuser.** The adversary is trying to put all kinds of doubt and fear in our minds so we will miss out on God's plan for us.

I was worried about all the broken pieces in my life and the lives of my family and was trying to fix and mend the broken pieces on my own strength. All kinds of distractions and doubts started to sneak up on me and I was unaware that I was so overwhelmed! Have you ever been there, where doubts and fear want to enter at every door in your life? But we have the authority to close all doors that will give access to the devil in the name of Jesus. It was during those moments that I asked God to let His Holy Ghost Fire burn out every negative setback, hindrance, and thought that would distract me from fulfilling my assignment.

We must remind ourselves that we are children of the Highest God, and the devil's weapons cannot harm us if we demolish them in the Mighty name of Jesus! So, I said, "Girl! Get up out of doubt and fear!" I asked myself, "Do you know whom you serve? Do you know who lives inside of you? Who is the King of your life? Who is your Heavenly Father who watches over you? Who is walking beside you every day?" *It is Jesus, our Lord and Savior, the Protector of the Universe! The one who is the ruler of Heaven and Earth! Do you know who your Abba Father is? The one who gave us privileges to be called sons of God! The one who says, "I am your Abba Father (see* **Galatians 4:1-7).** *I made you in My image; you are My child!" That's a HALLELUJAH praise, right there!*

All these amazing promises came alive in me, and suddenly, I felt complete assurance in the presence of the Lord. I gained full coverage of confidence in Jesus, my Lord, that He is my Father, and He will

Chapter 17: Yes! To the Call of God's Assignment After the Second Dream

guide me, even though the crooked side of the mountain. Father, I thank You for Your increased faith and confidence to stay steadfast in You. Holy Spirit, thanks for Your supernatural recall and for increasing my faith in Jehovah to pull me out of my comfort zone and fear so that I could rely on You. So, I prayed as I ought to pray, allowing God to have His way in my life, followed by fasting and so much more prayer from family and friends, as I depended on the leading of the Lord.

When Jesus told me to write this book, I was unaware that I would go through several years of difficulties and great testing before I could accomplish this assignment. **Now, I can say thank You, Lord, for this testing, learning, pruning, healing, and spiritual growth process through the journey of faith. Through it all, Jesus never leaves me. Just like in the dream, He was always beside me, protecting and guiding me. His promise is sure, and He will never break a promise.** Our God is faithful, and He is trustworthy in all He says and does. Peter reminds us, *"The Lord is not slack concerning his promise, as some men count slackness; but is longsuffering to us, not willing that any should perish, but that all should come to repentance"* (2 Peter 3:9).

Our God is true to His promises. His Word also tells us, *"If a son shall ask for bread of any of you that is a father, will he give him a stone? Or if he asks a fish, will he for a fish give him a serpent"* (Luke 11:11). God wants the best for us because He is our Father who cares for His own. He continues to extend His mercy, grace, and blessings to us every moment of the day. He will only give us the desires of our hearts if it is in His will to do so and when He chooses to grant them unto us. We need to wait and trust the God of the impossible to work the possible in our lives.

Even though it has been over eleven years since I had the dream of Heaven, it still stays fresh and powerful in my mind by the inspiration of the Holy Spirit. **Having that dream was one of my life's most defining and precious moments. My life felt like a broken cistern, seemingly unrepairable, at that time. EVERYTHING seemed to be broken or somewhat shattered, with so many pieces**

of clay all over the place. To me, it felt like the most puzzling and most complicated time of my life to be called for such an assignment from God. Maybe because I was trying to figure out all the missing pieces and trying to patch, mend, and fix things on my own. **We cannot do life on our own; in everything, we need to seek the guidance of God.** In my mind, I thought I was seeking God for everything, but deep down, I was not totally depending on Him! I was seeking Him but not waiting on Him as I ought to, so my strength could be renewed in Him. We cannot mount up in our strength to do anything (*see* Isaiah 40:30-31). Have you ever been there? Prophet Isaiah is telling us that when we seek and wait upon the Lord then we will be able to mount up like eagles, we will not get weary or faint. Seek God in everything. I know you will surely find Him!

We must thank God for being the Potter with the authentic material and blueprint of our shattered life that He is fixing daily. If not, we would be so splattered on the walls of the enemy's camp. We would be lost to the tricks and schemes of the adversary. Thank you, Jehovah, for coming to our rescue and delivering us right on time! We need Him more than ever because He is the Omniscient God! He is the Potter, and He knows how to mend the broken pieces and put them in their rightful places. He knows exactly how to mold and shape our shapeless hurting hearts back to their original shape and even at a better place in Him. **God can make our Spiritual hearts a BEAUTIFUL BLOOMING GARDEN; Filled with the fruits of the Spirit with so much LOVE to spread to the world. ONLY God can replace in us a HEART full of gratitude that will change us to search for our Christian attitude so that we can exemplify Christlike attributes. Then our hearts will blossom and bloom the fragrance of brotherly love, joy, peace, longsuffering, gentleness, goodness, faith, meekness, and temperance: against such there is no law** (*see* **Galatians 5:22-23). Hallelujah! God knows how to prepare our hearts for His assignment! He prepared my heart, and He will prepare your heart too.**

There were times when I would question God, "Why me, Lord?" At a time in my life when I was going through so much heartache and

Chapter 17: Yes! To the Call of God's Assignment After the Second Dream

pain, I asked, "How can I manage this assignment at this moment of my life?" But as I got into His Word and sought Him more, I realized that this was His will and plan for my life. So, I dare not question the plan and will of God over my life anymore. Instead, I seek Him for guidance and clarification on what to do and how to do it. Here comes the Holy Spirit, always ready to solve our problems with His strength and power. The Bible tells us in *Acts 1:8 (NLT)*, *"But you will receive power when the Holy Spirit has come upon you. And you will be my witnesses, telling people about me everywhere--in Jerusalem, throughout Judea, in Samaria, and to the ends of the earth."*

Jesus told us who to look to for help when He ascended to His Father. He left us the Comforter, who is our Earthly source. The Holy Spirit is here to manifest His power through us so we can gain the knowledge and wisdom of God to lead others to the kingdom of Heaven. The Bible also tells us that God is a spirit, and we MUST worship Him in Spirit and Truth (*see* John 4:23-24). God is the head of our life, but we can only go to the Father through His Son, Jesus Christ. Jesus is Superior to Creation and He is seated on the right side of His Father in Heaven. However, before Jesus ascended, He told His disciples that He would send the Holy Spirit, who comes with the power to ignite His fire in our lives. THE HOLY SPIRIT IS THE THIRD PERSON OF THE GODHEAD and He comes with fire to live in us, once we let Him in. He is here to help us in every area of our life, most of all, to lead us into God's truth!

With that being said, we have to remember that our Heavenly assignment was planned out by God even before conception took place in my mother's womb (See Psalm 139). We need to exercise our faith, and confidence and believe in God for His direction and His leading. He knows the Holy Spirit is here to be in partnership with us to help us accomplish what He assigned us to do. It is Solomon who says, *"A man's heart deviseth his way: but the Lord directeth his steps. The lot is cast into the lap; but the whole disposing thereof is of the Lord" (Proverb 16:9 & 33).* Our Sovereign God will lead and guide us through His assignment; just open up your heart to hear and yield to His voice on your journey.

Jesus Descending From The Golden Gates Of Heaven

Friends, I encourage you to trust in the Lord with all thine heart because He knows best, and He is the author and builder of your faith. God's purpose is to prosper us so we can be at peace and live in joy and happiness. However, the enemy is also on a mission to derail and destroy us so we will die without fulfilling the plan of God for our lives. Be determined and alert to the plot and scheme of the enemy. Do not let the spirit of doubt and fear steal your victory testimony. The adversary wants to deter and destroy you and lead you to the highway of destruction! Friends, stay on the resurrection street of glory with Jesus as your navigator, and He will lead you to the kingdom of Heaven. Do not let fear of the unknown creep up on you, causing you to question God's plan for your life. God got you covered, and He will not disappoint you or leave you comfortless!

I was somewhat hesitant because of my fear of the unknown! We all have experienced this kind of fear at some point in our lives! In those times, we must seek the Lord and depend on Him only. We should never think we are too independent and do not need the Lord as our guide and protector. We can NEVER make life worth living without the hands of our Savior leading, guiding, and protecting us! At the beginning of this assignment, I was in that place of doubt, fear, insecurity, and obscurity; however, our sweet and loving Savior reminded me that He was bigger than all my fears and doubts. **The adversary brings fear, but Jesus brings us faith.** Immediately, I was comforted by Philippians 4:13 *(KJV)*. The Apostle Paul encouraged the Philippians, and those words are still here to encourage us. He said, *"I can do all things through Christ which strengtheneth me."* In verse nineteen, he continued, *"But my God shall supply all your needs according to his riches in glory by Christ Jesus."* We serve a great and mighty God who continues to supply all our needs, lives inside us, and takes care of our circumstances. Depend on the wisdom and strength of The Omniscient God! He will never fail us!

My friend, only trust God. He will open the sea and roll back the water to take you to your next destination. He did it for Moses and the children of Israel over two thousand years ago, and He is the same Promise-Keeping God of yesterday, today, and forever. Trust God

Chapter 17: Yes! To the Call of God's Assignment After the Second Dream

and lean not unto your independence nor your understanding. **God has the MASTER LOCK and KEYS to unlock or open all the doors of our problems, breakthroughs, and victory. He also has all the gifts and talents safely secured and will distribute them to us in His way and in His own time.**

He is the Sovereign God who watches over us and continues to live within us. We need to give Him full access to be the head of our lives, allowing the Holy Spirit to be in partnership with all our daily plans. The Holy Spirit is our Earthly guide and Comforter, to assist us in every way. Do not ignore the Holy Spirit! He is ready and waiting to be our Spiritual support and Comforter in every area of our life. As Christians, we must be in partnership with the Holy Spirit to live according to God's will.

Now, looking back over the past years, I am so happy God directed me to write this book. Writing it pushed me to depend more on the Holy Spirit to help me as I researched and read the Bible even more. It was a sacred time to look forward to while building a closer and more intimate relationship with my Lord and Savior. It also made me realize that God had a different plan for my life regarding when and what type of message He wanted me to incorporate into this book. So, by the leading of the Holy Spirit, I ventured out trusting and believing in the Lord that He would see me through the end. I have confidence in the promises of God that if He says it, He will do it. **It does not matter how young or old we are; His plan over our lives stands forever and is always good and not evil. God had a plan for Moses's life when he encouraged and called him for the journey at the age of eighty (*see* Exodus 7:1-7). God called Abraham and promised Him blessings at the age of seventy-five (*see* Genesis 12:1-9). He also had a plan for King Jehoash who was crowned at the age of seven to be the King. He was the eighth King of Judah and he reigned for forty years (*see* 2 Kings 12:1-2 & 2 Chronicles 24:1-2).**

So, I beseech you, my friend, to hold on and keep your faith alive. God is preparing you to walk into your gift, dream, or assignment to edify others and glorify Him. It is never too late to avail yourself of the promises Of God over your life. Will you tap into your gift, talent, assignment, or calling today? **God will open your door of opportunity and He will extend your borders in many communities.**

Prayer--Seeking God's Direction and Guidance for the Assignment!

Our Dearest Father of Heaven and Earth. Holy be Your Mighty and Powerful Name throughout the World. We thank You that You are the Creator of this authentic and unique Universe. Heaven declares Your glory, and the sky proclaims the work of Your Mighty hands. No one can explain the perfectness and pureness that You established upon the Earth. I humbly come to You in glory, honor, and praise to lift Your Majestic name on high.

Dearest Father, I thank You for Your Son Jesus Christ who has divinely appeared to me and given me an assignment to write this book. I earnestly thank You for Your favor in my life and I will not measure or compare my assignment with others. Abba Father, I thank You for Your divine revelation as You lead and guide me in this chaotic and busy World. Father, I thank You for helping me to fight this battle, and I will keep the faith to the end. Lord, please give me the strength and faith to fight this battle so I can enter into my purpose in you. Dearest Father as I placed Your Words of Truth over my life, help me to stay steadfast in Your will and Your way. I placed Psalm 27, 2 Timothy 4:7, 1 Chronicles 4:9-10 & Genesis 32: 24-30) over my Life.

Father, I am asking You to remove the spirit of fear, anxiety, and worry as You cover me with Your Holy Spirit on this assignment. Let self be crucified as I depend on You for Your divine wisdom, knowledge, and understanding. Please open the eyes of my heart and remove any spiritual glaucoma or any defective cataract that will hinder my vision from seeing the plan You already set for my life. Remove everything that is unlike You from generational curse to my birth and even now in Jesus's name. Holy Ghost fire burns out everything that is unlike You from the root so that Your plan can be manifested in this assignment and throughout my life in Jesus's name. Father, detox me and flush out any liquid pollution from my body that will drown me in sin city. Place within me the body and mind of Christ so Your divine will, revelation, wisdom, knowledge, and understanding will flow as I pen every word.

Abba Father, please help me not to rush your assignment to meet my agenda but to stay committed to the timing of the Holy Spirit. Thank You for reminding me that my timing is not Your timing. Father, Your Word says that" ... *the race is not to the swift, nor the battle to the strong, neither yet the bread to the wise, nor yet riches to men of understanding, nor yet favor to men of skill; but time and chance happens to them all."* (Ecclesiastes 9:11 *KJV*). I thank You that Your timing doesn't have a clock with an alarm because Your timing is always right and ever so perfect. It is Peter the Apostle who reminds us, *"...be not ignorant of this one thing, that one day is with the Lord as a thousand years, and a thousand years as one day."* (2 Peter 3:8) Lord, help me to stay alert and focused as I follow the direction of the blessed Holy Spirit on this faith journey!

Father, I thank You for our biblical forefathers who kept the faith and centered their minds on completing the task that You set before them. Please, help me to not get tired or weary in completing this assignment, but to stay focused and endure to the end. I place Psalms 19 and 119 over my life to follow your lead. Thank you for helping me and others who are on their journey assignment to stay faithful and confident like our Father Abraham.

Father, I thank You for Your precious blood that gives me full coverage and protection in every area of my life. Your amazing blood that heals, saves, delivers, and sets me free from the hands of the enemy. I thank You for Your favor and blessings on me as I travel along the way. I give you thanks in Jesus's precious name. Amen.

Chapter 18: Jesus' Voice! My Strength, Power, and My Guide

"The majesty of the voice of the Lord."

"The voice of the Lord is upon the waters: the God of glory thundereth: the Lord is upon many waters. The voice of the Lord is powerful; the voice of the Lord is full of majesty. The voice of the Lord breaketh the cedars of Lebanon. The Lord will give strength unto his people; the Lord will bless his people with peace."

--Psalm 29:3-5 & 11 *KJV*

Then Jesus said to me, "Daughter, I am always with you!" A voice that is full of authority, assurance, and Majesty. A voice that I must listen to at all times. Most of all, being attentive to the *Dunamis* power coming to me in such a marvelous and commanding way! Jesus did not give me a date or a time to complete this assignment. However, He knew the answer to all my questions, and He also knew the answers to all your questions. God wants us to be courageous because He is our strength and our guide through the bright days and the dark days. Be not afraid of what the enemy might throw at you. Remember who is guiding you and living inside of you. Jesus encouraged me when He was walking beside me to be bold, confident, strong, and courageous when He told me to pick up the unicorn! We must learn to put action with our faith to make it work. If not, then our work is dead. We need to put total dependency and trust in the God of POWER that He will never leave us, nor will He fail us.

The Bible tells us that faith without work is dead. Faith and work go hand in hand (*see* James 2:14-26). Also, the Bible tells us in *Hebrews 11:6 (KJV)*, *"But without faith, it is impossible to please him: for he that cometh to God must believe that he is and that he is a rewarder of them that diligently seek him."* **God rewards those who diligently seek Him in**

Jesus Descending From The Golden Gates Of Heaven

faith prayer. We need to exercise faith and believe that He is the God of the impossible. Jesus is right beside you, shielding you and showing you the straight and narrow way to eternity if you let Him in! We cannot depend on our strength which will fail us, only in God can we find the strength to carry us through the journey. God will increase our faith so we can stay bold and strong in Him when we learn to remove fear. Fear is of the enemy which makes us terrified, but faith is of God and He will give us the power to endure and have a sound mind. The Bible tells us:

> *"For God did not give you a spirit of fear, But of power and of a sound mind."*
>
> --2 Timothy 1:7 *KJV*

Immediately, I said, "Father, I completely yield to Your will and Your ways as You lead and guide me. Thank You for giving me the power of a sound mind to concentrate and stay focused on this writing journey. God, I know You will help me conquer fear with faith through Your supernatural strength and power. My life belongs to You and I am safe and secure in Your Mighty and powerful hands. I know God will never give you a vision without giving you the maximum provision to tunnel your way through the process. It is God who placed different **gifts** in your life to propel you into your future and destiny for His glory. **There might be roadblocks and bumps on the way, but God is always in control, and He will steer us in the right direction and from the enemy.** We can always depend on God to give us the strength to carry us through to the expected end. He is our Jehovah Nissi, therefore, when we get tired or lonely on the journey, then He will place His complete banner of LOVE over us.

Also, while you are on your assignment, place the written Word of God upon the table of your heart, meditate on it day and night. So, I said today, God my Father, as I read Psalm 27, I am asking you to engraft every word in my heart as I meditate on You for full coverage protection. This is a Psalm of David, to gain strength, courage, assurance, and confidence in God our Father. Just like David, I

Chapter 18: Jesus' Voice! My Strength, Power, and My Guide

depend on God for complete strength, and I will not be afraid of any dart fire from the adversary. I will stand bold in the authority given to me by my Heavenly Father to crush the head of the enemy. I declare in the Mighty name of Jesus that on this writing assignment, I will stay confident, encouraged, and determined that You are my light and my salvation. I will put my trust in You to be positive and empowered that You will take me up and carry me through every unpaved road because You are my Shepherd, and I shall not want. You! Oh Lord, have a good and perfect plan for my life and I am standing on Your promises.

God is the most excellent Master Planner of the Universe, and we are a part of His plan. Therefore, He knows our desires and will give us the desire of our hearts in due season. Wait on the Lord; trust Him that He is the only one who knows all your thoughts, spoken and unspoken! He knows all about the gifts and talents He placed in our lives, and He wants us to use and share them only for His glory. Jesus wants us to build that relationship with Him and make Him the priority leader to make the right decisions for us. By doing so, He allows us to be of good service to others as we tell them of His goodness and His grace in our lives. Let Jesus lead the way to your purpose and your goal, he desires to prosper you, make you happy, and give you perfect peace! He will send destiny angels and helpers from the four corners of the earth to help you through your process to accomplish His purpose and plan in your life.

You will be amazed at the impossibilities that become possible when you disentangle yourself from the distraction of the world and listen to the voice of the Lord. God is ever so powerful, loving, and forgiving and that's why it is so important to get into a close relationship with the Lord. He wants us to depend on Him in every area of our lives. Our Father has so many good thoughts and plans for us and our family to succeed in every area that is pleasing to Him. He wants us to depend on Him, put our trust in Him and exercise FAITH so that He can remove the mountains of problems that are weighing us down.

We are serving a loving and generous God who wants to see us elevate and prosper from the good gifts around us and from the Heavenly blessings that He bestowed upon us. He has a matchless amount of favor and blessings for us to enjoy even as we wait for His royal return. He wants us to listen to His voice, obey His words, and apply it to our hearts every day. God is pouring out a multitude of blessings on His children all around the world. **One of the most amazing things is that these blessings will follow us, our children, and our grandchildren. God told Abraham that He would bless him and make him a great nation (***see* **Genesis 12).** His love for us is unfailing and selfless! Most of all His LOVE gives us the strength to face all the obstacles that we are facing in this cruel world. God's love never fails, and it is from everlasting to everlasting! Isn't He amazing to have so much love so He can spread it to all his children so generously? And that's one of the reasons why we need to trust Him with all our hearts and cling to his unchanging hands.

We cannot track, target, trace, or know His plan for our lives, but we can believe in Him as we give an ear to His voice and yield to His direction. Knowing that His plan is to see all His children prosper and excel at different levels is comforting. All things are possible when we tune in to the infinite mercies of God our Father. Sometimes, we cannot see it, because it is so big; but trust God and believe Him for the impossibility of great and mighty results coming our way. He is bigger than we can ever think or imagine! The Bible tells us about the greatness of God's power, wisdom, and His infinite understanding. The Mighty God who numbered the stars and knows them by name is our Jehovah Jireh. David says, *"He telleth the number of the stars; he calleth them all by their names. Great is our Lord, and of great power: his understanding is infinite"* (Psalm 147:4-5 *KJV*). How great thou art, Mighty God of Heaven and Earth and under the Earth. God, You are MIGHTY, STRONG, and POWERFUL!

Paul tells us that the Word of God is sharper than a two-edged sword (*see* Hebrews 4:12-13). God knew the intent of my heart, and in my mind, I was thinking of all kinds of reasons and excuses that could hinder me from fulfilling this assignment. However, God knows us

Chapter 18: Jesus' Voice! My Strength, Power, and My Guide

more than how we know ourselves. Paul tells us about the God we serve; He knows the biological framework of our body, Spirit, soul, joint, and marrow. We can look at each other and see just an image in the physical, but God sees through us and in us. No matter how many layers of clothes we put on, God still sees through us, and He knows our strengths and weaknesses. **The sharp two-edged sword of God is piercing through every movement we make. That's exactly how Jesus appeared to me in the dream; He was looking through every fiber of my being. There is nothing to hide when our Savior's flaming eyes of fire penetrate your mind, body, and soul.** I sensed it, and I felt it as His soul-searching eyes shone through us. Our body is like a magnifying see-through mirror open to the eyes of Jesus day and night.

The scripture tells us that,

> *"Daniel had a glorious vision." In which Daniel says, "Then I lifted mine eyes, and looked, and behold a certain man clothed in linen, whose lions were girded with fine gold of Uphaz: His body also was like beryl, and his face as the appearance of lightning, and his eyes as lamps of fire, and his arms and his feet like in color of polished brass, and the voice of his words like the voice of a multitude. And I Daniel alone saw the vision: for the men that were with me saw not the vision; but a great quaking fell upon them, so that they fled to hide themselves"* (Daniel 10:5-7).

We just cannot hide from God! That's why we should serve Him and fear Him because He is the only True and Living God with eyes as lamps of fire everywhere! We can never fathom who this great and Mighty God is! But we can acknowledge him as THE LIGHT OF THE WORLD! Therefore, we are naked images before Him at all times! It doesn't matter where you are; the Omnipresent God is always there, seeing, observing, and taking note of all our actions, good and bad. ***Yet, when He forgives, He cleans our slate and remembers our sins no more (see* Hebrews 8:12)**. We cannot live without Him, and we cannot dodge Him because He is the ruler of Heaven and Earth. We should love and appreciate such a God like this because He knows how to set your mind and heart at rest if you listen to His voice and cast your cares on Him. God is the one with all POWER and STRENGTH to guide us on our journey and to take us to our eternal end.

However, we have to be keen listeners to the voice of God and stay focused as we prepare to walk into our destiny. At once, I thought about Moses, the lawgiver of Israel who happened to be in my dream of Heaven. Moses was busy taking care of the flock at Horeb, the mountain of God when he noticed the burning bush. He became alert and curious, so he went over to get closer to see as he was listening. Suddenly, he heard the voice of God coming from the burning bush with different commands and assignments (*see* Exodus 3). From within a burning bush, God called Moses. God told Moses to remove his shoes because it was holy ground. Then God gave him the **assignment to face Pharaoh, the wicked ruler, and tell him, "...I AM hath sent me unto you"** (v14). Moses was afraid to face Pharaoh because he was depending on his strength and was thinking about his inability just like we do so many times. However, the Word of God reminds us not to fear because we know who is with us and watches over us. God said, be not dismayed because He will strengthen us and hold us up with His right hand (*see* Isaiah 41:10).

Moses questioned God about the assignment that seemed unattainable at the time, but God always has an answer to all our questions. (*see* Exodus 4:10-13). However, **God assured Moses as to who made man's mouth, reminding him that He would be with thy mouth and teach thee what thou shalt say!** Moses was fearful because he had a stuttering problem, but God looked beyond the speech impediment. God wants us to follow His command and His instruction, not the flaws that will distract us. So many times, we fall into that same fear, worrying about our inability and what people will say to make us look and think less of ourselves.

God cares for us, and He decides to use different people to assist us in completing the assignment that He placed before us. God had an agenda set out for Moses with destiny helpers, some were right

Chapter 18: Jesus' Voice! My Strength, Power, and My Guide

within his family, so too He got helpers to assist us with our assignment. We cannot excel with our strength or power; we need Jesus every step of the way to hold us up. God preordained different plans and assignments for us to fulfill and He will open doors for you that you never thought would be possible or thought to exist. However, He predestined it from the beginning of time for you to prosper and fulfill His plan for your life. He also promised that He will give His angels charge over you to assist and protect you to the finish line.

> *God does not look at your disability; He accepts your availability.*

Therefore, push your ability to depend on God's capability; He will make changes to meet you at your weakest moment. He has the strength and power to interrupt and change the shape and look of the mountain to scatter it and turn it into a plain flat land. The scripture tells us in Habakkuk 3:6, *"He stood, and measured the earth: he beheld, and drove asunder for the nation; and the everlasting mountains were scattered, the perpetual hills did bow: his ways are everlasting."*

God's power is from everlasting to everlasting and it supersedes the power of all man put together. He is God alone all by Himself. He is the "I AM God. "He is ready and willing to give us the strength to help us with his assignment. God just wants us to be willing and ready. **God is looking at the heart so that even when you feel fearful, He can use you because His strength is made perfect in our fear and weakness. Maybe, our disability and our dependency can be used so others can see God's capability in us.** We all experience some fears of the unknown at times. However, we must remember **that fear is the devil's tool to derail us, but faith is the evidence of the unseen power of God to see and do the impossible!**

I had fears in different areas of my life too, wondering if I was going to remember to say the correct thing or pronounce certain words correctly. Maybe, you asked yourself the same question or if people would understand our different accents. Perhaps, you have the same feelings or some other fears but remember God is bigger than ALL our fears put together. I thank God over the years I have learned to put complete trust in God and not in what man says or does because God sees the heart. God loves us so much and He wants us to accomplish goodness and not evil. **Learning to please God is much more comforting than trying to please man! It is better to displease man and please the great God who created all men!**

In the end, God is the only true Judge and He has the final say! So, if you are reading this book right now, do not be afraid of what man can do or say to distract you from fulfilling your purpose in life. **The same God that gives me strength to overcome fear will do the same for you, too! He is the same God who worked miracles in the lives of all the biblical warriors over two thousand years ago. God desires the sincerity of our hearts and the availability of our time to serve Him wholeheartedly.** I think about all the biblical warriors and their testimonies; they had different impediments and challenges in their lives too. However, God chose to use them to change the world and today we are encouraged by their testimonies to hold on to the hands of God.

The Word of God reminds us that we must fight against the odds and be brave. According to Joshua 1:9, the Bible repeats, *"Be strong and courageous."* God knows that we will face some perilous times and that fear will creep upon us which is coming from the adversary. So, He wants us to gain strength and power from His words of comfort. Today my friends, if you are feeling uncertain or fearful, remember God is covering you and He is protecting you from the schemes of the devil. We are more than conquerors in Jesus Christ, our Lord! Jesus is always beside us, and He will never leave us. His presence wipes away the spirit of fear and replaces it with POWER and FAITH in Christ our Lord!

God will protect and guide you as you journey on the road to complete His task and His assignment. God did the impossible for Moses, Joshua, Noah, Abraham, Elijah, Job, and many others, and so too will He do for us. **We are not alone; Jesus will stay with us to the end. Don't let negativity stain your heart and stop you from fulfilling your purpose. Our Father in Heaven will not reject you nor will He criticize you; instead, He will encourage you to go forward in fulfilling his purpose in your life.** Yes, you will face disappointments and difficulties during the process, but God will give you the strength and courage to carry on.

The Bible tells us also in *Deuteronomy 31:6, "Be strong and courageous. Do not be afraid or terrified because of them, for the Lord your God goes with you; he will never leave you nor forsake you."* Stand on the promises of God and listen to His voice. Feed on His word and place it upon the table of your heart. Keep fighting off fear of the unknown; do not let fear dominate your future or prevent you from walking into your purpose and destiny. **We must fight! But fight not alone! Again, we are encouraged to fight with the full armor of God!** We live in a world polluted with crime, violence, hatred, and savagery around us! Cruelty and assault are coming from all angles and the four corners of the earth! It is a time when people are forgetting that they should not be fighting and killing each other. Instead, we should be fighting off the attacks from the adversary who is filling our heads with so many lies of deceit and distaste.

Saints of God, we must lean on the STRENGTH of Jesus Christ to help us through this battlefield, a battlefield that will never cease to stop fighting until the Lord returns. However, we have JESUS as our CHIEF CORNERSTONE. **He is the warrior of all warriors and the Conquering Lion of the Tribe of Judah. We declare war against the enemy that we are Children of the King, and the devil will not deprive us of our kingly inheritance because of all his lies and his deceits.** We will fight fully armed with the Word of God! We are fighting against the forces of darkness, and we are on the winning side with Jesus as our Champion Warrior.

Soon after, I said yes to my Heavenly Father! I seek the Holy Spirit every step of the way for spiritual clarity and His divine wisdom and revelation to guide me through this process. During that time, I thought I was going through testing and chaos in my life. Little did I know that there would be many more difficulties to face as I took on this journey. They were coming like wildfire, storms, and tornadoes coming my way before the completion of this book. Even through the fire, He was there making sure that I didn't get any burns. I found assurance and comfort that Jesus would not leave me as I remember how He stayed beside me during the dream, which brought me peace and comfort.

I had no choice but to humble myself in several fasts and prayers before and during the writing phase, in total surrender. I continued to depend on God for wisdom in every area of my life. I was going through a complete spiritual detoxing of body, Spirit, and soul. There comes that season in our life when we must deny ourselves the physical food to receive the spiritual food because we desire more of God, a time of self-searching and sacrifice in humility before the merciful and gracious God for clarity and understanding!

There have been times when my valley seemed as if there was no bottom and my wilderness felt like it could not get any darker or any more isolated. But I continue to feel the presence of God so close, giving me the confidence to hold on. There were times when I felt like a loner, even though I knew I was never alone! I didn't wonder if God was near because I could feel His presence drawing me closer and closer into His arms of sweet deliverance. I am sure you have been there, experiencing that intimate moment with our Lord and Savior! **My friend, the God that we serve, never leaves us alone. He is always there, not as a standby, or an observer, or in reserve while we suffer. He is in the boat in the middle of the storm with us, saving us from the raging wind and waves.**

God loves us so much that He will never leave us to perish! He is always there, right by your side! He is always present. Even when we are in the valley of isolation, pain, and death, God is closer than even our next breath. His love for us will never cease, no matter what we are going through. We are sheltered, safe, and protected in the arms of our Savior as He cradles us in his big, loving, and welcoming

Chapter 18: Jesus' Voice! My Strength, Power, and My Guide

embrace. He is our Protector! We must exercise faith and have confidence in God that He is our refuge and strength and He will guide us to the end. According to Psalm 46:1-3, *"God is our refuge and strength, a very present help in trouble. Therefore, will not we fear, though the earth be removed and though the mountains be carried into the midst of the sea; Though the waters thereof roar and be troubled, though the mountains shake with the swelling thereof."* Because God is our refuge and our strength, we will stand on His promises that we are covered under His mighty wings sheltered and protected in His loving arms.

Although there were so many hindrances and setbacks, it was nothing compared to the deliverance and breakthrough blessings from above. God has been so merciful and faithful throughout the journey of this assignment, I have to continue to give Him all the praise. He is worthy of praise! He gave me the faith, strength, and courage to hold on to his unchanging hands as He led and guided me.

I always love to meditate on the power and glory of God's presence. However, since the dream, my desire has heightened to be in a closer and more intimate relationship with my Lord. Looking back and remembering the adrenaline rush with sweet euphoric sensation in His presence is unexplainable. It is such a wonderful feeling to relive the peace, assurance, joy, and contentment that I found in His presence, it is unspeakable happiness! Jesus has kept me covered and protected throughout my life, but in the dream, it felt so secret, comfortable, and safe. I have no desire to leave; I just want to be there in His presence! To hear His sweet voice over and over talking to me. Please don't get me wrong! I know we are always in the presence of the Lord. But being in the Heavenly presence with Him and having Him as my guide throughout the dream is unimaginable.

I just cannot find words to explain Jesus' power and His glory! There is that supernatural change in the atmosphere, which makes everything look and feel so much better! It was so amazing! I do not want to forget His powerful authoritative voice that even the intruder fled! It's a WOW! Beyond words and expressions that you cannot understand or comprehend because you are in the presence of the

King! Let Jesus be your strength and guide as you travel on life's journey. He is the good Shepherd that gives His life for his sheep. Today, let us listen and obey the voice that knows us and wants to save us. Jesus is the Door of the sheep (*see* John 10).

Prayer--Thanking God for Being My Strength, Power, And My Guide!

Gracious and loving Father, Creator of Heaven and Earth. I come to You in the name of Jesus, to give You glory, honor, and praise. Father, according to Psalm 46:1-3, I want to thank You that You *"are our refuge and strength, a very present help in trouble. Therefore, will not we fear, though the earth be removed, and though the mountains be carried into the midst of the sea; Though the water thereof roar and be troubled, though the mountains shake with the swelling thereof."* We acknowledge that You are the God of the mountain and the sea and we have confidence that You are our refuge, strength, and guide!

Dearest Father, Your Word reminds us that we should, "Fear thou not, for I am with thee: be not dismayed; for I am thy God: I will strengthen thee; for I am thy God: I will strengthen thee: yea, I will help thee: yea, I will uphold thee with the right hand of my righteousness" (Isaiah 41:10 KJV). Father, today I will join in with Moses to sing to You, *"Lord is my strength and song, and he is become my salvation: he is my God, and I will prepare him for an inhabitation; my father's God and I will exalt him. The Lord is a man of war: the Lord is his name" (Exodus 15:2-3 KJV).* Father, we thank You for redeeming us and calling us out by our names. Abba Father, You promised that You would be with us through the water, the fire, and through the rivers so we would not be destroyed. You, Oh Lord, gave Egypt for our ransom, and we thank Thee (*see* Isaiah 43:1-3). Your voice makes all the difference in my life.

Dearest Father, we thank You that we find complete safety and protection in You that when we are at our weakest, You are at Your strongest. Thank You for Your multitude of mercies and Your loving kindness. We give You thanks in Jesus's name! Amen!

Chapter 19: Every Gift from God Has a Significant Meaning

Use Your Gift to Glorify God

"As every man hath received the gifts, even so minister the same one to another, as good stewards of the manifold grace of God. If any man speak, let him speak as the oracles of God; if any man minister, let him do it as of the ability which God giveth: that God in all things may be glorified through Jesus Christ, to whom be praise and dominion for ever and ever. Amen. "

– 1 Peter 4:10-11 KJV

(Also see 1 Peter Chapter 4 for scriptural references)

We are living in a chaotic world of turmoil, and all kinds of rebellion and confusion are everywhere; there is crime and rumors of wars throughout the world. The Apostle Peter is encouraging us to live according to the commands and will of Jesus Christ because the end is drawing near. Even though Peter spoke these words over two thousand years ago, we can see that we are encountering some perilous times throughout the world and in all nations. Although we are experiencing hardship, trials, and tribulations everywhere, our suffering is not in vain because everything in this world is temporary. God promises us a glorious end to spend eternity with Him in Heaven if we trust and obey him in all our ways. It is during times like these that we can remind ourselves that Jesus suffered for us when He took our sins to the cross, but arose on the third day to set us free to live with Him forever. Even though we are Christians, we know that we will experience suffering sometimes, but God can see us through.

Peter continued to encourage us to be sober, watch, pray, love, and

Chapter 19: Every Gift from God Has a Significant Meaning

be obedient to God our Father and turn from our wicked ways. As Christians, we know that we are in "Partnership in Christ's suffering." Furthermore, He says in v15, "Yet if any man suffers as a Christian, let him not be ashamed; but let him glorify God on his behalf." This is so encouraging because Peter is telling us to be alert and focused as we watch, pray, and live a new life in Christ. We should aim to be Christlike, so the world can see Christ in us. Now, that old things are dead and have passed away and now we are living in the new spirit of Christ. He also stated, "Above all things have fervent charity among yourselves: for charity shall cover the multitude of sins. Used hospitality one to another without grudging" (1 Peter 4:8-9).

For this chapter, I would like to focus on our assignments and our gifts from God and how He would like us to use these wonderful gifts to encourage one another. According to the above scripture in verses 10-11, God wants us to be good and faithful stewards when we are operating in these gifts. It is only through God's grace that we receive these wonderful gifts which He gave us according to our ability. God wants us to be satisfied with our gifts, we should not compare, hide, or bury our gifts. Instead, we should use these gifts with the right mindset because they are God's possessions which He lends to us to use to edify others and to glorify Him through Jesus Christ. We all have different kinds of gifts, some through speaking and some through ministering but they all work together in the body of Christ through our faith in action. God wants us to present our bodies as living sacrifices; by doing so we can show love and respect to the church as we fellowship one with another (**see** Romans 12, 1 Corinthians 12).

The Bible also tells us in James 1:17-18, *"Every good gift and every perfect gift is from above, and cometh down from the Father of lights, with whom there is no variableness, neither shadow of turning. Of his own will begat he us with the word of truth, that we should be a kind of first fruits of his creatures."* These are promises of God that are laid out for His children. **We are considered the First Fruits of His creatures! Glory to God! I implore you to appreciate the gift that God planted in your**

life. His gifts and plans for us are perfect and will last forever. Do not underrate, worry, or compare your gift with others. God called out your name and marked your gift with a unique print even before you were conceived in your mother's womb. We are all special in the sight of God and He wants everything good for us, so He grants us gifts out of His love and grace for us.

Trust God first and believe in Him always. Thank God for your gift; use it to honor God! Do not manipulate or misuse the gift or gifts God placed into your life, nor be a man-pleaser with your gift. A reminder from the Bible, *"For do I now persuade men, or God? or do I seek to please men? for if I yet please men, I should not be the servant of Christ"* (Galatians 1:10). We can only be servants of truth by using the gifts that God gave us for His glory. In doing so, we would be pleasing God and not man. Are we pleasing God with our gifts?

In life, getting an education is vital so we can excel and have a stable life in society, enabling us to fulfill our basic human needs and take care of our family independently. However, the words of God tell us that a man's gift will make room for him. Therefore, we all have some form of gifts that the Holy Spirit will inspire in us to use for the glory of God. Ask the Holy Spirit to stir up the gifts in you which could also be a career gift that you can use to gain souls for the Kingdom. Don't let your gift and calling stay dormant. Ask the Lord to show you so you can share them with the universe.

We serve an awesome and Mighty God who chooses to give us different assignments and gifts that He placed into our lives. He is the one who decides what or who He wants to use to fulfill His assignment and the gifts He places in our lives. For instance, in the story of Balaam when God allows the donkey to speak to his master who responds in a negative and mean way to the faithful donkey, the master wasn't aware that the donkey was protecting him from danger. Who would think the donkey would talk to his master and the master respond without seeing the whole picture, until the angel responded? At the time, the master did not understand why the donkey was acting strange (*see* Numbers 22:21-35). So, too, God can

Chapter 19: Every Gift from God Has a Significant Meaning

use different people, animals, or things to help us along the way. **God never makes a mistake, even when things seem puzzling to us; never underestimate the power or purpose of God. We often see things in the natural. However, we serve a God that is supernatural.** We just need to be attentive and sensitive to His commanding voice. He also does the impossible, and He sees the invisible.

God can and will use anything to show His power to mankind which could be a crucial time for you to operate in your assignment or your gift. Jesus gave me a special bronze unicorn in my Heavenly Dream, and I will never forget the miraculous encounter with that beautiful creature. Neither can I forget the sweet authoritative voice coming from Jesus as He gives it to me. In all my life, I never thought I would dream of seeing a unicorn, but I am so happy I did because telling others about the miraculous scene that took place, it blesses them in **many different ways. This is another way to share God's Word about Jesus to increase the Kingdom of Heaven.** I will always hold this experience dear to my heart. Should we question God about our gifts? No! God has the final say in our mundane life, all He wants us to do is to trust and believe in Him.

However, we must be spiritually alert to discern what the Holy Spirit shows us. As Christians, there are times when we would question God about everything instead of waiting patiently for His truth to come alive. Yes! At times, we would wonder and ponder over things that we are so unsure about; but we need to trust and exercise faith in the Omniscient God. We need to have confidence in God and believe that He can do the impossible and use the unusable. We should remember that we are serving the all-knowing God whom we can trust in every area of our lives!

For instance, Jesus is right there; even the donkey is paying attention. **If the donkey is listening to God and obeying Him, then what about us? We are looking for the answers and breakthroughs, sometimes in the wrong place.** Today, I encourage you to look to Jesus. He has all the answers to our questions and also the world's questions. There was a time in my life when I had so many questions for God. It was so overwhelming and frustrating! God said to me, "Daughter, I have more answers than you have questions! I have ALL the questions and answers to the world!" (*see* Job 38-39) God asked Job over seventy rhetorical questions that Job could not answer, and neither do we have the answers. Now, I learned to stop worrying, because I will never get all the answers to my questions and for sure I don't need to know. I have learned to be satisfied with whatever God wants His answer to be for my life. Let His will be done and not my will. He is the one with the gifts and plans for our life. His plan is always good, and it is perfect!

Whom can Jesus use to fulfill His plans? He is the creator of everyone. His words declared that He allowed His spirit to fall on all flesh. He made us in His likeness and image. Therefore, if He chooses to assign you to a task, it doesn't matter if you are rich or poor, young, or old, black, or white, unusable, disfigured or disabled. He can use you for His service and for His glory. He decided to use you, even before you were born, even though we sometimes feel as if we are too full of sin and shame. Oh No! We all have sinned! For instance, who would think Rahab would want to protect the spies? Again, as Christians, we tend to be judgmental, not only toward others but also to ourselves. Let God be the judge of everyone (*see* Joshua. 2:1-16). **The God we serve is Omnipresent and Omniscient; He sees us and He knows all our flaws. Will you walk away from Satan's camp of negativity and step into God's camp of positivity? Give God total control over your life because He is always beside you!**

Even though Jesus was still in midair looking down at the world, I could feel that He was closer than my next breath. I could see and feel His presence, such fullness of joy! According to Isaiah 66:1, *"Thus saith the Lord, the heaven is my throne, and the earth is my footstool: where is the house that he would build unto me? And where is the place of my rest."* Jesus is building a place of rest for His children, but while we are here on Earth, He wants us to use our gifts to build His kingdom. Are we ready to make the sacrifice to leave the world and the things of this world so we can follow Jesus even through the suffering? Are you ready to stop worrying about your age, step out in faith, and use your

Chapter 19: Every Gift from God Has a Significant Meaning

gift to build the kingdom of Heaven?

For example, the Bible tells us God spoke to Moses through the burning bush (*see* Exodus 3). Moses was eighty years old, busy attending to the flock when God called him. God wants our full and undivided attention so we can focus on the plan that He has set out for us. God has a set goal for all His children to be used by Him for His glory and His purpose. It could be a season in your life when you least expect that call, then you will hear that voice or see that sign! You will see it in the physical, in the spiritual, or both!

Do not ignore His call upon your life! God will pull you out from anywhere He chooses to call you from! You could be up on the mountain or down in the valley. He will come and pick you out! You see, God has a plan and a purpose for all His children and His plan is the greatest! It is a good plan because He said so; all we need to do is believe it and let God direct us as we listen to His voice and his calling! It is such a joy to know that God has a plan for every one of His children, and He wants us to excel and advance in the plan of our life. So amazing! (*see* Jeremiah 29:10-13).

Even though God has plans for us, we sometimes seek to trust man's plan *vs.* God's plan and that's wrong. We should seek Him to lead and guide us in every area of our lives. Man's plan over your life is temporary and it may harm you, but God plans to prosper you and to take you to eternity with Him. We must exercise our confidence, faith, and trust in God; do not waver or get derailed by the tricks of the enemy.

I was uncertain and hesitant to start this assignment, but then I realized it was fear of the unknown that wanted to block my faith in God. So, I had to seek God's direction and guidance through fasting and prayer. Even though these are things that we sometimes do not want to do because of the weakness of the flesh, it is essential to our spiritual growth and maturity. Making the sacrifice to fast and pray helps us to stay focused on the assignment that God planned for us and our spiritual stability on the journey. Jesus made the ultimate sacrifice for us when He died for our sins. He was also in the wilderness fasting for forty days and forty nights, and He was tempted by the devil during and after His fast. However, He kept on rebuking the devil (*see* James 4:7).

Please, do not let the enemy hinder you from setting aside time to spend secret time with your Savior. We know that the flesh and the spirit are fighting every day, but we must kill the flesh and die daily to the flesh's desire so we can walk in the spirit. Daily, we try to eat and enjoy our nutritious meals for physical growth and development. We also need our spiritual food for spiritual growth so we can fight against the adversary. Therefore, we must fast, pray, and feed on the word of God, which will help us to put on the full Armor of God as we walk with Him daily.

He didn't have to do so, but He was here on Earth to do His Father's will and fulfill the assignment that was set before Him. When He came down to Earth in human form, He too was faced with all kinds of challenges and temptations. Jesus experienced the hardest and most cruel time of His life. He faced these battles alone, and most of all, He was blameless of all the sins and shame that He suffered for us. Jesus stayed focused and continued to do His Father's will and complete His assignment when He went to the cross for our sins. We must keep our eyes centered on the finish line that Jesus is going to take us to the expected end, even through trials and tribulations. We must exercise faith and endurance through this process, remembering that we cannot please God without faith! Are we following in the footsteps of our Savior?

I have confidence in the promises of God that if He said it, then He will do it. It does not matter how young or how old we are; God had a plan for Moses's life when he was called at the age of eighty and God encouraged him for the journey (*see* Exodus 7:7). God got a plan for you too to tap into; start praying for the revelation of his gift to birth in you and through you!

While we are waiting, God continues to fulfill His plan and promises to us through gifts, which are without repentance. We must be submissive to the Spirit of God as we walk in humility to fulfill His plan through the different gifts He placed into our lives! The Bible tells us that "The gifts and calling of God are without repentance" (Romans 11:29). God will not take His gift away from us; He planted gifts in us so we can excel and shine through to the world so they can see Jesus' light in us.

Even though we sometimes do not deserve such favor, He extends His compassion toward us because of His grace and mercies. Psalm 116:5 says, "Gracious is the LORD, and righteous; yea, our God is merciful." Our God never runs out of compassion; His love and compassion for us fail not! Our Heavenly Father, the giver of all good gifts around us, continues to give us precious gifts from Heaven above! You are never too young nor too old to be used by God. Today is the day and the hour to tap into your destiny with angels on assignment knocking at your door of availability, opportunity, and purpose. Will you tap into God's special gift for you today?

Prayer of Thanks for Gifts and Talents!

Our dear Heavenly Father, holy and righteous be thy name in Heaven, on Earth, and underneath the Earth. Today, we praise You in the beauty of holiness, peace, and joy. We magnify Your holy name because You, Oh Lord, are worthy to be praised. Father, we want to first thank You for your special Gift of Your Son Jesus Christ. Jesus, we want to thank You for coming down to us as servants to die for our sins upon the cross of Calvary. Through the shedding of Your blood, there is remission of sins. Thank You, Jesus, for taking my sins to the old rugged cross. Thank You for the salvation plan that You brought down to man, setting us free from the plan of the enemy. Thank You also for the good thoughts and plans that You have for our future (*see* Jeremiah 29:11).

Thank You, Father, for allowing Your spirit to fall upon all flesh. Thank You for the gifts and calling that You placed upon Your children. We will use these gifts only for Your kingdom. Abba Father, I want to give You thanks for all the beautiful gifts that You bestowed on us throughout our lives. We do not have enough words to show You how much we appreciate You for the gifts and talents that You allowed us. Father, I acknowledge that we should use these gifts to glory You and to edify those around us. Please, help us to be trustworthy and honest when using Your gift. Remove from us the spirit of Ananias and Sapphira so we will not rob or lie to the Holy Spirit. Take away the spirit of pride when using or acting in the demonstration of our gifts. Help us to be grateful for Your love and Your kindness as You generously divided Your gifts among us. Father, I am praying that we will be happy and content with the gifts that You give unto us according to Your plan (*see* Romans 12:6). Let us commit thy works unto You, oh Lord, so that thy thoughts will be established in us.

Prayer of Thanks for Gifts and Talents!

Father, thank You for giving us the faith and confidence that You are going to change the impossible to possible because we believe in You. Father, we believe through increased faith in You that everything that the enemy devours from us will come back triple and quadruple fold in the Mighty Name of Jesus. Father, we thank You also for the restoration of gifts and talents that we lost along the way. We are taking back everything stolen or hiding gifts from us and our parents by force in the Mighty Name of Jesus.

Thank You, God, for all the wonderful gifts around us which are sent from Heaven above. Please, let us use these to honor and glory You and for the edification of those around us. Father, we give thee thanks in Jesus' Name. Amen!

Part 4: Inspiration of Biblical Heroes in the Dreams

Chapter 20: Faith Exercised by Jesus and Biblical Heroes

Faith is Defined and Illustrated Through the Lives of Old Testament Heroes

(*see* Hebrews Chapters 11&12)

The above scripture is telling us of the unfailing faith that was exercised by these biblical characters in the Old Testament which we are now reading and living in the New Testament. The Word of God is active and will remain alive and active forever because it is the breath of God! As we read through Hebrews Chapters 11 and 12, we see how we are encouraged to keep the faith just like Jesus and all these biblical heroes. They look unto Jesus as their role model because they know that He is the author and finisher of their faith. They know that Jesus is sitting down at the right hand of God intervening for them (Hebrew 12). Even though their lives were tested and tried in many different ways and some even stumbled and fell along the way, they remained faithful to God to the end. They got back up and continued the Christian journey as they endured and stayed faithful to the assignment that God allotted to them. Today, we too can be encouraged as we learn some important lessons from their lives and testimonies and how they stuck with God as their leader and guide.

The Bible tells us of the Heavenly inheritance that is laid up in Heaven for those who serve the Lord wholeheartedly. I was so happy and overjoyed to see all these biblical heroes at Heaven's Golden Gate. These patriots were all looking so young, handsome, happy, and full of joy! They were all wearing the expression of sheer peace, calm, and tranquility that seemed indescribable. They were beautifully dressed in robes of unique designs more charming than any royal attire on Earth! In addition, their robes had several different shades of colors far beyond our naked eyes. They were standing beside the King; The ruler of Heaven and Earth; His Majesty! King Jesus! The King of Glory! The Seed of Jesse, The Balm in Gilead, The Bright and Morning Star, The Fairest of Ten Thousand to our Souls, The Lily of the Valley! JESUS our Lord, our great Messiah! My friend, keep on calling those wonderful names of Jesus. It will bring comfort and joy to your heart. Hallelujah!

Furthermore, they were looking at me with eyes that spoke of a magnitude of Heavenly contentment. It felt like a family reunion with Jesus and His welcoming party, ready to say, "Come in, my child, and partake of all the Heavenly inheritance here waiting for you. "This scene before my eyes was far beyond human comprehension! So much more than any reunion here on Earth. Words are just inadequate to comprehend or explain the volume of holiness and beauty surrounding the magnificent scenery before my eyes.

Even though some of them didn't get to go to the Promised Land during and after their assignment on Earth, God had something greater planned for them, which is everlasting life, and living with him in the kingdom of Heaven is one of His promises to us. We have access to the kingdom of God, our Father (*see* Psalm 145:10-13).

These biblical warriors that were at the Golden Gates of Heaven standing beside King Jesus were at one time here on Earth where they suffered and experienced many perilous times in their lives. However, they stayed focused and faithful to God, even in aches, pains, tests, and trials; they exercised faith as they were going through the process, somewhat like what we are experiencing today; but the same faithful God who brought them through the flood and out of the fire is the same God that is still working in us today.

Seeing Father Abraham, Moses, Elijah, and David standing beside Jesus was a profound and divine revelation that I cannot forget. I don't know what role they will be playing when Jesus returns; however, seeing and recognizing them was enough for me to gasp with excitement, joy, and unexplainable happiness to be in their presence. Can you imagine that those warriors may be at the Gates of Heaven to welcome us when Jesus returns? It is unimaginable and surreal! However, this gives us hope to stay strong in the battle of the Lord because He is the Mighty force against the adversary that we are facing every day. Jesus is the Mighty Warrior in the battle of Armageddon! The army of God will win, and I am encouraged to be on the Lord's side because He never loses a battle, and He never will. Daily we are encouraged by the different biblical heroes who exercised faith throughout their faith journey as they depended on the Lord to guide and protect them. We are soldiers of God's army, and we need to stay FOCUSED and be in tune with our relationship with Jesus the Warrior of all Warriors.

FAITHFUL BIBLICAL HEROES

Jesus will return and take us to the mansion that He has gone to prepare for us. We will see those Prophets that have gone before us. They were here on Earth over two thousand years ago, going through trials and tribulations, but they leaned on the Lord and persevered to the end. Now they are spending their eternity in the presence of the Lord because they held onto their faith, belief, and trust. They also feared the Lord and depended on Him for everything. For instance, Father Abraham endured some trying times while he was on his assignment, but he stayed faithful to the end. Because of his faithfulness, he was called righteous. We are the seed of Father Abraham; let us stay faithful to God our Father as we put our complete trust and faith in Him.

Moses had to face the wicked ruler Pharaoh several times during his assignment. He never gave up; even though he got frustrated at times, he held onto the true God! He brought the children of Israel out of bondage by the power of the Lord. He met with God several times, how amazing is that! Now, he is standing beside Jesus at Heaven's Gate looking young, fearless, and strong.

Prophet Elijah was brave and persistent when he had to face the most wicked King Ahab and his wicked wife Jezebel, but he kept on praying until the power of God came down in several miraculous ways. For example, he prayed for rain to stop, fire to come down, and he prayed for the dead boy to come back to life. Everything he prayed for then happened, and many lives were changed. People started to serve the true God. However, there was a time when Elijah feared for his life because Jezebel wanted to kill him, and he ran away into the wilderness, but the Lord took care of him and provided for him. He was caught up in a whirlwind of fire in Heaven to be with the Lord (*see* 2 Kings 2).

Another great hero of the Bible was King David, a great man of valor and war, who depended on the strength of God to lead him all the way. Even though he messed up several times, just like we do in our daily lives, he continued to seek God in prayer and fasting. God said he is a man "after my own heart" (*see* 1 Samuel 13:14).

We are encouraged today by the life of these biblical warriors who kept the faith and persevered through the most challenging time of their lives. **God kept them through all the tests and trials over two thousand years ago, and He is still delivering His chosen people just the same today.**

My friend, we have an anchor in Jesus Christ, which assures us that we are safe in the arms of God. I am encouraging you to anchor your life in the hands of Jesus Christ. As Christians, we should always be prepared to face different battles but do remember, that the battle is not ours to fight alone. We are living in a world that is full of so much deception and deceits from the adversary. Therefore, we must put on The Whole Armor of God (*see* Ephesians 6:10-11). We also know that the enemy, Satan, doesn't like the fact that he lost one soldier to Christ. So, he is busy night and day trying to steal our joy and destroy our relationship with the Lord (*see* John 10:10-11). The enemy comes to kill us, but Jesus comes to save us and give us eternal life. Hence, we must be ready and prepared for the unexpected guest and punch him out with the word of God, we are more than conquerors (*see* Romans 8:37-39).

Jesus laid down His precious life for us, giving us full access to the kingdom of Heaven. Our kingdom inheritance depends on our

Chapter 20: Faith Exercised by Jesus and Biblical Heroes

relationship with the Lord. We cannot receive from the Lord if He doesn't know who we are, so go ahead and build a stable and strong relationship with the One who died to save you. The enemy may come like a thief in the night, but we come in the NAME of JESUS to pull down Satan's kingdom. We will demolish Satan, his army, and his plans against us and our family–in the name of Jesus.

We will not lose focus or be distracted by the cunning tactics of the devil's tricks anymore. Remind yourself daily that when you cross off your name from Satan's book then God is entering your name in His Book of Eternal Life. Glory to God! We will not continue to be a slave to the adversary; we will be a radical servant of the Lord. You will have fights with the adversary daily, but we must stand strong as Christian soldiers in the army of the Lord. Jesus will never leave you and He also gives His angels charge over you in every area of your life. We were in darkness but now we are experiencing the marvelous Light of Jesus Christ. So, our spiritual eyes must be alert so we can see in the spiritual realms (*see* 1 Peter 2:9).

Friends, we must be persistent in prayer and fasting. We should feast on His words daily so we can be spiritually prepared to fight the good fight of faith. The avenger is not giving up; he is always throwing darts in our direction, trying so hard to kill us! And not you alone, but your entire family, friends, and everyone connected to you! It is spiritual warfare. Therefore, if you get knocked down, **GET UP!** Throw your punches at the devil with the Word of God. Remember, Jesus is our **NUMBER ONE CHAMPION WARRIOR** and He is fighting alongside you, with you, and for you. Don't forget, the devil wants to distract you so he can kill you! That is why we must stay spiritually awake, alert, and fully armed with the Gospel of Truth at all times.

We have to be prepared soldiers who are ready to fight in the spiritual realms against principalities, and powers, against the rulers of darkness in high places (*see* Ephesians 6:12). The devil is living in the four corners of the world, and he is working in every region and nation trying to pull us into a destruction pit. However, we are

Christian soldiers fighting together in the name of JESUS, and we will stand together and burn down his kingdom. Yes! The adversary, the devil, the liar, the deceiver, the slew foot, the thief, the conniving demon is trying to put us down day and night! We are called in these perilous times to keep our spiritual eyes open because we can easily be deceived by the tricks of the enemy. Saints of God, let us be humble in the sight of God and stay focused as we cast all our care upon Him. Now is the time to look unto God, seek Him daily, and let us stay steadfast as we WATCH and PRAY!

Peter told us:

> *"Be sober, be vigilant; because your adversary the devil, as a roaring lion, walketh about, seeking whom he may devour."*
>
> --1 Peter 5:8 *KJV*

We need to keep our eyes focused on Jesus so we will not sink into the sea of sin or the ocean of deception. The devil cannot come as any roaring lion when we are fully armed with the Word! We are coming with Jesus, who is THE CONQUERING LION OF THE TRIBE OF JUDAH, and He is coming back to judge the world (*see* Revelation 5:1-5). We must focus on the great light of this world, which is Jesus Christ our Lord, who is on the winning side. He never lost a fight, and He never will! He is the King of Glory who endured the cross for us, taking our guilt and shame. Jesus carried the weight of our sins upon His shoulders and also the physical weight of the cross which was over one hundred and sixty pounds.

Jesus could have called legions of angels to set Him free, but for you and me, He bore the pain on the cross to set us free (*see* Matthew 26:53). This great man, Jesus, endured the pain from the crown of thorns, the scourging whip (flagrum), the sword, and the nails that pierced through His hands and feet. Jesus went through physical, psychological, and emotional abuse because of His extraordinary love for us (*see* Mark 15). Jesus died on the cruel cross to set the captive free. Surely, He is Jesus, the King of Kings and Lord of Lords!

I am encouraging you to put Jesus first in your life. Remember, He is the author and finisher of our faith. The following Bible verse tells us who to look to:

> *"Looking unto Jesus, the author and finisher of our faith, who for the joy that was set before Him endured the cross, despising the shame, and has sat down at the right hand of the throne of God."*
>
> --Hebrews 12:2 *KJV*

Jesus is our Number One role model in every area of our lives, and we should look to Him for everything. The One who endured the burden of the cross (despised the shame) also sits at the right hand of God, interceding for you and me. Will you build a stable and strong relationship with Christ the King?

We need to feed on the Word of God so we can get spiritually stronger in this journey. We should crave that intimate moment and relationship with our Father so we can get closer to the knowledge and wisdom of God. He wants us to live right so we can pursue His righteousness and His holiness through the Holy Spirit. He loved us so much that He chose to make us in His likeness, His image, and His beauty. God, our Father, makes us to serve and worship Him in the spirit of holiness.

How can we do that?

We MUST be in obedience to the Holy Spirit. He will teach us the truth of God, how we should live and serve God in Spirit, and His Truth. When we got saved, we became a part of the family of God, and now we are joint heirs with King Jesus. We are the King's children; royalty is in us to live an upright life that is pleasing to King Jesus. We now gain access to the Throne of Grace. Can you imagine the magnitude of this Kingly relationship that we inherited through the shedding of the blood of Jesus Christ? We now have a stamp of approval on our Passport to Heaven! Hallelujah! Therefore, our Christian life should exemplify the characteristics of The King of Glory! **His fatherly love, thoughts, feelings, and plans for us never change. There are times when we disappoint and disobey our Creator and Life-Giver, but His love for us remains. He is the same**

yesterday, today, and forever. The Bible tells us, *"For I am the Lord, I change not; therefore, ye sons of Jacob are not consumed"* (Malachi 3:6 KJV).

This fast-paced world we live in is forever changing; it is becoming more like a microwave with different technologies that speed up our lives and make things easier. This has affected our way of life and our thinking in so many ways. However, as Christians, we need to focus on the Creator of the world and not the distractor. Try not to get distracted by the things of the world. We cannot hide away from the different trials and tribulations that we will face at times in our lives. Why? Because **we are living in a world where the flesh and the spirit are always fighting! But the spirit of God is in partnership with the Holy Spirit to teach us the truth as we continue to kill the flesh, which will deceive us daily.**

Therefore, we need to be wise and alert that these things can derail us from the promise and purpose of God in our lives. Just remember whom you should focus on, so you won't get sidetracked or bombarded by the devil and his evil agents. In every situation, the Lord is protecting us and shielding us from the attack of the enemy. God desires us to be happy and free from the bondage of sin, and neither does He want us to be consumed by the world's distractions. **God wants us to be fully sanctified and saturated by His Word of Truth, so we can have His joy and fulfillment in us (*see* John 17:13-19).**

God tells us that we must live and serve Him in Spirit and Truth, and exercise faith in Him. Jesus set the stage and example to live and serve His Father according to His Father's will. We are also encouraged to let the truth of God be our daily bread. He is the one who gives and sustains life; He chose to lend us His breath, and He can retrieve His breath anytime. Therefore, we should not abuse the gift of life. Instead, we should serve Him with our whole heart, mind, body, and soul. We should not partake in the things of this world or try to be like others in this sinful world. We cannot be a friend of the world and be a friend of God. We are chosen and set apart to be in the royal family of God. We are representatives and ambassadors of Jesus.

Therefore, we must try to live a holy and righteous life that lines up with the truth of God. We must remind ourselves that the old life we lived was to please the devil, but the new life that we now live is to please God through the ministry of reconciliation through Jesus Christ (*see* 2 Corinthians 5:17-21).

Jesus had several different experiences with family and friends when He was on Earth. However, He knew no sin, nor did He commit any sins! Instead, *"He hath made him to be sin for us, who knew no sin; that we might be made the righteousness of God in him"* (2 Corinthians 5:21). Glory be to God! There were times in His life when He was in the company of the Pharisees and tax collectors about different matters, but He refused to be a hypocrite. Instead, He would rebuke them and tell them what they needed to do to change their lives (*see* Luke 18:9-14). Jesus was also among people who were afflicted with different diseases, and mental and physiological problems. His heart ached with their situations, and He is still concerned with our griefs and sorrows. Because of His earthly experiences, He understands our pain and grief; most of all, He cares about our feelings. That's why He extends love and compassion for the different circumstances that we are facing daily. Jesus is touched by the feeling of our infirmities and our sorrows (*see* Hebrews 4: 14-16).

Even though Jesus was faced with many challenges in His life, He was sent to do His Father's business. His Father was pleased with Him and said, *"...This is my beloved Son, in whom I am well pleased"* (Matthew 3:17 *KJV*). Jesus' life and testimony are the main examples for us to follow in our Christian walk. A life without Christ is like receiving the most priceless gift from a friend and never saying, thank you! How do you think that friend feels? How often do we say this? "Thank you, God, for the gift of your Son." Or "Thank you, Jesus, for dying for my sins. "You can say that right now and acknowledge Jesus as your Lord and Savior. **Please take a moment and think about the great LOVE that Jesus has for the world. That same kind of love I saw on our Savior's face as He descended from the right side of Heaven's Golden gates. Jesus' face was filled with compassion, mercies, grace, and endless love.**

Do not let the adversary derail you from the promises of God. The enemy will always try to distract you from the truth of God; just remember that the Lord is always with you. There were times when Satan tempted Jesus, but He rebuked the devil with the Word of God as seen in Luke 4:8:

> *"And Jesus answered and said unto him, Get thee behind me, Satan: For it is written, thou shalt worship the Lord thy God, and him only shalt thou serve."*

Can you imagine the boldness of the devil trying to tempt Jesus during fasting and even after He goes off fasting? Jesus responded with the Word of God. We too, are tempted daily by the fierceness of the adversary who keeps tugging at our backs with lies and deceits. But we too, like Jesus, have the tool to equip our spiritual life with the Word of God to crush the enemy's head.

We must be fully clothed in the Wisdom of God as we wear His armor daily so that we can stand up against the wiles of the enemy. Jesus stood firm and was grounded in the Word of God until He completed His assignment. No matter what we are going through, stay connected to God. The devil will try to ride our back every moment to get us off track. However, as Christians we need to stand on the Solid Rock of Jesus; He will help us prevail against the scheme of the enemy. We have confidence in God that His grace is sufficient to keep us even in our weakest moments (*see* 2 Corinthians 12:9). Friends, let the power of Christ rest in us to stay faithful and strong, just like those faithful warriors of long ago.

Prayer– Thanking God For Biblical Heroes!

Our dearest Father in Heaven. Holy be Your matchless name. The Creator of everything and everyone. We give You glory, honor, and praise for Your precious Son Jesus Christ who died on the cruel cross to save the world. We exalt You, as we worship and adore You in Spirit and Truth. Abba Father, I thank You for Your beautiful love letter to us that brings forth You in every word! Beautiful Words that come alive and active in our daily lives.

Holy Spirit, we thank You for being our Advocate, Navigator, Teacher, Counselor, and Comforter in every area of our lives. Father, we will seek holiness and righteousness so that we will be prepared and ready to meet King Jesus in Heaven. Oh! What a sweet and glorious day that will be. Oh! Father, I am overwhelmed with all Your power and Your awesomeness that I see in Your handy works each day! How great You are, my God and my King! Every day, I am reliving the Heavenly bliss of the everlasting peace and joy that I experienced in that supernatural encounter with my Savior. Such experiential wisdom and knowledge could only be given and attained by the power of God Almighty during that divine revelation. It is Job who said," *Wisdom is with aged men, with long life is understanding."* Job 12:12. Father, I thank You for Your favor.

I will forever give You all the glory, honor, and praise for Your all-sufficient peace and love. Thank You, Father, for showing me Jesus and all those biblical heroes who stand in faith and confidence in completing the assignment that You placed into their hands. Father, I am so encouraged by the life of those heroes that You lead and guide them through all the trials and tribulations that they faced here on Earth. We are so encouraged by their faith lives and what they accomplished through Your leadership and guidance.

Father, help us to exercise the faith and fortitude to stay on the Christian path as we journey on the road that leads to eternity. Father, I know, just like You did for them You promise that You will never leave us nor will You forsake us. Even when we are walking through the valley of the shadow of death, we shall fear no evil, for You are with us. (See Psalm 23). Today, we crucify every spirit of Goliath, Saul, Pharaoh, Jezebel, and any other spirit that will hinder us from fulfilling our Heavenly assignment in the name of Jesus.

Father, thank You for Your increased faith in the things that are impossible to man but possible to You. Thank You, God, for the plan that You have for us to prosper and not to harm us, and the plan to give us hope and a future. Father, I thank You that my hope is in You and I will always look to You as the great and mighty author of my life and my faith.

We shall live and declare the works of the Lord as we stand flatfoot as soldiers in the army of the Lord. Some sweet day we shall see King Jesus and these biblical heroes as we sit around the throne of God. Oh! what a glory that will be in the sweet and New Jerusalem. Dearest Father, thank You for Your love, grace, and Your mercies. We give You the glory and tell **You thanks in Jesus's Name. Amen!**

Chapter 21: Appreciating the King of Glory

An overall picture of Jesus' Descension and Ascension

LOVING AND APPRECIATING OUR HEAVENLY FATHER.

ONE LORD, ONE FAITH, ONE BAPTISM.

> "There is one body, and one Spirit, even as ye are called in one hope of your calling; One Lord, One faith, one baptism, One God and Father of all, who is above all, and through all, and in you all. But unto every one of us is given grace according to the measure of the gift of Christ. Wherefore he saith, When he ascended up on high, he led captivity captive and gave gifts unto men. (Now that he ascended, what is it but that he also descended first into the lower parts of the earth? He that descended is the same also that ascended up far above all heavens, that he might fill all things.")
>
> -- Ephesians 4:4-10 *KJV (see also the Book of Ephesians for scriptural references in the following chapter)*

I joined with the Apostle Paul in Ephesians, when he states that we should show love and appreciation to our Heavenly Father who is one Lord, one faith, one baptism. God is the greatest Father of all who loves us with an everlasting love that is infinite and knows no boundary. Also, His love has no limit to time or space because He is from everlasting to everlasting, the one who is Alpha and Omega, the Beginning and the End! He is the CEO of the universe, and He is worthy to be praised, loved, and appreciated. Why? Because He is the "One God and Father of all." Yes, God exalted Jesus with the highest authority and final decision in our mundane life. Paul also states that" Christ is the model of humility" *(see Colossians 1: 15-23 KJV)*. Therefore, as Christians, we should exercise the attributes and characteristics of Jesus Christ in our daily lives. "Children of God "should shine as light (Ephesians 5). Let God be the Father in our life so we can shine so bright that even "in a crooked and perverse nation," we will outshine the world's darkness (*see* Philippians 2:1-18).

God chooses to meet with all His children day after day, anytime, anywhere, and through various ways. Most of all, for different reasons and with numerous assignments. He also chooses to have divine encounters with some of us through visions, dreams, or His appearance through angels, just like He did over two thousand years ago.

Several people in the Bible had divine encounters with God in different stages of their lives such as Abraham, (*see* Genesis 18), Moses, (*see* Exodus 3), Elijah, (*see* 1 Kings 19), Mary, (*see* Luke 1:26-45), just to name a few. This great God will continue to have divine visitations with His people all over the world until He returns. As I said before, some of my encounters are through dreams. The most profound dream was seeing Jesus, the Son of the living God, swiftly and suddenly bursting out from the glorious cloud of Heaven. My body was in severe shock mode as I kept my eyes glued to His holiness before me! As I continued to look at my Savior's face, this sweet Jesus, that saved me and you by His grace, such marvelous grace that washed away ALL the sins of the world, unlocking the doors of heaven to let us in, I felt my body trembling because I was bursting with exuberant joy and excitement. As my wandering eyes gazed at the dimension of light that glowed from and around my Savior's face, the smile, and love that was flowing on His face were breathtaking, sincere, pure, and holy. His eyes were full of divine truth with such revelation of light that shone through His entire being. Oh, how I love and appreciate King Jesus!

Paul's prayer says in Ephesians 3:14-21, "That the love of God be appreciated." How can we not love our Father of all Fathers? The outpouring fountain of love that was flowing from Jesus shook my body like an electrical shock without pain or words. I screamed: JESUS! JESUS! JESUS! I was experiencing such a great euphoric desire

Chapter 21: Appreciating the King of Glory

to run and bow down and worship the Messiah. However, Jesus had me in midair position as He continued to smile at me with such unquestioning love. It felt surreal, knowing that Jesus the Messiah was right there high in the cloud, in front of me. I continued to look at my Savior who glowed with this Heavenly glow and this breathtaking glory around Him. I was so overwhelmed with utter excitement. I felt like I was a little child. I was dumbfounded by numerous questions; however, I was experiencing this awesome telepathic communication between my Savior and me. So, there was no need to ask any questions because I was transfixed and glued to His holiness and His righteousness. Glory shone all around Him!

Oftentimes, I wonder, how could we not appreciate this great Messiah who is filled with so much love for the world? In life, we show our appreciation to so many people and generally forget to love and appreciate our Savior as we go about our daily activities. Are we forgetting to love the one God and Father of us all? Together, we are one unified body only by the grace of God, given to us by the measure of the gift of Jesus Christ.

According to the Merriam-Webster dictionary, the word "appreciate" has several meanings of which I listed a few: *1a. to grasp the nature, worth, quality, or significance of, b. to value or admire highly, d. to recognize with gratitude. 2: to increase the value of.* These meanings hold a high degree of ways in which we can show our love and appreciation to each other. However, I want to look at *1a.* For us to grasp the nature, worth, and quality of God's love for us is unimaginable and immeasurable. God is the worthiest one who is set above all others to have our undivided attention at all times! His power and authority supersede all the leaders of the world put together (Matthew 28:18). He is not only the Number One King, but He is the King above all Kings who will bring everything together under His authority. His majesty rules the Heavens and the Earth (*see* Ephesians 1:10). As Christians, we need to build a stable love relationship with our Heavenly Father.

The Apostle Paul continues to say in Ephesians 3, *"For this cause I bow my knees unto the Father of our Lord Jesus Christ, of whom the whole family in heaven and earth is named" (vs 14&15).* We cannot comprehend the nature of God, nor can we understand His worth or quality because He is God all by Himself. No one can compute or calculate the manifold wisdom of God, but if we learn to pray as Paul encourages us to do when he says, "That Christ may dwell in your heart by faith; so, we can be rooted and grounded in love" (*v* 17). Believe and exercise faith in Jesus Christ because He is the only one who can keep us rooted and grounded in His love. God in His infinite love and mercy sent His only begotten Son down to Earth to die to set humanity free from sin. Jesus came and bridged the gap for us with His redemption plan so we can have access as citizens to the kingdom of Heaven (*see* Ephesians 4:8-10).

King Jesus is our PASSPORT to the Kingdom of Heaven. Not only does He stamp the approval to enter His Kingdom, but we are now Kingdom kids, giving us full access to be joint heirs with Him (*see* Romans 8:17). Hallelujah! Isn't that amazing? Jesus returned to Heaven and He left the Holy Spirit to comfort us, lead us, teach us, and guide us. Jesus also promised His disciples that He is coming back for them, which includes us because we are also adopted into God's kingdom by His grace and through the love of Jesus Christ. His love for us NEVER fails, and His promises are from everlasting to everlasting. He is not slack concerning His promise as men often do (*see* 2 Peter 3:9).

Now that we know that we are Kingdom kids, we need to operate as children of the Highest God as we listen and obey the King daily. There is no need to be deceived and tossed to and fro by every false doctrine and craftiness of men when we walk in the light. The Apostle Paul wrote letters to the Christians to encourage them to walk worthy in the calling of the Lord. He wants them to endeavor to keep unity of spirit in the bond of peace, unity in faith and in the knowledge of God. God wants us to know that the church is the BRIDE of Christ and also the BODY of Christ with Him being the Father of us all. With that being said, we should put off the old self and put on the NEW self as we die daily. We are followers and servants of God; therefore, we should live circumspectly and walk as children of LIGHT and not as children of darkness. When we get saved and accept the Lord as our Savior, we die to the flesh and receive the spirit of the living God who is the light of the world to dwell within us. Killing the flesh daily will help us shine because the flesh and the Spirit are always fighting against each other.

There is a big spiritual warfare going on in the atmosphere around us every day. In all this chaos, don't be discouraged, distracted or derailed by the cunning attack of the enemy. Let us stand firm and strong in the army of the Lord. Let us, therefore, exercise Heavenly thoughts and desires that Jesus is coming back to take us to our eternal home. Let us shun away from the things of this world so we can center our focus on King Jesus.

Jesus had a wonderful relationship with His disciples, and He blessed them before He was carried up into Heaven, leaving them a promise that He would not leave them comfortless and that He would return. See the following scripture:

> *"And he led them out as far as to Bethany, and he lifted his hands, and blessed them. And it came to pass, while he blessed them, he was parted from them, and carried up into heaven. And they worshiped him and returned to Jerusalem with great joy: And were continually in the temple, praising and blessing God. Amen."*
>
> --Luke 24:50-53 *KJV*

The above scripture describes the scene with Jesus and His disciples when He took them to Bethany, the place where His ascension took place. Have you ever pictured King Jesus ascending into Heaven and imagining the glorious supernatural power and magnificent beauty of such a scene? Soon after Jesus finished His work here on Earth, He transitioned from the Earth back to Heaven to be with His Father and to prepare a place for us. The apostles and disciples were in awe and **total shock during Jesus' ascension! That must have been an amazing and exciting experience to behold as they looked towards Heaven in this astonishing ascension, as a cloud received Him out of their sight** (*see* Acts 1:9-11). They were in awe! Watching in astonishment! I can just imagine the jaw-dropping stare, moment of surprise, and bewilderment with eyes gazing in disbelief and wonder! I am sure I would be in shock and disbelief too, just to behold this awesome transition of our Lord Jesus Christ. He is God in the flesh. The incarnated God of the world is worthy to be praised!

The Apostle John spoke about the pre-existence of Jesus Christ in John 1:1-18. **John explains that Jesus is God's Word made flesh.** He said, **"In the beginning was the Word (Jesus), and the Word (Jesus) was with God, and the Word (Jesus) was God. The same was in the beginning with God"** (*vs* 1&2). Isn't this amazing? Tell me who can fathom the knowledge and wisdom of God the Father, God the Son, and God the Holy Spirit? No one! That's why it is imperative to serve this Holy and Righteous God of the Universe!

Although Jesus is from the beginning to the end of time, there were Old Testament heroes who wrote about Him and were looking forward with anticipation to King Jesus. The Bible tells us that Jesus is the seed of Abraham! (*see* Galatians 3:15-29). He is also the seed of Jesse! (*see* Isaiah 11:1). Jesus Christ is the perfect seed that flourishes to multiply from nation to nation through the true and living Vine. Jesus even foretold His death as He took the sins of the world upon His shoulders, while drawing all men unto Him (*see* John 12:23-36). Jesus, the Lord is returning with a loud shout and with the voice of the archangel (*see* 1 Thessalonians 4:16-17). He is coming back as the only true Judge, the Eternal King of Kings, and Lord of Lords. Are we preparing to meet Christ, the King?

Meeting The Queen and The Duke of England

I can still remember, even though I was about seven years old when the Queen and Duke of England visited Jamaica in 1966. I was super excited that my school was among the groups selected to go and see this royal family. Several weeks before their arrival, our principal told us to get our best uniforms, shoes, and other attire ready for the special bus trip. Even though I was so young, it seemed as if I could not contain my excitement as I anxiously awaited their arrival, oftentimes reminding my mother to get my uniform ready for the grand occasion. For weeks on the radio, television, and in the daily newspaper, the reporters continued to announce that the Queen and Duke were coming. That seemed to be the daily topic in every parish, town, city, and street, just about everywhere. Everyone was busy mending and fixing everything and anything. They were waiting in joyous anticipation for the grand arrival of the royal family. They were preparing from the House of Parliament to the Mayor's house, even to your own house. From the highways to the byways, workers were busy making everything cleaner and more attractive. There was beautiful landscaping all over with flower gardens looking their best with all kinds and types of flowers. The spirit of festivity was evident everywhere. Everyone seemed excited, happy, and cheerful, reminding each other of the date for this special event.

After preparing for several weeks, the day finally arrived, and several buses headed off to the destination to welcome the Queen and Duke. Each school had a designated spot to stay in line with their teachers and watch the procession and different forms of entertainment. I was so excited and happy that day to feed my curious little mind. I had seen several pictures before of the royal family and heard so many stories about their beautiful Palace, which made me more excited. I can still remember all the school children looking so beautiful in their uniforms standing patiently in line with great expectation. The joy and happiness showed on all the excited and curious smiling faces as we patiently waited for the helicopter to circle and land. I noticed that all the police and soldiers were busy in their tailored stiff uniforms serving in their respective places. After several gun salutes, which I am sure the royal family grew accustomed to hearing as they traveled around the world, there was an "aha" and historic moment as they stepped off the helicopter to face the large and excited crowd. Everyone cheered them with a warm welcome and several rounds of applause. The crowd seemed so happy and excited as the royal family waved and shook hands with some of the dignitaries.

There were different kinds of performances to welcome and entertain the royal family who were seated on a huge platform facing the crowd. From a distance, we waved and shouted at the royal family, bubbling with joy and happiness, just to get a glimpse of them. They continued to wave and smile at the crowd. They seemed to enjoy every moment of the festivity that was put together by the different schools and other entertainment groups. The atmosphere was filled with excitement, joy, and sheer happiness on everyone's faces! There, in their private section with security guards around them, the royal family was joyfully entertained by the beautiful people of Jamaica. Unfortunately, several people, including children, didn't get a chance to personally greet them. Neither did we get the opportunity to shake their hands due to the safety protocol that surrounded them, which I do understand now.

Several years went by and I thought about that specific celebration. Reminding myself, how I saw the Queen and Duke as a child–at a distance- even though I didn't get to greet them personally. I can still recall how happy and excited I was at that moment in time, and I could hardly contain my enthusiasm. The encounter made me happy but also saddened me and many of my friends because we did not get a chance to make close contact or talk to them. I remember going back home shortly after that with mixed emotions and many unanswered questions.

Many years went by, and I questioned how we put so much effort into preparing to meet the Royal family, the Pope, Presidents, Prime Ministers, movie stars, and many other dignitaries from all over the world. I do understand that these meetings and celebrations for those leaders are necessary. Also, we should honor those that God sets over us. Nevertheless, are we appreciating and honoring King Jesus like we do to these leaders? Are we looking forward to the return of the King of Kings and Lord of Lords of the universe? **Are we loving this great King who extends His love, grace, and mercies to us every day? Are we the excited bride who is anxiously waiting as the wife of the Lamb of God? (*see* Revelation 19:5-9; Ephesians 5:21-33).** If we can take the time to prepare for kings and queens and other dignitaries who are leaders and rulers on Earth, then why are we hesitant to prepare for King Jesus? These Earthly leaders can only rule and lead for some time but King Jesus rules and reigns forever. His Lordship governs all kings, queens, and other leaders of the world. Yet, we hesitate to love, appreciate, and adore Jesus.

Going back to the Apostle Paul's prayer that the love of God should be appreciated. Are we taking the King of Glory for granted? Are we giving the earthly leaders priority in our lives and forgetting who is the true King that we should honor and obey? Friends, NOW is the time to seek ye the Lord, while He is near and call upon Him before it is too late. Jesus is coming back, not only as the King but also as the JUDGE of the world. **There will be great noise in Heaven as the Messiah prepares to reign forever and ever (*see* Revelation 11:15).** Are you ready to stand before the Judge of the world? Are we getting our hearts, souls, and minds ready for the returning king? I was somewhat perplexed and perturbed for a long time about the complexity of how we treat Jesus, the King of Glory, *vs.* the kings on Earth who will one day bow to the King of Glory. Jesus is the son of the living God whose name is above all names! God gave Him all the authority over Heaven and Earth.

As I got older and started to learn more about King Jesus, the great Messiah, I sometimes wondered: shouldn't we make special time to prepare for His royal return? Although this happened many years ago, it still amazed me how only a few people got a chance to shake the hands of the royal family. Yet, everyone seemed so happy and overjoyed about the opportunity to meet them even from a distance. Friends, it is high time to wake up from our sleep and open the eyes of our hearts to acknowledge who Jesus is to us! Jesus Christ, the King who had to purge Himself of our sins, sat down on the right hand of the Majesty on high (*see* Hebrews 1:3). He is the only true King with healing in His wings! Revelation 19:16 *KJV* says, *"And he hath on his vesture and on his thigh a name written, KINGS OF KINGS AND LORD OF LORDS."*

This JESUS, who appears to me from the Golden Gates, is so glorious and holy to be praised. During the dream, all my heart desired was to stay in His presence forever in the Heavenly realms. He was my central focus throughout the dream as His Spirit kept on pulling me more and more to His glorious presence. I wish you were there on this heavenly journey with me and our Savior! However, I hope you are excited as you prepare to meet Him on His royal return. Jesus, the Messiah, born from the virgin Mary is coming back as the WARRIOR, RULER, and JUDGE of all nations. Matthew 1:21, *"And she shall bring forth a son, and thou shalt call his name JESUS: for he shall save his people from their sins."* Jesus is the true vine, and we are His seed, woven into His DNA. He came to save the world and set the captive free. Today, will you let Jesus free you from your burden of sins?

Chapter 22: Preparing to Meet the Returning King

David talks about "The King of Glory."

Let us read together:

> *"The earth is the Lord's, and the fullness thereof; the world and they that dwell therein. For he hath founded it upon the seas and established it upon the floods. Who shall ascend into the hill of the Lord? or who shall stand in his holy place? He that hath clean hands, and a pure heart; who hath not lifted up his soul unto vanity, nor sworn deceitfully. He shall receive blessings from the Lord, and righteousness from the God of his salvation. This is the generation of them that seek him, that seek thy face, O Jacob. Lift up your heads, O ye gates and be ye lifted up, ye everlasting door; and the King of glory shall come in, Who is the King of glory? The Lord strong and mighty, the Lord mighty in battle. Lift up your heads, O ye gates; even lift them up, ye everlasting doors; and the King of glory shall come in. Who is the King of glory? The Lord of host, he is the King of glory. "*
>
> --Psalm 24 (KJV). (See also the book of James for scriptural references for the following chapter)

My question for us today is, "Do you know who is the King of glory? The Bible clearly states, "...he that hath seen me hath seen the Father; and how sayest thou then, Shew us the Father? (John 14:9). Are you spending more time getting to know your friends here on earth and less time getting to know your Heavenly Father? James states in the title of Chapter 4," Friends of the world are enemies of God." I encourage you to let Jesus be the Number One priority (FRIEND) in your life. Jesus Christ laid down his life for his friends (*see* John 15:9-

15). Jesus is the true friend that sticks closer than a brother, so let us stick to Him wholeheartedly.

We should try to live one moment at a time basking in the presence of the Lord as we build a stable relationship with him. Are we boasting about tomorrow instead of exercising patience and endurance until the Ruler and Judge of the world returns? (*see* James 4:13-17, 5:7-12). Jesus is the ONLY Judge who sits on the Judgment seat? Chapter 4:12 says, *"There is one lawgiver, who can save and to destroy; who art thou that judgest another?* "Are we preparing to face this great Judge who has all the authority over Heaven and Earth to save and destroy? We do not have the authority to oppress those in need or talk evil against each other because we have Jesus who is the Judge and He has the final say in our lives.

Chapter 3:1-12 also, talks about the importance of controlling the tongue, which can be a dangerous weapon to ourselves and others. Let us seek Heavenly wisdom in our daily conversation as we prepare for His return. *James says, "...the wisdom that is from above is first pure, then peaceable, gentle, and easy to be entreated, full of mercy and good fruits, without partiality, and without hypocrisy. And the fruit of righteousness is sown in peace of them that make peace"* (Chapter 3:17-18). James states in his content, *"To merely say we have faith is insufficient."* He stresses to say that we must have faith that manifests itself in the action of good works." He also provides a dramatic account of the faith of Elijah. We know from the biblical history of Prophet Elijah that he stayed constantly in prayer which resulted in several miracles. Are we showing love and exercising the faith of our Fathers who are now in Heaven?

God wants us to show love to each other and share our wealth with those in need. We are encouraged to pray for strength and healing for our brothers and sisters all over the world. Friends, there is no distance in prayer and God wants us to pray one for another (*see* James 5:16). We need to be hearers and doers of the Word of God as we practice to walk worthy in the calling of God. The King of Glory is coming back with open arms to welcome us to our permanent home, but we must stay ready as we practice to do His will daily. We don't have to set an appointment to meet with this King because He is always knocking at our heart's door! He is saying to us today, "Come as you are. There is room at the cross for you!" It doesn't take weeks of preparation to let Him into our lives. Jesus just wants a repentant heart and someone who believes that He is the Savior of the world. We are encouraged to build a relationship with Jesus the King so that we will not only see Him face to face, but we will live with Him forever because He loves us. Are you anticipating meeting "The Lord of hosts; he is the King of glory?" (Psalm 24:6). He is coming back for CLEAN HANDS and PURE HEARTS!

Friends, there is no King on Earth to compare to the Lord of hosts! **He is so powerful and mighty that He can embrace everyone in the world altogether! He is the King who loves us equally.** There is no injustice or unfairness in Him. He does not manipulate or abuse His authority to rule and govern the world. He is the only true and just God with all the authority to rule the Universe. The Bible clearly states, *"Let every soul be subject unto the higher powers. For there is no power but of God: the powers that be are ordained of God" (Romans 13:1 KJV).* God sets the rules and regulations for us to follow; however, the sinful nature of man tends to ignore the Spirit of God. Man continues to reject and disobey the authority and laws given to us from the beginning of time by our first parents (*see* Genesis 3). It was Adam and Eve who disobeyed the law and command of God in the Garden of Eden, pulling forth the spirit of disobedience upon us. Because of their disobedience, the Bible tells us that we ALL have sinned and come short of the glory of God (*see* Romans 3:23). However, God loves us so much that He sent His only begotten Son, Jesus, to Earth to die to save us from our sins if we repent. Jesus willingly came from Heaven, not to condemn us, but to save us so we too can live with Him forever, giving us a promise and access to eternal life (*see* John 3:16-17).

God our Father in Heaven continues to extend His love, grace, and mercies to us daily. He desires that none should perish. However, He gives us a free will to love Him first, love our neighbors, seek Him first, and worship Him in Spirit and Truth (*see* Matthew 6:33, Matthew 22:37-39, & John 4:24). God gave us life and He also has a good plan for our life. **God is concerned with how we live this life while we are using His breath on His clock. What we do between birth and death matters to God because He desires us to live according to His will and His way so He can get the glory.** Yes, we mess up so many times along the way and come short of the glory of God. However, we serve a forgiving God who wants us to love Him, repent, and turn to Him now not tomorrow. Do not be deceived by the enemy and stay in sin. The enemy does not want us to be close to God because he knows that God has plans for us!

The adversary has been around for thousands of years, and he knows the Bible and he knows Jesus came to give us abundant life. Therefore, the adversary will try to do anything to deceive us and hinder us from having a good relationship with God. The devil also has a plan to destroy us and our loved ones. No one wants to be a friend of the devil because he is a murderer. He comes to kill, steal, and destroy because he is our enemy (*see* John 10:10-19). Seek Jesus as your friend today; He will add all the good things to you and give you eternal life. The adversary is our enemy, and he will add all the bad things to our lives that will send us to the destruction highway. The devil plans to derail, destroy, and distract us and our family from the blessings of the Lord! Seek the Lord today, tomorrow maybe too late!

The question is asked: What are we doing with our time here on Earth? **God chose to give us different lengths of time, but the amazing thing about this time is that we all are experiencing the same twenty-four hours in one day!** It doesn't matter where we are in the four corners of the world; we have the same number of hours in a day. Are we putting God first on our daily timetable? Is He first on our agenda as we start our day? Now is the time to put God first on your daily schedule.

Can you imagine King Jesus sitting on His throne, daily giving us His breath? Yet, we greet others before we seek Him and greet Him FIRST when we wake up. I believe Jesus is looking down at us and saying,

Chapter 22: Preparing to Meet the Returning King

"They forgot to talk with me first or ever talk with me today." Jesus wants us to seek Him first in everything and anything! Therefore, let us try to start our day by talking to God first. Taking the time to greet the Trinity first before getting out of bed should be one of our daily routines. After all, **He didn't have to give us His precious breath, but He did because He loved us. So, why not thank Him first for allowing us to use His wonderful breath of life?**

My friend, we can take this moment to say thank You, God, for lending me Your breath of life. Please let me use Your breath wisely as I go about my daily activities. I love You; I adore You, and I appreciate You, God my Father. Today, I will give You my timetable so You can lead me and guide me through this chaotic world. Our Father wants us to talk with Him constantly about everything. Sometimes, we might have to make changes in our schedule, but try to make PRAYER one of your daily priorities. **A life without prayer is a life without Christ because PRAYER is our main mode of communicating and connecting with God our Father. Would you go about the day ignoring your family and friends, especially if they are living in your home? No! We should not forget about the Holy Spirit that lives inside of us. God wants us to talk with Him every day.** He is waiting to hear your voice; He alone knows what is best for you as you propel your way through this confused world. Today make Jesus your FIRST choice. Acknowledge Him in your conversations and all your decisions.

We are living in a world of so much hatred and crime just about everywhere. Nations against nations, so much civil unrest in different countries, states, communities, cities, schools, colleges, etc. We are up against so much spiritual wickedness, even in the minds of the young generations because the adversary wants to pollute their minds from a young age. It is imperative to continue in warfare prayer for your loved one, especially the young ones because they are the generation for tomorrow. It is high time to be alert and stay awake because we are living in a world of sin, shame, and disgrace and the enemy is not sleeping. Jesus told us in Matthew 24 to watch and pray because perilous times will come, and many false prophets will try to steer us in the wrong direction. Some will turn away from the faith and fight against others. Therefore, **we must be fully covered daily with the powerful blood of Jesus Christ, which will save us from the plan of the enemy to stand firm for the Lord.**

Yes! We will suffer at times, but it will all be to the glory of God because these afflictions are only for a moment. This suffering is pale compared to the glorious time we will have in Heaven, just stay faithful to God our Father even when we are persecuted, let it be for the glory of God (*see* 2 Corinthians 4). Some sweet day, the Son of God will appear, and we shall see Him bursting out from the cloud of Heaven. Friends, get ready and stay ready for the returning King of Glory, the One who died on the cross to set you free from your burden of sins. Jesus is the only One who shed His PRECIOUS BLOOD on the cross to set the world free from sin. It is all about the BLOOD of Jesus which washes, cleanses, and makes us clean. Please, place it on the doorpost of your heart every day as you await His royal return. Make time for Jesus because He took time for us when He was nailed to the cross.

I thank God for the blessed Holy Spirit, the Spirit of Truth, for counseling me, guiding me, and directing me to seek God first for everything and anything. He sticks closer than a brother and He reminds me of all the things I need to know (*see* John 14:26). The more you start seeking God first, the more you depend on Him for everything. Also, the sooner you realize that you cannot make life without Him, the more you are prepared to serve Him and look forward to meeting Him in glory. I am still in awe of seeing the magnificent light and Heavenly glow around my Lord and Savior as He descended from the clouds. His wonderful face is filled with so much love, compassion, and grace, the wonderful grace that pardoned and washed away all our sins. While we wait on the Lord let us love and pray for each other.

We are so blessed to have a King who provides for the just and the unjust, the rich and the poor, the black and the white, and any color, creed, or race. He is our Jehovah Jireh, our Great Provider! **No matter**

Chapter 22: Preparing to Meet the Returning King

how excellent, powerful, smart, or educated you are, you will always be second to the King of the Universe and He is our Father! Jesus was scourged and crowned with thorns as the King of the Jews when He died on the cross for our sins. (*see* John chapter 19). His death as King was painful because He suffered, bled, and spat upon as He died an innocent death for you and me. Jesus fulfilled His Father's assignment which pleased God as the" ...heavens opened and the Spirit descended on him like a dove..." (*see* Mark 1:9-13). After His baptism, He was tested and tried as the enemy came to tempt Him. Despite everything, Jesus stayed firm and strong in the word and prayed as He depended on His Father to lead Him all the way.

God is searching our hearts every day and He is looking through every cell that makes up our body, making note of all our mistakes, and still loving us unconditionally. That is one of the many reasons why you should make Him the FIRST priority in your life. Let Him be the central focus of your daily life, so we can have a prosperous and purposeful life with Him. We need to live for Him and obey Him, even when we think everything is going well. Jesus is coming back soon for those who are ready to meet Him in the air.

These dreams and revelations that I experienced were so phenomenal and vivid, they encouraged me to look forward to the glorious return of Jesus with joy and gladness. I hope you are too! Just to think about it, is unimaginable! **A day when every knee shall bow before the Lord God, our maker. We need to do daily self-searching because there is a Great Day coming when we shall stand before King Jesus! Will our name be in the BOOK OF LIFE? We must do a spiritual self-examination and crucify the flesh daily because we are nothing but filthy rags (*see* Isaiah 64:6).** So, stop being prideful and seek Jesus and try to live according to His will and His way! All glory belongs to the One who gives us the ability to perform in our daily activities and different roles. It is God's grace that allows us to function and have hope for tomorrow. We are nothing without God and we cannot do anything without Him! However, we are EVERYTHING with God when we put Him first because every impossibility becomes possible through Jesus Christ, our Lord.

We should live each day with Heavenly thoughts and desires, seeking things which are above, where Christ our Lord is sitting on the right hand of God (*see* Colossians 3). Therefore, we should aim to be understanding to the feelings of others and encourage them that Jesus loves and cares for them in every area of their lives. Be humble, be kind, be sweet, be sincere, and stay positive as you shine the light of Christ everywhere you go. Strive to show love and mercy to each other as you keep a MERRY and JOYFUL HEART to be the STEWARD God wants you to be for His glory. Remove yourself from the BROKEN spirit because it will dry up your bones and make you and others unhappy! Gravitate to wise advice spoken by King Solomon (*see* Proverb 17). Most of all, we are encouraged to seek the wisdom, knowledge and understanding from JESUS the King of Glory! God wants us to have clean hands and pure hearts (*see* Psalm 23:4-5).

It is King David who wrote Psalm 24, which is a song of praise about the great and Mighty King of the Universe. God the Creator of Heaven and Earth and everything under the Earth is the Redeeming King of glory. The question is asked several times: *Who is the King of glory?* The word of God declares, *"The Lord strong and mighty, The Lord mighty in battle. The Lord of hosts; He is the king of glory."* He is the King sent down from Heaven to Earth with clean hands and a pure heart to save and satisfy our empty souls. He is the All-Knowing and All-Powerful God who reigns forever. There is none before Him, and there is none beside Him nor after Him. Please, open your heart's door and let the King into all your plans so He can give you the desires of your heart. How can we walk away or turn our back from God our Father? Our lives belong to Him because He only lends us His breath for a while. What are we doing with this borrowed life from birth to death? Jesus loves us so much and He wants to live inside of us, a dwelling place of praise.

Are we a generation that seeks after the King, preparing to meet Him in His Kingdom? Today the Psalmist is asking, "Who is the King of

Chapter 22: Preparing to Meet the Returning King

Glory?" Do you know Him as your returning King? My friends, this King who brings eternal life is the one who died to set us free from all condemnation. Seek Him today and you will surely find Him. Jesus is unlike the kings and queens who only reign and rule on earth for a short period. Jesus is the only King who has power and dominion in Heaven and on Earth forever! I am so happy and excited to know that the Messiah is my King, and He is your King too. Are you happy to know that we are joint heirs with Jesus and He gave us access to be in His Kingdom? (*see* Romans 8:16-17). Hallelujah! He is the Omniscient God and He is our Savior who says, *"Behold, I stand at the door, and knock: if any man hears my voice, and open the door, I will come into him, and will sup with him, and he with Me"* (Revelation 3:20 *KJV*).

There is so much to receive from the promises of God. You shall receive blessing from the Lord and righteousness from the God of His salvation. Seek ye this day whom you will serve! Will you serve the strong and mighty King who fights every battle and wins them all because He is The Mighty Warrior? God sent His son Jesus Christ to be the propitiation for our sins (*see* 1 John 4:7-12). Jesus came willingly to set us free when He died the cruel death on the cross for our salvation, giving us a great redemption plan. There are no human beings on earth to express this magnitude of love or who can give you so much love as the Love of God through His son, Jesus.

In the dream, it felt like I was engulfed in a Universe of never-ending love and compassion. I cannot find any words to describe His power and how strong His presence felt. It was so amazing, powerful, sincere, and glorious. Our Savior is all *Dunamis* power, and He is the mighty force beyond human comprehension! At times in the dream, **I was astonished by the Heavenly scenery of the Golden Gates, the flowing curtains, the presence of the biblical heroes, and David's enormous golden harp. Most of all, God's authority, and mighty power to have EVERYONE and EVERYTHING in control, peace, and in order.** Surely, He is not an author of confusion (*see* 1 Corinthians 14:33). I prayed everyone could have this wonderful experience. One cannot measure or embrace the enormity of such divine love, a love beyond measure, limit, or boundary! We are encouraged to seek Him and serve Him in the Spirit of holiness, gratitude, and appreciation for all the many blessings He bestowed on us each day.

He is unexplainable, indescribable, and unforgettable. This is Jesus, who is the Chief Commander, Judge, and King in the Kingdom of Heaven. He is always with you, protecting you and carrying you away from the danger zone every day of your life. Jesus chose to forgive and forget the sins of our past when we let Him into our lives. **He is Alpha and Omega, The Beginning, and The End. He is the only wise God and the forgiving Father! He is the Chief Executive Officer (CEO) of the Universe!** The only Sovereign God of the World! The Cornerstone! The Creator of Heaven and Earth, and I love Him with all my heart, mind, body, and soul! He knows everything about us from the beginning of time until now! David tells us in Psalm 139 that our substance was not "hidden from thee." He knows about our actions, attitudes, and our mistakes; even if we make our beds in hell, He is there to rescue us. This great and mighty God wove us into every fiber of His DNA and made us in His image in our mother's womb. Therefore, we cannot hide from Him, nor can we run from Him. We are always on Jesus' mind. The Great God is always thinking about us, even when we forget to say a prayer, He continues to love us unconditionally.

Jesus arose from the grave on the third day with a Mighty triumph of His own. Glory, hallelujah! The grave could not hold Him captive; death had no power over the Messiah, who came back and continued to work wonders and miracles, then ascended to His Father after forty days. While Jesus was on Earth, He experienced some trying and crucial times; even the disciples fell asleep when He needed them to pray with Him (*see* Matthew 26:37, Hebrew 2:17&18, 4:16). The Bible tells us that not even His brothers believed in Him (*see* John 7:5). There is nothing that we are going through that Jesus did not experience. However, His earthly testing was a divine process to fulfill the will of His Father, and He did so with honor so that mankind could have access to the Throne of Grace. God knows what we are facing in this cruel and sinful world and that we cannot fight off the enemy on our

Chapter 22: Preparing to Meet the Returning King

own. The Bible tells us that we are troubled on every side, but there is hope because Jesus never leaves us alone (*see* 2 Corinthians 4:8-10).

God wants the best for us and He also knows the enemy wants to kill us and rob us of the privilege to spend eternity with our Father which is in Heaven. Our suffering here on Earth is only temporary; we must put our hope in God and try to persevere through this suffering (*see* Romans 5:3-5). Let us believe in Jesus and stand on His promises that He is the One who is the Way, the Truth, and the Life! (*see* John 14:1-7). Jesus is encouraging us not to let our hearts be troubled; He wants us to BELIEVE in Him and take Him at His word. He is knocking at **your heart's door. Will you let Him in?** (*see* Revelation 3:20-22 *KJV*). This is an open invitation to everyone to be joint heirs with Jesus. Come to Jesus as you are. He comes to save you, deliver you, and set you free. James, the brother of Jesus, is telling us that, "There is no place for discrimination or greed in the life of a committed believer." James continued to say, "Favoritism should not be shown" (*see* James 2:1-8). Jesus's love for us is pure and genuine, it is unfailing and unlimited. He wants us to be committed believers and to serve Him in Spirit and in Truth. James encourages us to live a Christlike life.

Seek Jesus today as your Number One Spiritual Navigator to guide and lead you through this pilgrim journey. Jesus is my Governing Prince of Salvation (GPS). He can be your GPS too because He is the only Way to the Father, Salvation, and Heaven. Saints of God, let us pray for each other and continue to show love to each other. Jesus wants unity and solidarity among believers and unbelievers. Jesus said, *"I came not to call the righteous, but sinners to repentance"* (Luke 5:32 *KJV*). Let us be the light to others who are in darkness so they can see the light of Jesus in us.

There are several reasons why we should not turn our backs on the Lord! First, **we need Him more than we could ever imagine! We need Him because He knows more about us than we know about ourselves. We are not our own; we all belong to God! He is our Father, and we are His children. Most of all, His love for us never ceases or fails; it is from everlasting to everlasting** (*see*

Lamentations 3:22). He created us in such a special and unique way so we can look like Him. He desires for us to serve Him and Him alone. He is the only one with the authentic copy and manual of our framework. He existed before us and will always be here because He is the Alpha and Omega, the Beginning, and the End (*see* Revelation 1:8). The Earth belongs to the Lord, also everyone and everything belongs to Him. Not only did He make us, but He plans our lives, knows about our past, present, and future, and always takes care of us. Just to be alive is more than enough reason to serve the Omnipresent God. He is always present, never absent. The scripture tells us, *"The eyes of the Lord are in every place, beholding the evil and the good"* (Proverbs 15:3 KJV).

My friend, we serve such an awesome and mighty God; It doesn't matter where you are on the face of the Earth; He's there with us. He takes account of all our actions and deeds. The Bible tells us in Jeremiah 23:23-24, *"Am I a God at hand, saith the Lord, and not a God afar off? Can any hide himself in secret places that I shall not see him? saith the Lord. Do not I fill heaven and earth? saith the Lord."* **We cannot hide or run from God, so that's enough for us to serve Him in Spirit and in Truth!** He is the great and mighty Creator who made us, and He desires the best for us; even when we don't deserve His love and mercy, He still grants it to us.

This is the same wonderful and awesome God who sits upon the circle of the Earth, observing us day after day. There is no secret place to hide. We may be able to hide our activities from man, whether good or bad, but we sure cannot hide from God. **He is JESUS CHRIST the LORD, and He will be returning as the great Magistrate and Ruler of the World! He is the only true Commander and Chief of our busy life.** He has the POWER, STRENGTH, and ABILITY to INTERRUPT, INTERJECT, and DISRUPT all our daily activities any time He chooses to do so! Jesus spoke to me during the walk and His voice was full of POWER and AUTHORITY. Even though softly spoken, His commanding voice was enough to shake every fiber of my being! He is the God of POWER, THUNDER, and LIGHTNING. The Bible tells us in Psalm 77:18, *"The voice of thy*

Chapter 22: Preparing to Meet the Returning King

thunder was in the heaven: the lightnings lightened the world: the earth trembled and shook." That is the voice of the Lord which can make Heaven tremble and shake with His authoritative voice.

The Ruler of the Universe! Psalm 95 tells us about the great King above all gods, a great and Mighty God worthy of all praise, one to whom we need to give thanks. He's a merciful God who grieved because of our disobedience, yet, in His mercy, His compassion fails not. Our daily prayer should be to thank our Lord Jesus Christ for dying on the cross to save us from eternal doom. Jesus granted us access so we can enjoy our Heavenly inheritance just like those biblical heroes of long ago.

As I said before, **Heaven is God's Kingdom, and it is mentioned over SEVEN HUNDRED times in the Bible. Also, the second coming of the Lord is mentioned EIGHTEEN HUNDRED times in the Bible.** Therefore, God wants us to know about Heaven, and He wants us to know about the coming of the Lord. I am encouraged by the Word of God (His love letter to us) to have Heavenly thoughts and desires as **I prepare my heart and soul for the returning King.** Heaven is God's Kingdom, a really beautiful place where God wants all His children who obey Him to live with Him forever. This Heavenly home that we inherited through His son Jesus Christ. Authentically designed and prepared by the hands of God just for those who do His will.

Let us be steadfast and vigilant in our daily walk as we continue to humble ourselves in prayer and fasting and meditate on His words. Let us be READY and waiting as we WATCH and PRAY, for we know not the hour when Jesus shall appear. Matthew 24:36-51 talks about *"The unknown day and hour. But of that day and hour knoweth no man, no, not the angels of heaven, but my Father only. Watch, therefore: for ye know not what hour your Lord doth come. Therefore, be ye also ready: for in such an hour as he thinks not the son of man cometh"* (vs 36,42 & 44).

Hell is also real. *Matthew 25:41 & 46, says, "Then shall he say unto them on the left hand, depart from me, ye cursed, into everlasting fire, prepare for the devil and his angels. And these shall go away into everlasting punishment: but the righteous into life eternal."* **This is the word of God,** and His word stands forever. "Be not deceived." God cannot accept sinners into His kingdom, nor can unrighteousness be in the presence of God (*see* 1 Corinthians 6:9-11). He doesn't lie, and He never changes any of His promises. Today, you are encouraged to REPENT and seek God's righteousness.

Now is the time to walk, talk, and live holy. We should strive to live according to the will of God. If we continue to disobey and refuse to live according to God's LOVE LETTER (the BIBLE), then we become short of the glory of God. Jesus is coming back as the Judge. *"For the wrath of God is revealed from heaven against all ungodliness and unrighteousness of men, who hold the truth in unrighteousness;" Our great God reveals Himself in His creation." "God gives man up to his unrighteousness." "God judges sin impartially"* (*see* Romans 1:18-32, 2:1-16). We need to seek after righteousness and godliness as we prepare for the returning King. The good NEWS is, Jesus Christ is coming back "with a shout, with the voice of the archangel, and the trump of God: and the dead in Christ shall rise first. Then we who are alive and remain shall be caught together with them in the clouds, to meet him the Lord: and so, shall we ever be with the Lord" (*see* 1 Thessalonians 4:13-18).

Are you looking forward to spending eternity with Jesus and all the biblical heroes of the Bible? After so many years, I am still excited and continually reliving that Heavenly encounter. I am still in shock and awe at seeing Jesus along with those biblical warriors and the beautiful Heavenly scenery that was revealed to me. **I am still trying to digest the miraculous growth of the magnificent UNICORN and the swiftness of his power, strength, and speed that took place right before my eyes. I was still clinging to the final words before the unicorn took me home when JESUS said, "PICK IT UP! I GAVE IT TO YOU. IT IS YOURS TO TAKE YOU ANYWHERE YOU ARE GOING!" That is exactly what happened in the flash of a moment. The unicorn grew into a huge animal full of power and vigor and swiftly took me home.**

Today, don't let the adversary prevent you from picking up all the

Chapter 22: Preparing to Meet the Returning King

good gifts and talents that the Lord placed into your life. **God has a good plan for YOU to claim and tap into.** Remember, all good gifts around us are sent from our Heavenly Father to use for His glory and to edify others. Put your FAITH with action before your fear and anxiety. God will send all the destiny angels to assist you during the process because he **LOVES** You and he cares about our achievements.

Today, through the help and inspiration of the Holy Spirit, which brought to memory these wonderful dreams in detail, I was able to finish this assignment as I write and share these encounters with you. I hope and pray that your hearts will be immensely blessed as you wait and prepare for the return of the Messiah to take us home. Are you preparing to meet the King? Arise! Pick up the cross and follow the King. The one who was nailed to the cross for our sins. Are you ready to worship Him on His Golden Throne? Heaven is beautiful and it is real. Don't turn away from God for his wrath you will feel. Jesus is coming back as the Judge and King. Please open your heart and let Christ in. Jesus is the King of Kings and Lord of Lords. I saw Him descending from the clouds of glory. Let us be READY and waiting as we WATCH and PRAY for we know not the hour when Jesus shall appear. Will you be the wise virgin or the foolish virgin? Don't bury your talent and come up with frivolous excuses! Will you be the selected sheep (righteous believers on the right side), or will you be the departed from me goats (unrighteous unbelievers on the left side)? (*see* Matthew 25). Now is the time to seek salvation. Jesus is coming back for PREPARED people to take to His PREPARED home in glory!

ARE YOU PREPARING FOR KING JESUS ROYAL RETURN?

Jesus Descending From The Golden Gates Of Heaven

Poem: Are You Ready to See Jesus The King?

Are you ready and waiting to see Jesus the Eternal King?
He is the King of Glory, salvation and new life He brings!
He is the only true Champion Warrior of all Warriors!
Fighting our battles and removing our sinful barriers!

Repent from your sins and let Christ into your heart!
Jesus will stay close beside you, and He will never depart!
The Bible tells us that the wages of sin is death!
But Jesus paid it all on the cross with no regrets!

Can you imagine Jesus leaving His Heavenly Throne above?
He suffered severe pain because of His unconditional love!
A love so great, He took our sin, guilt, disgrace, and shame!
Beaten, mocked, and spat upon as He stooped to take our blame!

Yet! For you and me, He endured the pain, on the cross He died!
I thought about His gracious love and I often wondered, why!
But He was sent by His Father to fulfill His Earthly assignment!
For this reason, JESUS the Messiah brought to us His atonement!

Friends, are you preparing to see King Jesus that set us free?
Our Sovereign Savior and Lord that was nailed to the tree!
He died and was even buried in a borrowed tomb!
Taking away all our sins, shame, and impending doom!

Thorns upon His head, with several wounds He bled!
He is the first after three days to be raised from the dead!

Poem: Are You Ready to See Jesus The King?

Hallelujah! With *Dunamis* power, He arose on the third day!
Proclaiming the world and setting us free, the total price He paid!

Are you anxious to see the Miracle-working King of Kings?
From His resurrection, we must believe in the new life He brings!
In the Kingdom of Heaven, His glorious face you and I shall see!
Jesus Christ, The Mighty Redeemer who was born to set us free!

After Jesus's baptism, the spirit of God flew upon Him like a dove!
This great King Jesus ascended to His Heavenly Father above!
He is our Savior and He is coming back as the Eternal King.
Glory! Glory! Hallelujah! We shall shout, worship, and sing!

Are your garments spotless? Are they white as snow?
Jesus is coming back shining with His Heavenly glow!
You cannot afford to miss this Holy and Royal Jubilee!
It is free for everyone who repents, trusts, and believes!

Upon His head, He shall wear the beautiful, Golden Crown!
As we praise, worship, and gather around His Royal Throne!
The glorious Kingdom of Heaven will shine so brightly!
The Heavenly host will sing, "Holy! Holy! Lord God Almighty!"

Hallelujah! Hallelujah! Holy is the LORD God Almighty;
The whole Earth is full of His glory and splendor!
Glory Hallelujah! Hallelujah! He is the Lord of Host;
His glory filled the whole Earth! Yes! He is Lord God Almighty!

Jesus Descending From The Golden Gates Of Heaven

Prayer--The Great Day of Separation!

(see Matthew 25:31-34)

Dearest Father in Heaven, holy be Your beautiful and wonderful name. Your wonderful name is above all names. Today, we come to You in praise, worship, and adoration, acknowledging that You are the PROPHET, PRIEST, and KING. Father, we love You, we appreciate You, and adore You. Sweet Jesus, You are the King of all Kings, Lord of all Lords, and Judge of all Judges. We praise You because You are the Father of the Heavens and the Earth. You are our Emanuel, a God who is always with us and for us. We are looking forward to Your glorious appearance from Heaven above.

Heavenly Father, we thank You for sending Your precious Son Jesus Christ, the Messiah. Jesus, we thank You for willingly leaving Your home in Heaven to come down to attend to humanity's needs. Thank You for laying down Your life to redeem us from this sinful world of shame and disgrace. Jesus, You came down with Your perfect self to take up the imperfection of this sinful world. Thank You, Jesus, for bridging the gap between Heaven and hell and setting us free, giving us Your ROYAL PASSPORT with the ROYAL CITIZENSHIP to enter into the kingdom of Heaven. Father, I thank You for the beautiful dream of Heaven and seeing Jesus Christ, our soon-coming King, also for the dream to write this book. I thank you for granting me this favor and that I will stay steadfast and in tune with your voice.

Father, you said that Jesus is coming back as the Judge of the world to judge everyone according to their works. Help us to repent and separate ourselves from the things of this world so we can live in peace and love with each other. Enable us to be of great encouragement to Your people near and far.

Prayer--The Great Day of Separation!

Today, sweet Jesus, as we repent, let us change from a goat to a sheep, so we can be on the right side to see Your glorious face. Thank You, Father, for giving us a seat at Your table where we can partake and fellowship with You in Your house forever. Help us to be steadfast, faithful, and obedient to Your will and Your ways so we can be the chosen sheep You desire us to be. Abba Father, even at this moment, we are asking You to search us and purify our hearts from the things of this world. Please, remove from us known and unknown sins. Father, deliver us from hypocritical thinking and any carnal weakness that is blocking our breakthrough and our growth in You. Please remove from us any generational curses, barriers, obstacles, or setbacks from any of our ancestors in Jesus's name. Wash us with hyssop and purge us from every evil that will separate us from You. Detox us from the things that will hinder us from entering into Your kingdom. Father, help us to be obedient to the Lordship of Jesus Christ, the great Messiah, as we depend on the Holy Spirit to be our guide and Counselor.

Lord, help us to realize that we cannot go to Heaven by our good works or good deeds BUT only by true repentance and Your grace and mercies. Father, lead and guide us to stay committed to reading Your word and applying it to our lives daily. Today, we put our complete trust, faith, belief, and confidence in You, thou, Lamb of Calvary. I pray that we will be ready to meet Your Son, Jesus Christ when He stretched forth His right hand to receive us into Your kingdom. We decree and declare that we are children of the Most High God and we will walk as children of light and not as children of darkness. Father, we are looking forward to Jesus's return with great anticipation to be with Christ our Redeemer, the high Priest.

This priceless Heavenly inheritance that we can never afford, no matter how rich we think we are because it was paid for in full by the precious blood of the Lamb. Father, we know that we cannot pay our way into Heaven because Jesus paid it all when He died on the old rugged cross to set us free. We thank You for all the surprises, blessings, and inheritance that You are preparing for us in Your Kingdom. Our hearts are rejoicing, thinking about our eternal home where we shall spend eternity with You and the Heavenly host of glory! Even though we are living in a world that is the epitome of Sodom and Gomorrah, we shall stay focused so we will not be separated from your love. A love that is beyond measure that you decided to create us in Your image as Your creative masterpiece. **This beautiful image can only be made by Your nail-printed hand and authentically designed by God our Father. This human blueprint compacts with your awesome DNA, which consists of love, grace, and mercies toward us.**

Dearest Father, we will stand as Soldiers of the Cross, ready to fight off the adversary who is trying to derail and ambush us off guard. We aim to die daily as we pray against the distractions of this world. Father, we recognize that the world is polluted with sin, shame, and disgrace in every corner. However, we are holding onto Your mighty and powerful hands to lead and guide us into Your wisdom, knowledge, and understanding. We will not give up but will keep our focus on You because You are our Solid Rock of Ages. Father, You promise that You will never leave us, nor will You forsake us. We are standing on Your promises until eternity ends. We know that You will lead us to victory, just like You did for all the biblical heroes of long ago.

Father, I know there are times when we need to hold our peace and let You fight the battle, according to Exodus 14:14, knowing that when we are at our weakest, you Oh Lord, you are at your strongest! Because of your strength, power, and might, we do not need to fear the adversary. **Thank You for removing the spirit of fear and replacing it with faith, power, love, and a sound mind.** Today, even through heartache and pain, we declare that we are victorious in Jesus' name. Thank You, Father, for the comfort we found in Your promise that says, *"Who shall change our vile body, that it may be fashioned like unto his glorious body, according to the working whereby he is able even to subdue all things unto himself."* (Philippians 3:21 *KJV*). Father, we thank you for your power to subdue all things unto yourself.

Abba Father, thank You for my friends who are saying this prayer that their souls will be blessed in every area of their lives. I pray that they will find perfect peace, total deliverance, and unspeakable comfort in Your loving arms. Today, we join with the Apostle Paul when he says," *I was with you in weakness, and in fear, and in much trembling. And my speech and my preaching were not with enticing words of man's wisdom, but in demonstration of the Spirit and of power: that your faith should not stand in the wisdom of men, but in the power of God"* (1 Corinthians 2:3-5 *KJV*). I pray that You will stand as the sheep God wants you to be. Most of all, you will experience increased wisdom, knowledge, and understanding in the things of God and not of men.

Thank You, Father, for Your continued grace that gives us the confidence and tenacity to keep faith alive. You are our PROVIDER, DELIVER, PROTECTOR, and WAYMAKER, and we are standing on Your promise that You are coming back to receive us into Your kingdom. Thank You for being the GOOD SHEPHERD who watches over us as we await Your royal return. I give You all the glory, honor, and praise. In Jesus' Holy and matchless Name, I pray!

AMEN!

Jesus Descending From The Golden Gates Of Heaven

Song: King Jesus Is Coming

King Jesus is coming! Yes, my friend!
King Jesus is coming! Yes, my friend!
King Jesus is coming; Yes, He is coming back again!
He is the only King who forever will reign!
And he is coming; He's coming back again! (Repeat)

Jesus is coming with outstretched hands and open arms!
He will embrace you with peace and give you eternal calm!
No more sadness or pain coming from your heart.
Friends! Lean on Jesus and stay on the Christian part!
For King Jesus is coming. He is coming back again!

Jesus is coming back; He is the pure and holy bridegroom.
The great Messiah may come in the morning, night, or noon.
Behold, I come quickly to take you to the prepared place!
Children guard your heart and endure the Christian race!
For King Jesus is coming. He is coming back again!
Read Revelation 22:12-14 at the end of the song followed by singing the chorus two-three times.
"And, behold, I come quickly; and my reward is with me,
to give every man according as his work shall be.
 I am Alpha and Omega,
the beginning and the end,
the first and the last.
Blessed are they that do his commandments, that they may have right to the tree of life, and may enter in through the gates into the city."

Pamalyn Lalor

About The Author

Pamalyn Lalor, affectionately called, "Mother Pam," was born and raised on the beautiful island of Jamaica. She is a writer who started writing poems, songs, prayers and skits at the tender age of eight to encourage and motivate family members and friends to be the best they could be. She attended the Bethel Mennonite Church in Jamaica for thirty years, where she assisted in many different roles. She migrated from Jamaica in 1989 to Hartford, Connecticut, where she lived and worked in the medical field for over twenty-six years. She enjoys taking care of children and was a foster mother for fifteen years. She has volunteered in several outreach programs as a nurse and a mentor in Hospitals, Skilled Nursing facilities, clinics, health fairs, halfway homes, and shelters.

While in Hartford, Connecticut, she attended the Trinity Community Church where she served in many capacities for twenty-six years. She also attended Crossroads Community Church in East Hartford, Connecticut for two years where she was a student in their school of ministry, and also participated in their drama production. She now resides in North Carolina with her daughter, son-in-law, and her three beautiful granddaughters. She attends the Bethel Temple Faith Church in Concord, North Carolina under the leadership of Bishop Bertram D. Hinton, Jr., and First Lady Nickie L. Hinton. She is a devoted member and one of the church's mothers. She is a committed and militant prayer warrior who continues to empower the lives of many through prayer and encouragement as she wages war against the plot and schemes of the adversary.

She holds a Diploma in Business Administration from Stewarts Comprehensive College in Jamaica, an Associate's Degree in Nursing from Capital Community College in Hartford, Connecticut, and a Bachelor of Science in Nursing from the University of Hartford, Connecticut. She holds Certificates in Acts of the Apostle, Hermeneutics 1, Old Testament, and Pastoral Ministry from the Crossroads Community International Bible Institute. East Hartford, Connecticut.

She desires to see everyone get connected to God our Father and stay in His Word, His Will, and His Way while daily building a relationship with Him. The primary goal is to decrease the kingdom of hell and increase the Kingdom of Heaven by working together as Christian Soldiers of the Cross!

She enjoys acting, cooking, sewing, singing, and writing, but most of all, traveling and spending time with family and friends.

From the Author

I thank you for coming along with me on this Heavenly tour led by Jesus Christ the Author and finisher of your FAITH. He is our Shepherd and the Governing Prince of Salvation (GPS). Jesus loves and cares for you with an EVERLASTING LOVE.

I do hope you enjoyed these dreams and that you are inspired to have Heavenly Thoughts and Desires. Thanks for sharing with your family and friends.

For additional copies of this book go to Amazon.com.

To schedule "The Dream Presentation" or Poetry Recitals email:

Pamalynlalor@gmail.com

Jesus Descending From The Golden Gates Of Heaven

www.ingramcontent.com/pod-product-compliance
Lightning Source LLC
Chambersburg PA
CBHW050518100526
44581CB00001B/27